Microcomputer Aided Design
For Architects and Designers

Gerhard Schmitt

WILEY

A Wiley-Interscience Publication
John Wiley & Sons
New York • Chichester • Brisbane • Toronto • Singapore

Copyright © 1988 by John Wiley & Sons, Inc.

All rights reserved. Published simultaneously in Canada.

Reproduction or translation of any part of this work
beyond that permitted by Section 107 or 108 of the
1976 United States Copyright Act without the permission
of the copyright owner is unlawful. Requests for
permission or further information should be addressed to
the Permissions Department, John Wiley & Sons, Inc.

Library of Congress Cataloging in Publication Data:

Schmitt, Gerhard, 1953-
   Microcomputer aided design for architects and designers
   Gerhard Schmitt.
"A Wiley-Interscience publication."
Includes index.
ISBN 0-471-60075-X
ISBN 0-471-61876-4 (pbk)
1. Architectural design—Data processing. 2. Computer-aided
design. I. Title.
NA2728.S36 1988
720'.28'4285—dc 19

Printed in the United States of America

10 9 8 7 6 5 4 3 2 1

Microcomputer Aided Design

For Architects and Designers

Meinen Eltern

PREFACE

This book aims to remove the unnecessary mystique surrounding the use of computers for architects and designers. Written as a user's introduction to architectural microcomputer-aided design, it addresses how microcomputers can be applied to the design process. The assumption is that the reader is interested in using or understanding a CAD system but has little or no knowledge of how the computer operates and produces results.

Research areas such as computer graphics and computer modeling have matured to a degree where the results are implemented in most of the commercial or university CAD systems. This book will therefore not elaborate on them. Other issues that are prime research topics today—the use of Artificial Intelligence techniques in design and the formalization of the design process itself—will be dealt with in more detail as they promise to be significant.

This book will define present and possible future uses of microcomputers in the design process. It describes the two fundamental directions of computer programs: to enhance and expedite the traditional and manual design activities and to open new design possibilities by exploring the particular capabilities of the microcomputer and innovative programming paradigms. As design relies heavily on graphical interaction, examples of this type and the necessary programming steps are included. This book is intended for use by the following groups:

1. **Architecture and Design Students.** These students have an interest in becoming competent program users and have access to a microcomputer environment at home or in their university. They are not afraid of computers and are also creative and willing to investigate new

ways of design exploration. The first part of this book will help students to become familiar with basic concepts; the second part is aimed at students interested in advanced topics.

2. **Architecture and Design Teachers.** These teachers have an interest in using the microcomputer-based CAD systems to their maximum potential and to integrate them in a meaningful way in the curriculum. They are not afraid of the new machines and also not afraid of using state-of-the-art commercial software that has been developed outside the academic environment. Rather, they will use this software for what it is best suited and build more interesting applications on top of existing programs. The second part and appendix of the book should be of particular interest to this group.

3. **Architects and Designers.** These architects and designers should already own or plan to own a microcomputer. They can see some positive impact of these machines on their practice—through administrative support, for example—and are willing to explore some of the graphics and database capabilities as well. They are interested in the practical use of the new machines and want to tailor them to fit their own idiosyncratic needs. For this group, the first part of the book is an example of what they can expect from current programs; the second part should familiarize them with the next generation of computer-aided design systems.

Obviously, the important time factor must be considered. The techniques and principles described will be with the design profession for a long time, but the equipment will change. All work presented in this book can be executed on machines with 68000 or 80286 microprocessors, a hard disk with at least 20-megabyte storage capacity, graphic tablet or mouse, medium-sized plotter, commercial drafting package, and some knowledge about macro operations and batch files, that is, very basic programming skills. With a few listed exceptions, most images were produced with the AutoCAD [AutoCAD87] and AutoLISP [AutoLISP87] program on an IBM AT with 640 kilobytes of RAM and a 20-megabyte hard disk. In the near future, the storage problem will virtually disappear and programming skills will be less crucial for the successful use of CAD in design, as there will be more powerful and user-friendly interfaces.

The purpose of this book will be fulfilled if the reader reaches an understanding of CAD as an advanced drafting tool in Part One; and if Part Two inspires the exploration of innovative uses of computers and programs as possible amplifiers of human design intelligence.

GERHARD SCHMITT

Schönberg im Westerwald

ACKNOWLEDGMENTS

I thank the people who have contributed to this book through their work and drawings. I am most grateful to Laura Ann Lee who accompanied the book through its different stages for her numerous suggestions, corrections, and drawings. Special thanks to Christopher Alexander, Charles Moore, Peter Eisenman, Ulrich Flemming, Bill Jepson, Yehuda Kalay, Paul Laseau, Robin Liggett, Patricia MacIntosh, William Mitchell, Antonino Saggio, George Stiny, and Robert Woodbury, who in their function as my teachers, colleagues, and critiques helped to make the writing of this book an exciting experience. I am also thankful to Anna Matyas, who helped in the final editing, and the students who contributed through their illustrations. They are, in the order of their appearance in the text: Adam Stoller, Jean Christophe Robert, Nancy Barton, Donatella Orazi, Joel Murray, Brett Ligo, Clemente Duran-Ballen, Daniel Blander, Michael Gehr, Tassoula Hadjiyanni, Robert Hering, Alexander Biagioli, Richard Cobti, Norman Larson, Anastasia Haidos, Cynthia Massagli, Aaron Levin, Mark Aufdemberge, George Zaglakas, Chen Cheng Chen, Heng Jung Hsiung, Gen Shong Lo, Fang Yuan Chih, and Weiguang Zhang.

CONTENTS

Introduction / 1

PART ONE: MICROCOMPUTERS IN THE TRADITIONAL DESIGN APPROACH   3

1. A Traditional Design Process / 5

    1.1. Microcomputers in the Traditional Design Process / 6

2. Basic Skills / 11

    2.1. Points and Lines / 12
    2.2. Tracing / 18
    2.3. Sketching / 25

3. Representation / 29

    3.1. Scale / 30
    3.2. Plans / 34
    3.3. Sections / 39
    3.4. Elevations / 44
    3.5. Axonometric and Oblique Projections / 52
    3.6. Perspective Projection / 59

4. Manipulation / 69

    4.1. Transformation / 70
    4.2. Repetition / 75
    4.3. Extrusion / 79

PART TWO: INNOVATIVE DESIGN APPROACHES 83

5. A New Design Approach / 85
   5.1. Computer-assisted Architectural Design / 86

6. Abstraction / 89
   6.1. Architectural Language / 90
   6.2. Vocabulary / 95
   6.3. Relations / 99
   6.4. Rules / 102
   6.5. Grammar / 107
   6.6. Programming / 114

7. Discovery / 121
   7.1. Search in Architectural Design / 122
   7.2. Representation of Architectural Design / 126
   7.3. Inference and Reasoning in Architecture / 129

8. Creativity / 133
   8.1. Architectural Creativity / 134
   8.2. Support Utilities / 136
   8.3. Fractals / 141

9. Evaluation / 151
   9.1. Energy Performance Evaluation / 153
   9.2. Cost Evaluation / 158
   9.3. Structural Evaluation / 160
   9.4. Integration of Design Evaluations / 164

Appendix A. Sample Programs in AutoLISP / 171
   A.1. Three Programs to Draw Windows / 172
   A.2. CCURVE.LSP: A Program to Build C-Curves / 179
   A.3. Three Simple Shape Grammar Programs / 182
   A.4. Two Programs to Draw Three-dimensional Vaults and Domes / 190

Bibliography / 197

Index / 205

Introduction

Since the advent of the digital computer, the potential to model, predict, and analyze future reality has taken a quantum leap. Similar to other disciplines, architecture and design have begun to take advantage of the availability of increasing computing power to create, examine, and assess design alternatives in the context of an underlying model. Analysis and predictions based on a model are valid if the model embodies the causal relationships observed in reality. If such models can be integrated in the design decision-making process, improvements in efficiency and design quality may exceed present standards. Visual communication between external media and the designer is fundamental to the design process. Consequently, the graphical capabilities of microcomputers and the operations on the underlying mathematical and knowledge-based models are the main focus of this book.

Conceptual frameworks for the use of graphic representation can be of major benefit in the architectural design process. The approaches developed in the past concentrated on the use of manual and semiautomated tools. With the introduction of inexpensive and powerful microcomputers came a new set of possibilities to develop and present architectural design. Since the middle of the 1980s, a paradigm change in architectural computing has taken place. This development has been predicted for the last 20 years. However, the rapid pace and tremendous impact on the architectural profession are surprising. The wave of new software and hardware creates the need for a new conceptual framework to integrate the new tool in the design process. The second part of this book outlines such a new framework.

As in the past, the new technology is primarily used to accomplish the same results as the old technology in less time and with less effort. Most of the present architectural computer programs do exactly that. The first part of the book will describe this development. Needless to say, the capabilities of the new machines would be wasted if they would not be applied to new, unexpected tasks. The same holds true for applications that were not considered before because the present tools are not suited to achieve them or due to the fact the new machines are used mainly by nonarchitects. The second part of the book will explore these innovative uses of the new machines.

PART ONE

Microcomputers in the Traditional Design Approach

1
A Traditional Design Process

Universities and professionals are beginning to integrate microcomputers in the teaching of design and in the individual design process in ways that range from ad hoc pragmatic decisions to carefully planned approaches [Kemper85]. Simply by implementation, computers have become a part of the traditional design process over the last few years [Stoller87]. The adapted view for the first part of this book defines design as a rational decision-making and problem-solving process in which graphical representation is a necessary vehicle for recording ideas and different design stages.

According to this view, the design process is a procedure whereby a given architectural program is translated into built form. The result of the process should satisfy a number of criteria, namely, client satisfaction and contextual integrity. In architectural practice, the process is traditionally broken down into the following steps:

1. Program development,
2. Schematic design,
3. Preliminary design,
4. Design development,
5. Contract documents,
6. Shop drawings,
7. Construction.

Successful progression from one step to the next requires effective problem-solving techniques. One possible problem-solving model is the following five-step procedure [Laseau80]:

1. *Problem and Design Objectives Definition.* The limits of the problem to be solved are identified. The problem is decomposed into parts and then analyzed. Constraints and resources are evaluated. Design objectives are established.
2. *Development of Alternatives.* The designer explores several solutions and develops viable alternatives.
3. *Evaluation.* Design evaluation criteria are applied according to the design objectives. Alternative solutions are rated using the design criteria and appropriate weighting factors.
4. *Selection.* One alternative is selected based on the results of the evaluation. Often, there is no overall best alternative. In this case, successful parts of several alternatives may be combined. This requires a reevaluation.
5. *Communication.* The final solution to the problem must be described in an appropriate way, that is, it must be usable for the integration into the next design step and for presentation to the client.

Traditionally, the development from initial sketches to a completed design solution was performed as a process of stepwise refinement, using external media to record and represent intermediate and final stages of design. This chapter begins to explore how microcomputers can support the tasks of problem definition, development of alternatives, evaluation, selection, and communication.

1.1 MICROCOMPUTERS IN THE TRADITIONAL DESIGN PROCESS

If the traditional process of design was perfectly organized and needed no further improvement, the necessity to introduce computers into the architectural office and teaching environment would be questionable. However, more than four fifths of the architecture offices in the United States use computers in some capacity. Given the capital-intensive nature of computers, the decision to buy expensive equipment must promise some benefit to architects and educators. What are these benefits and in which areas of the design process are they applicable? It is of paramount importance in the traditional design process that each step be explained and reevaluated. A more detailed look at the individual design stages will reveal differences and benefits in using the computer as compared to the traditional methods:

1. **Problem and Design Objectives Definition.** The main advantage of the computer in this stage is its use as an organizational aid, able to perform quick references and comparisons to define needs, constraints, and resources. Word processing, spread sheet, and database operations are typical applications. Word processing programs have reached high-quality standards at very low cost. The electronic spread sheet, a relatively new invention, has penetrated the market in less than half a decade and made its main distributor one of the largest software companies. Its benefits for simple what-if calculations and for looking at data graphically are unquestionable. Database management systems have migrated from mainframes to microcomputers and are useful tools to manage large quantities of data.

2. **Development of Alternatives.** Paint systems are popular tools to express design ideas in their very early stage. These programs allow the user to quickly develop alternatives by sketching ideas in black and white or in color, using a stylus, light pen, or mouse as input devices. It is interesting to note that students develop impressive drawing skills with the new input devices. There is still a missing high-quality commercial link between the sketching process and the transformation into an exact two- or three-dimensional model, although research in this area has a 20-year history. Drafting programs allow the user to easily manipulate a well-defined geometric representation of a building. Modification and manipulation of one solution is the single most useful application. Chapter 4 addresses this issue in particular. The consistent storage of different alternatives and their use in later design stages is guaranteed if sufficient mass storage is available.

3. **Evaluation.** The evaluation of design alternatives, a critical activity in the design process, is only now becoming computerized. Chapter 9 is dedicated to this issue. However, the necessary analyses on which evaluations are based offer application areas for microcomputers. Computers are strongest in performing quantitative analysis, such as energy or cost analysis. Available tools are generic commercial software packages or dedicated analysis programs. Templates for spread sheet and database management programs fall into the first category, whereas complex structural analysis programs fall into the second category. The application of microcomputers in the evaluation process requires the existence of a framework and the definition of appropriate criteria, such as energy budgets or costs. Without this framework, the benefits of using microcomputers in the evaluation phase will be marginal because no programs exist yet that produce an integrated assessment of the quality of a particular design proposal.

4. **Selection.** Decision support systems can help select one alternative, based on direct numerical comparisons and heuristics, previous experiences, and rules of thumb. It is unlikely, however, that complete

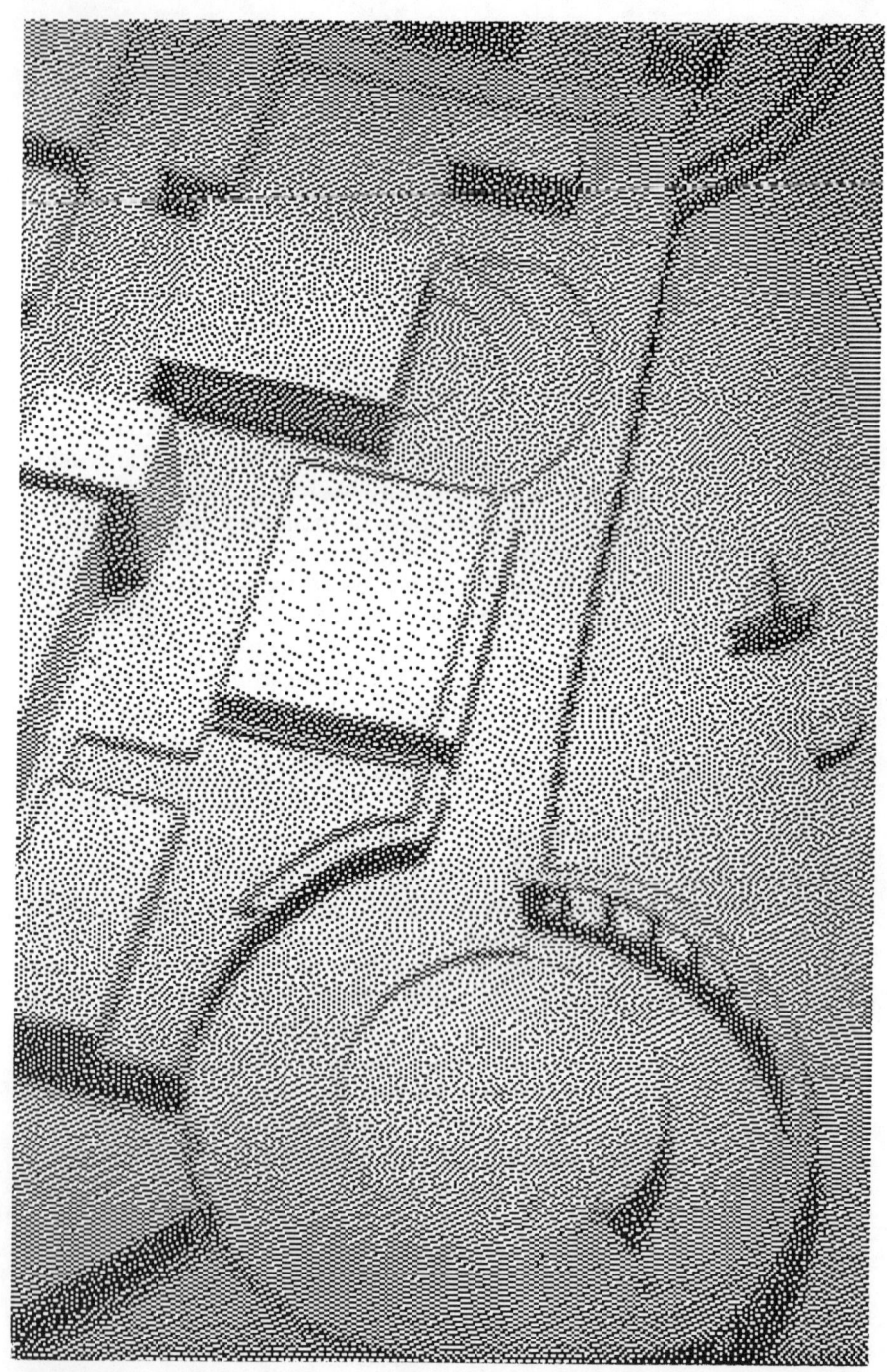

Figure 1.1a View of a manually built massing model transferred to MacPaint from MacVision.

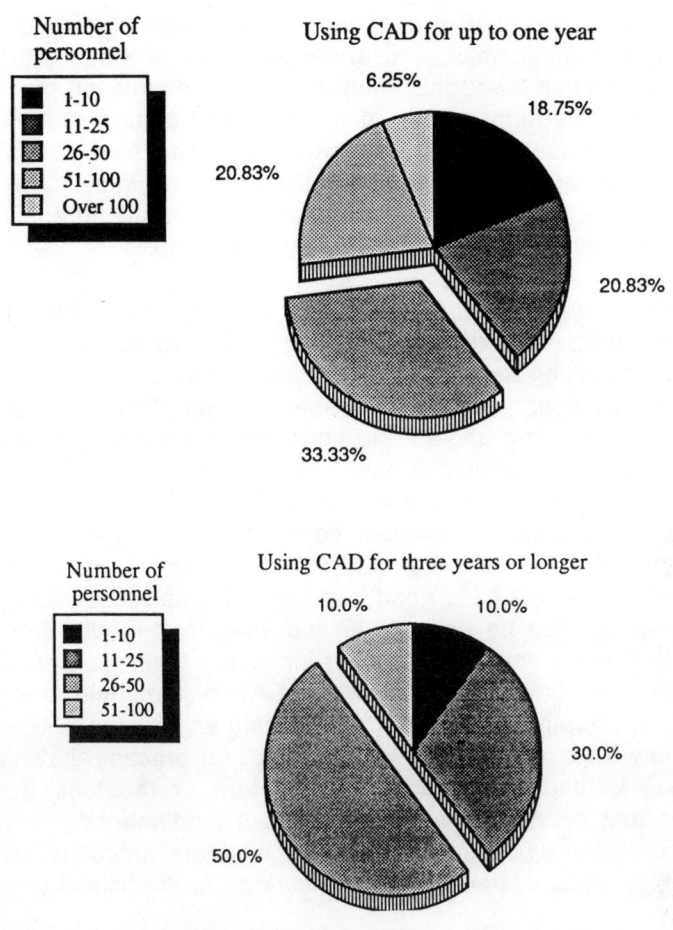

Figure 1.1b Size of architectural firms having used CAD for up to 1 year (top), and for 3 years or longer (bottom). Adam Stoller.

decision support systems will be available for the average architect or student in the near future. The excessive amount of decision objects, operations, and rules required hinders the development of an architectural decision support system to select design alternatives that could equal or outperform humans. Although dozens of commercial decision support systems or shells to construct such systems are on the market, there are few architectural applications that go beyond the solution of toy problems. Evaluation and selection are closely related and should be computationally integrated.

5. **Communication.** This involves communication between clients and partners of the design team, as well as communication between the designer and the representation of the design in its different stages.

Microcomputers are able to expedite the exchange of information: Text is sent by electronic mail, and entire sketches or small drawings are transmitted through electronic channels. The presentation process itself improves with the high degree of accuracy and editing capabilities that most microcomputer drafting programs offer. The possibilities of color use and visual effects are virtually unlimited (see Figure 1.1a). Limitations do exist in the size of the screens; there are still no equivalents to large and beautifully rendered architectural drawings.

In reality, these five steps will not be executed so rigidly. The creative design process lives from breaking certain rules, redefining objectives, and assigning new weighting factors. With the exception of quick what-if calculations in spread sheet applications, or automatic redefinition of viewing angles, the computer will produce results slower than experienced humans. It has, however, the advantage of requiring decision making that is explicit and explainable.

In the architectural profession, computers are increasingly used in small firms. Previous to 1983, only 10% of all firms installing computer-aided design systems (CAD) had less than 10 employees. This percentage almost doubled between 1983 and 1986 (see Figure 1.1b). Firms with more than 50 employees further increased their use of CAD. More than 80% of the firms presently owning CAD systems intend to increase their use of computers, particularly in drafting and design [Stoller87].

The new tools are introduced into a design process that has developed over centuries. Based on the nature of the tool, it must be expected that computers will gradually, but fundamentally, change the traditional design process. The following chapters speculate on how this change may occur in the given framework of the traditional design process.

2
Basic Skills

The use of microcomputers will free architects and designers from many routine tasks. However, a set of basic drawing and drafting skills are necessary to produce clear and attractive computer-generated drawings. In the first phase of introducing microcomputers in the design environment, it is useful to compare the three traditional design-related activities of drafting, tracing, and sketching with their equivalent in the new design environment. The question of where these traditional activities fit into the new design process will be addressed in the second part of this book.

Section 2.1 deals with drawing points and lines using computer programs. All current commercial microcomputer drafting packages offer this capability. Although the computer-generated lines may contain similar attributes to the manually produced lines, they contain completely different information. Computer-generated lines are defined by the coordinates of their end points, thus expressing the line as an abstract object. Manually drawn points and lines actually have substance and structure; they consist of graphite or ink. Only when the computer-generated lines are translated from their temporary and abstract existence on a display screen to paper, they become similar to traditional lines. This abstract character of points and lines offers many new possibilities of manipulation.

Section 2.2 addresses tracing, an important activity to represent any form of existing context. Tracing with manual methods is relatively easy and straightforward. It requires, however, constant decisions of selection and omission. Only relevant parts of the context are translated into new drawings. Microcomputers offer a range of possibilities to support and partially replace the traditional process.

Section 2.3 addresses sketching. The traditional sketching process involves selecting the object, observing it, making decisions about the critical and less important elements, and then drawing it in a multiple-step process. Orthogonal, axonometric, or perspective sketches are the result. Microcomputers do not support a direct equivalent of this process. However, there are some techniques that could improve the traditional sketching process.

2.1 POINTS AND LINES

Points and lines are the fundamental building blocks of most architectural drawings. Drawing points and lines as a means of graphic communication is a basic skill that most people learn at an early age, thus, it becomes a natural part of education and personal expression. In the past, all drawings were permanently recorded on some kind of external medium, most often on paper. Such permanent records can be produced with computer programs as well in the form of prints or computer plots. The interaction with the drawing—editing and visual feedback—happens mainly on the computer screen. The points and lines appearing on the computer screen are not permanent and will disappear with the termination of the program. The information they represent, however, can be recorded in the computer's permanent memory, the disk.

Lines are differentiated by attributes such as thickness, type, color, and intensity. These attributes have some equivalent on the computer screen:

1. **Line Thickness.** The equivalent of using pens of varying thickness (see Figure 2.1a) is to change the thickness of a line on the screen by highlighting a greater number or fewer pixels between two points. If the resolution of the screen is high, the pixels will not appear as individual "boxes" but will form a smooth line of varying thickness. The resolution of a computer screen is measured by the number of pixels displayed in the x and y direction. A second measure is the size of the pixel, sometimes referred to as "dots per inch." The more dots per inch displayed, the higher the resolution. Acceptable resolutions start with 640 by 480 pixels on a 13-inch screen (see Figure 2.1b).

2. **Line Type.** The equivalent of using different line types on paper (see Figure 2.1a) is to highlight only certain parts of a line on the computer screen. The consistency of different line types is sometimes difficult to maintain manually. For this reason, templates are available. On the computer screen, these consistency problems do not exist once the line type has been defined. The equivalent to traditional templates are computer menus for different line types.

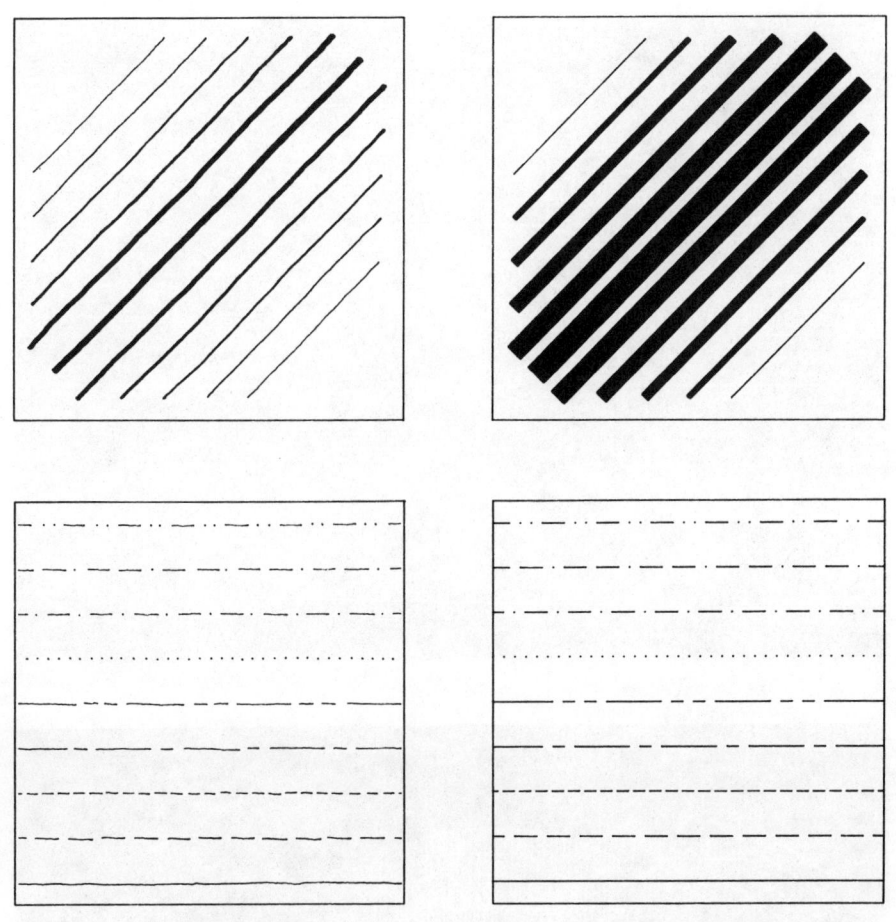

Figure 2.1a Freehand lines of varying thickness (top left), computer-generated lines of varying thickness (top right), freehand lines of varying line type (bottom left), computer-generated lines of different line type (bottom right).

3. **Line Color.** The equivalent of drawing a color line on a piece of paper is to display a colored line on a color graphics display. Different color lines can also vary in thickness and line type. Depending on the screen and graphics processor type, the simultaneous display from 2 to more than 256 different colors is possible, out of a palette of several million.

4. **Line intensity.** Different line intensities are easily achieved through some traditional drawing media by applying greater or less force of a pencil on paper. The equivalent on the computer screen is to highlight certain lines by increasing their intensity (see Figure 2.1c). Line intensity is a particularly important issue for programs that display the drawing background in black. Most programs allow the user to choose the screen background color.

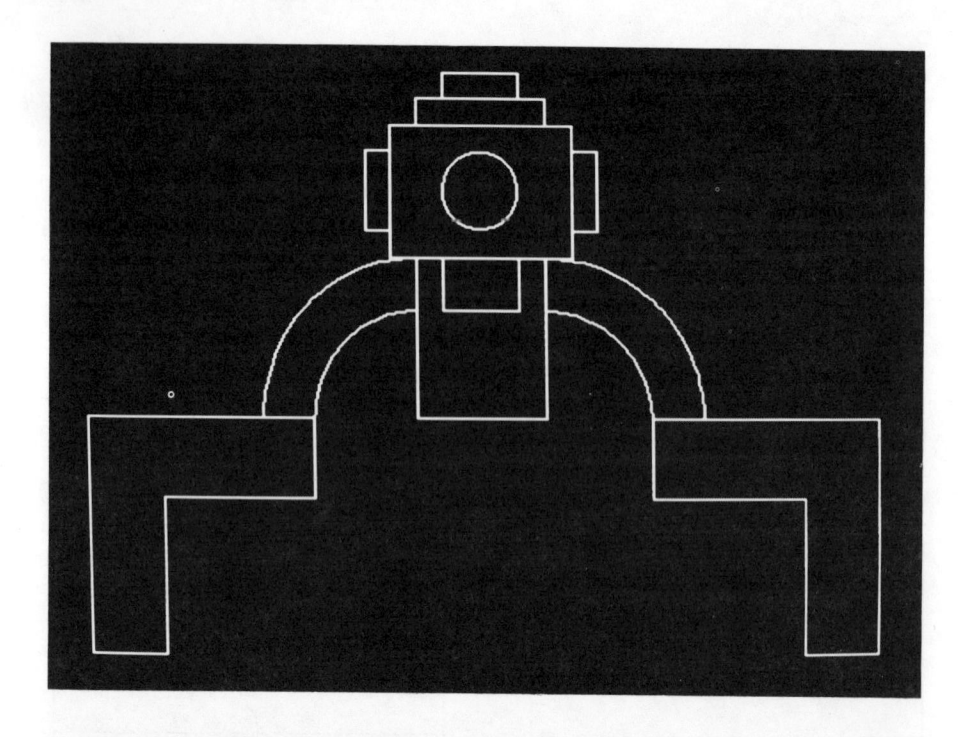

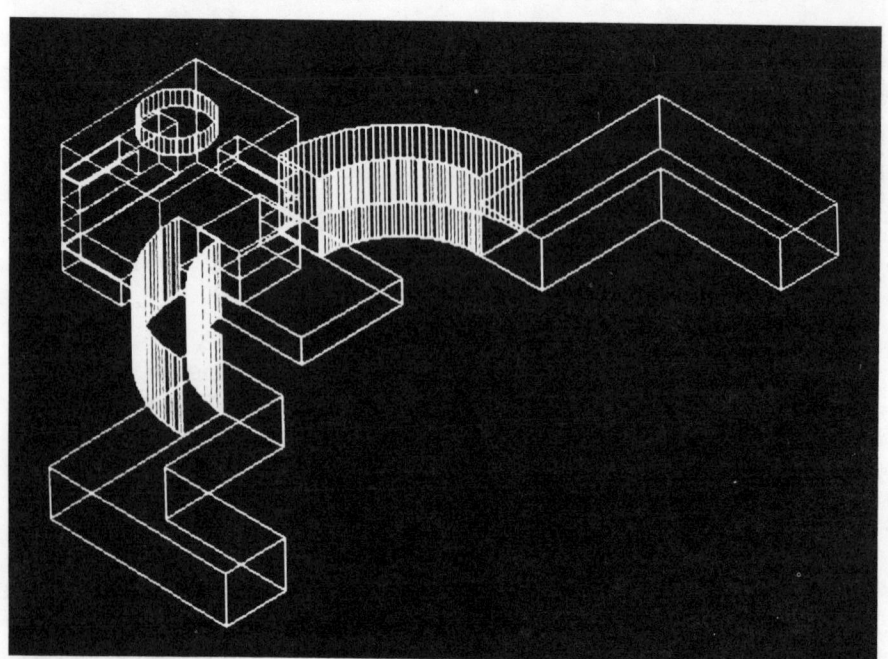

Figure 2.1b Palladian Villa wireframe. White lines on a high-resolution computer screen produced with DRAW. Jean Christophe Robert.

Figure 2.1c Top: varying line intensity to simulate light and shadow. Bottom: varying line intensity to highlight ornaments on the screen. Nancy Barton.

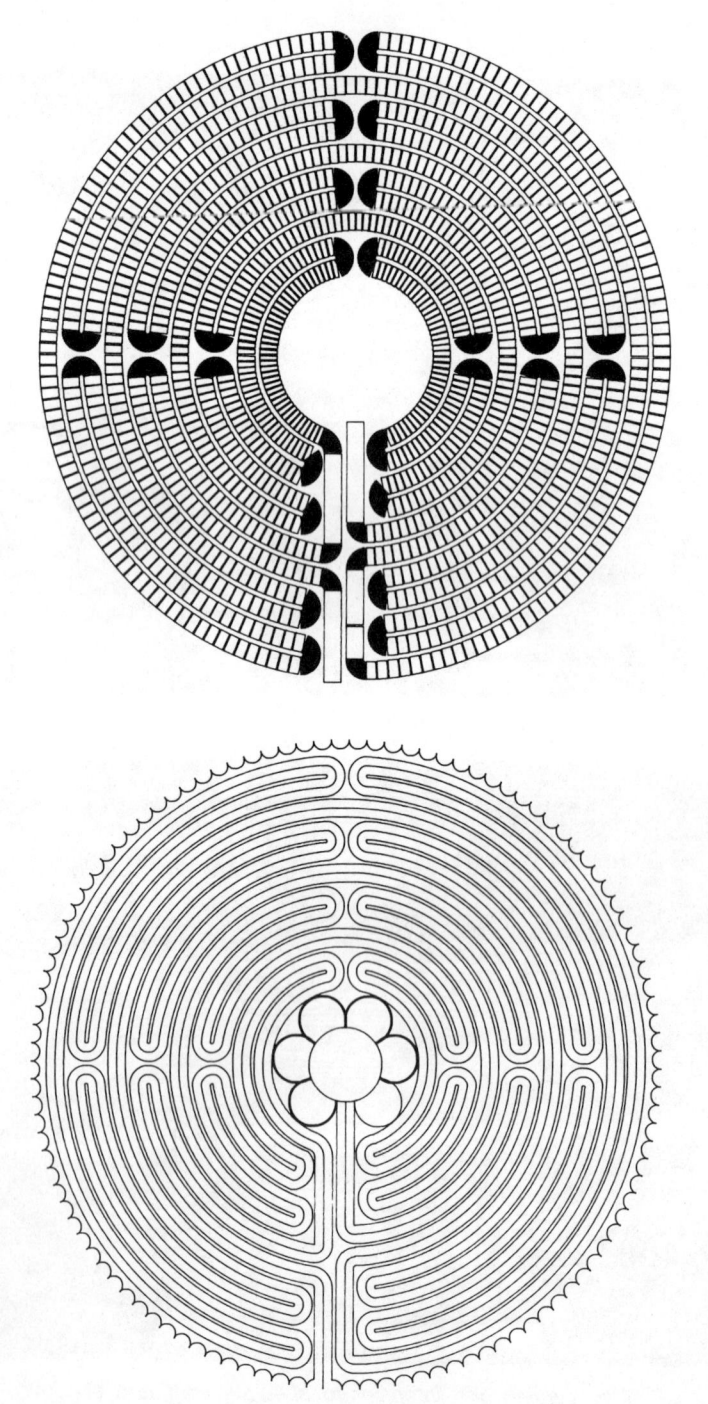

Figure 2.1d   Two drawings of the Labyrinth in the cathedral of Chartres (12th century): examples of computer accuracy and line quality.

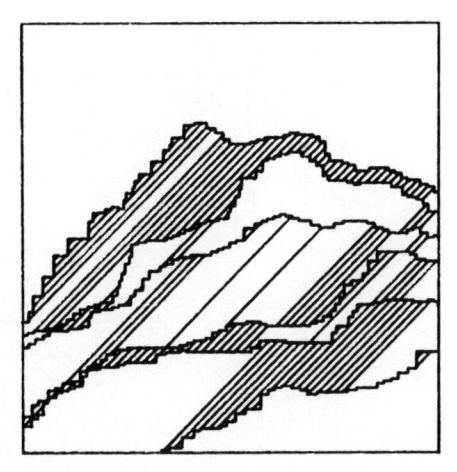

Figure 2.1e Manual sketch of mountains (left), computer sketch of mountains using hatching (right).

Although on the surface manual and computer techniques seem to have similar results and capabilities, some fundamental differences must be addressed:

1. The initial capital invested to draw points and lines with traditional media, such as pencil and paper, is much less than the capital invested to achieve the equivalent on the computer. The difference becomes particularly apparent when color and high-resolution screens and plotter or printer output are needed. However, the quality and accuracy of lines, in particular curves, can be greatly enhanced with the computer (see Figure 2.1d).
2. The display on a computer screen is temporary. To record points and lines permanently on a computer, they must be stored in a file in a set format. The content of the file is not usually transparent for the user. This does not usually present a problem, though the risk of losing a file exists in the case of physical damage to the disk.
3. To replicate a traditional drawing by printing or plotting the equivalent with the computer requires an additional investment. Plotters and printers can produce high-quality point and line drawings at a price proportional to the output quality.
4. Some characteristics of manual drawings cannot yet be replicated easily with microcomputers, such as freehand lines (see Figure 2.1e) or lines with varying thickness and intensity. Although some programs offer options such as "overshooting" lines, there presently is no true equivalent on the microcomputer to a high-quality freehand drawing, neither in size nor resolution.

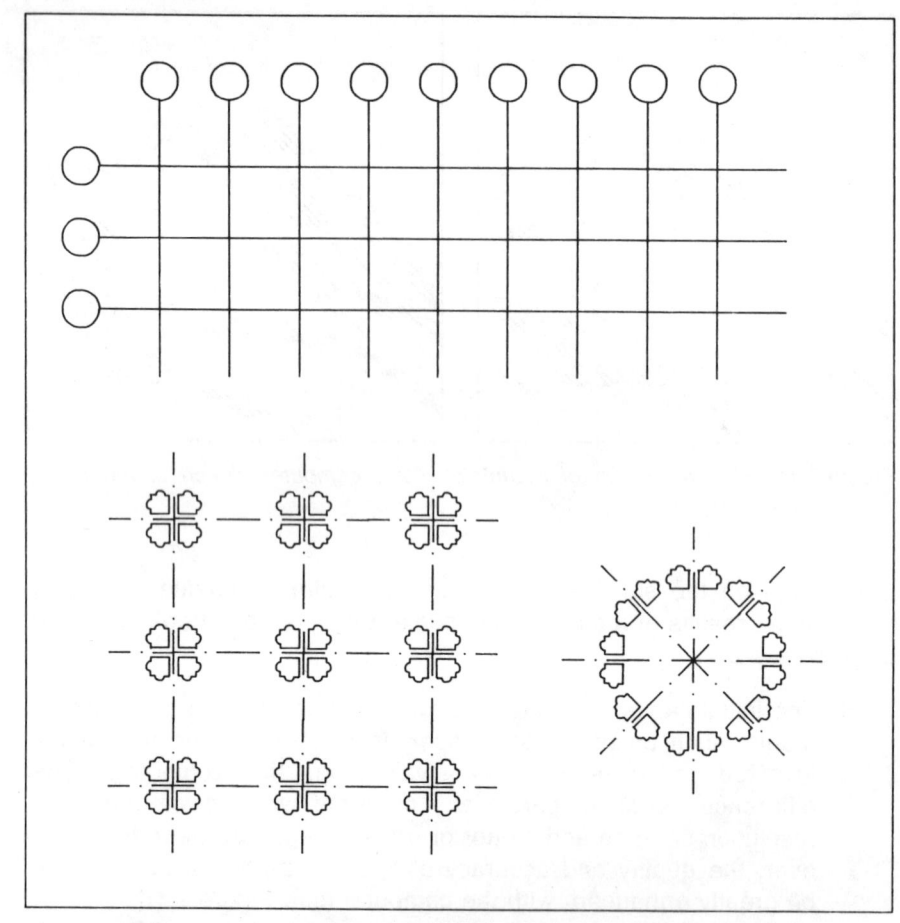

Figure 2.1f Using points and lines as underlying grids and axes.

Points and lines can function as underlying grids and axes. This task is often difficult to achieve manually but can be easily handled with most microcomputers. Once the grid spacing and the number of rows and columns are defined, the grid can be created as an underlay (see Figure 2.1f). As points and lines are fundamental primitives in many drawings, they act as a basis for the applications described in the following sections.

2.2 TRACING

Tracing describes a technique to selectively or completely transfer a previously drawn document or photograph to a new drawing. With the existing building stock growing each year and the resulting increase of

Figure 2.2a Entrance to the Villa Rotonda. Computer "tracing" or scanning with ThunderScan. Antonino Saggio.

renovation and remodeling activities, intelligent tracing takes on an important support role in the design process.

Tracing is a form of interpretation whereby only a selected part of the image information is transferred. Traditional tracing requires the use of transparent or translucent media to be placed over the original. Important parts of the image to be traced can be highlighted by varying line thickness or line type. Tracing is particularly important for permanent storage of standard details that can then be used repeatedly.

The microcomputer offers two distinct procedures as an equivalent to tracing: semiautomatic digitizing and automatic scanning. The first technique requires the original to be placed on a digitizer. The original is followed line by line, marking each end of a line by pushing a button or by clicking with the stylus. As the original is entered on the digitizer, the corresponding lines appear on the screen and can later be edited. A major advantage of digitizing is that the translated drawing may be supplied with attributes in the digitizing process.

The second technique of tracing an original line drawing is scanning, the process of optically evaluating an original drawing, pixel by pixel, and of then storing the result in the computer's memory (see Figure 2.2a). Thus, lines on the original drawing can be translated into lines on the screen. Scanning is a computing and memory-intensive procedure. Advanced scanning devices allow the vectorization of the drawing, meaning that the pixels encountered on the original drawing are evaluated for their continuity, and are connected to lines if they are continuous. New and sophisticated scanning devices also allow the selective recording of an image, that is, only vertical lines or lines of a certain thickness or another selected specification will be transferred.

Figure 2.2b Photograph of the Willow II chair by Charles Rennie Mackintosh. Atelier International.

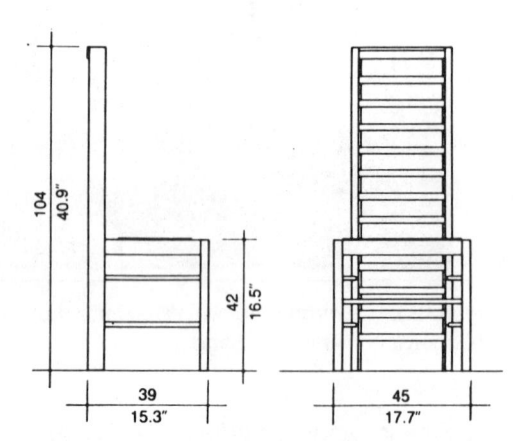

Figure 2.2c Dimensioned side and front elevation of the Willow II chair by Charles Rennie Mackintosh. Atelier International.

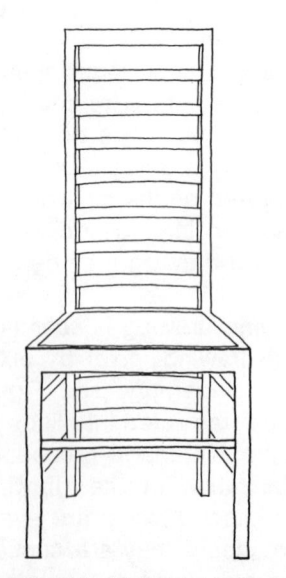

Figure 2.2d Manual tracing of the Willow II chair front elevation. Laura Ann Lee.

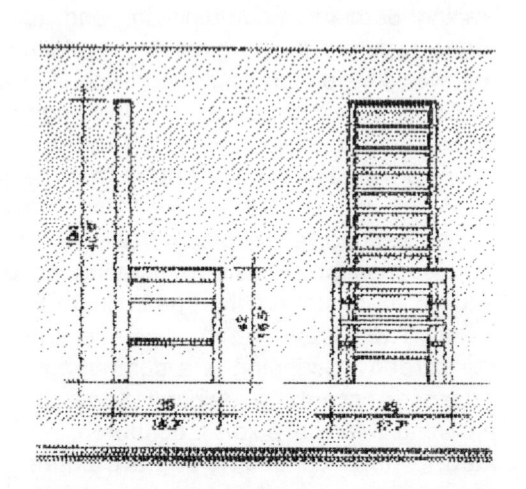

Figure 2.2e Computer tracing of the Willow II chair with ThunderScan.

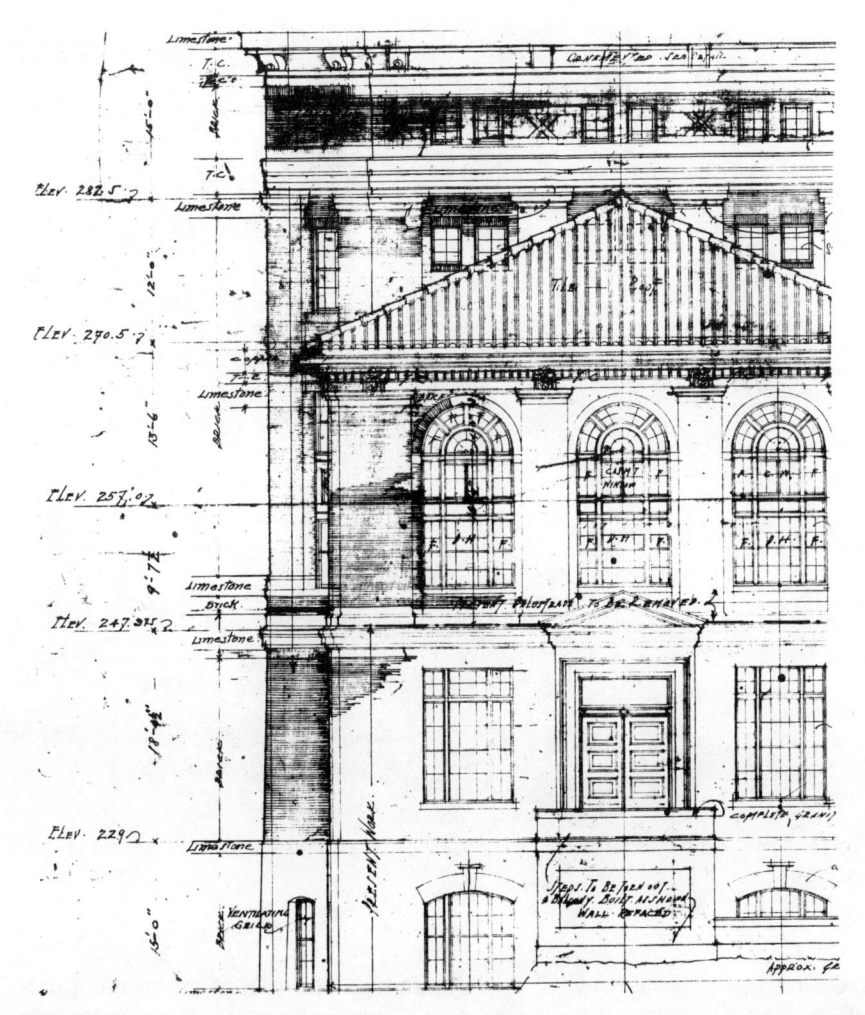

Figure 2.2f   A blueprint of the original elevation of Hamerschlag Hall, Carnegie Mellon University, by Henry Hornbostel.

Figure 2.2b shows a photograph of the Willow II Chair by Charles Rennie Mackintosh. Figure 2.2c is a set of dimensioned orthogonal projections of the same object, produced by measuring the real chair. Figure 2.2d is an attempt to improve the three-dimensional readability of the two-dimensional projection by tracing. The parts closer to the viewer are drawn in a heavier line weight, the parts further away in a lighter line weight. Lines belonging to parts further away do not touch the lines in the foreground to strengthen the impression of depth. Computer programs exist that employ the same visual "trick" [Emde87]. The result of a computer scanning operation of the dimensioned orthogonal views is shown in Figure 2.2e. The scanner operates by sensing light and dark

Figure 2.2g Hamerschlag Hall. Using a low-resolution scanner to trace the original blueprint.

spots on the original drawing and sends the information to the computer, which in turn displays it on the screen [ThunderScan85]. Due to the resolution of the scanner, straight lines in the original become a series of dots, with the result that numbers and thin lines are difficult to read. Manual editing of the scanned image can dramatically improve the result.

Figure 2.2f is the blueprint of an original construction drawing for an engineering building by Henry Hornbostel produced in 1913. The attempt to scan the elevation results in Figure 2.2g. Manual editing could improve the results, but obviously the delicacy of the original drawing imposes limits: Some of the original lines are thinner than the smallest increments in the scanning device and are therefore difficult to represent with pixels. Figure 2.2h is the result of digitizing. The original was placed on the digitizer, a reference origin was established, and the drawing was selectively input. In this case, a combination of direct input

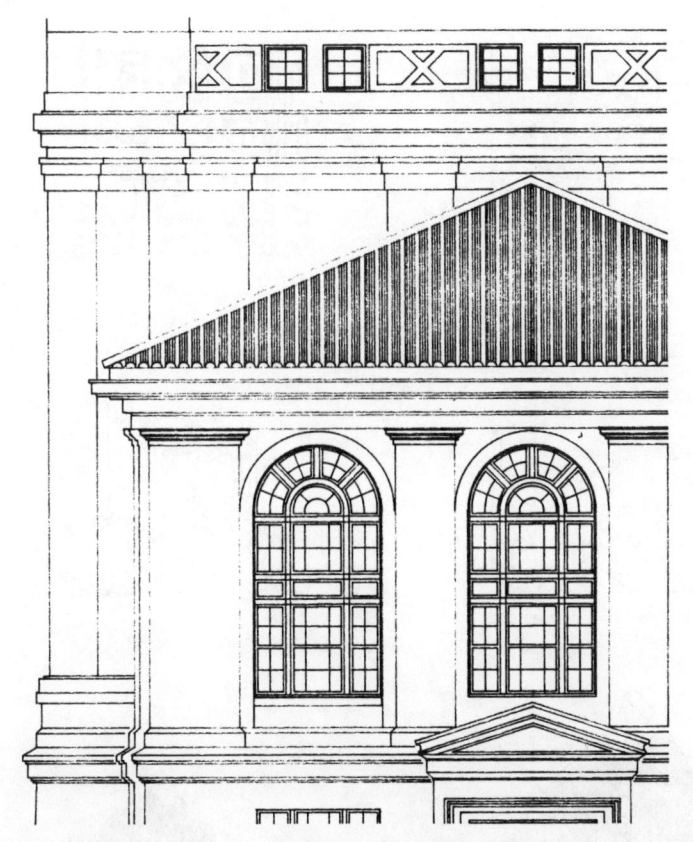

Figure 2.2h Hamerschlag Hall. Computer-generated plot of digitized elevation.

and digitizing techniques was used: Absolute dimensions were input where they appear on the original elevation to guarantee the accuracy of the traced drawing. In addition, the original elevation contains a number of symmetrical and repetitive elements. These properties were used to further simplify the tracing process. After one side of the repetitive elements, such as the windows, was digitized, it was mirrored and then repeated. This technique will be described in depth later.

The examples demonstrate some of the strengths and weaknesses of computer-aided tracing techniques. An ideal computer tool would support a combination of very high resolution scanning (up to 3000 dots per inch), vectorization, digitizing, and direct input. It is realistic to expect such tools in the near future. The strength of computer-aided scanning lies in the ability to transfer images onto the screen (see Figure 2.2i). All operations described in the following chapters may be performed from this point on.

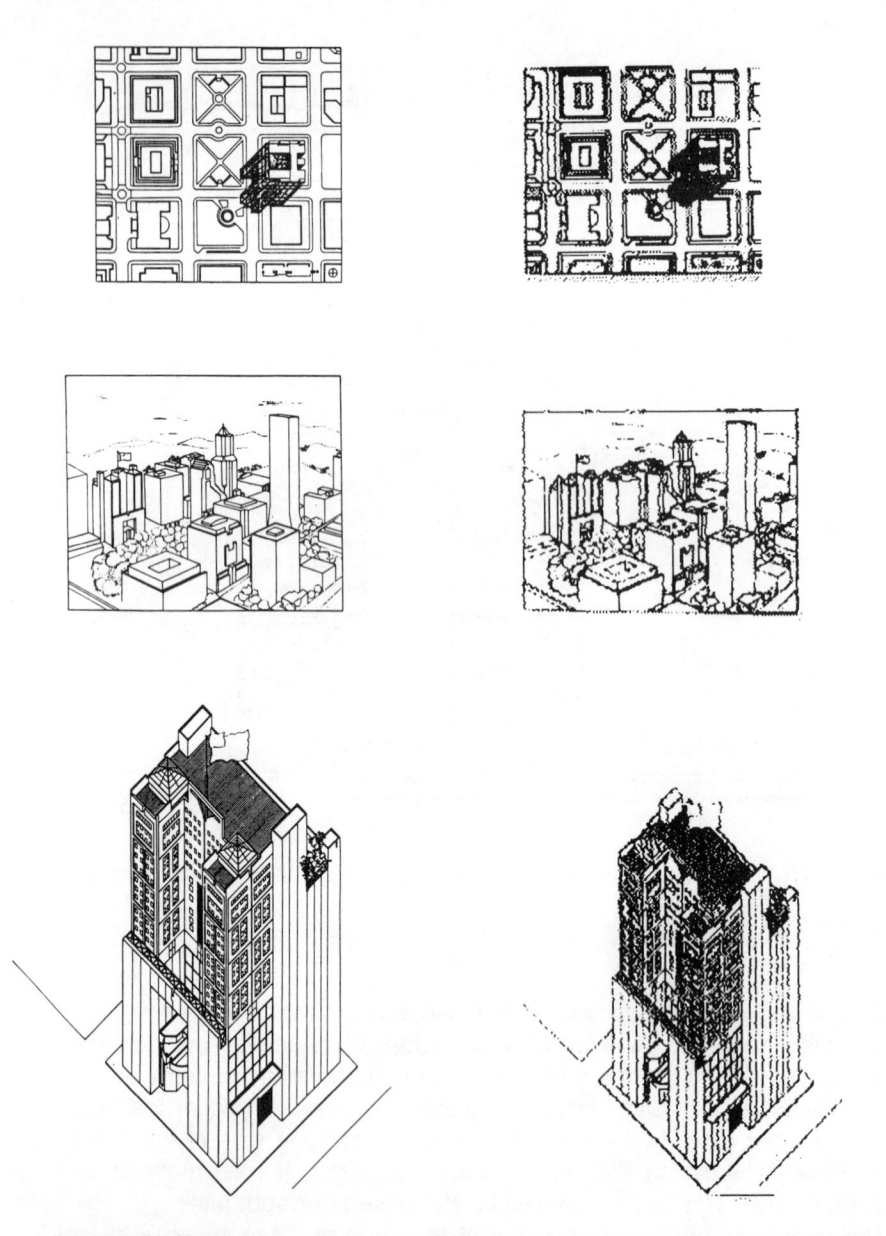

Figure 2.2i Downtown Portland, Oregon. Manual drawing and computer-scanned plan (top), manual drawing and computer-scanned perspective (center), manual drawing and computer-scanned axonometric of a proposed building for Portland using ThunderScan. Donatella Orazi.

2.3 SKETCHING

It could be argued that manual tracing is an almost mechanical mapping activity from a two-dimensional original to a two-dimensional interpretation and is therefore easily imitated by computers. Manual sketching, however, requires highly developed skills of seeing an object, processing this three-dimensional information, and drawing a two-dimensional representation. In terms of visual information processing, this is a formidable task that no computer has yet solved to perfection. Relevant research areas in computer vision and the interpretation of three-dimensional sceneries have not matured to a point where they are commercially available for microcomputers at acceptable prices.

Various manual techniques have emerged that are helpful in building a sketch. Upon the selection of an appropriate viewpoint, basic sketching involves a three-step procedure: building the basic structure, filling in the tones, and finally adding details [Laseau80].

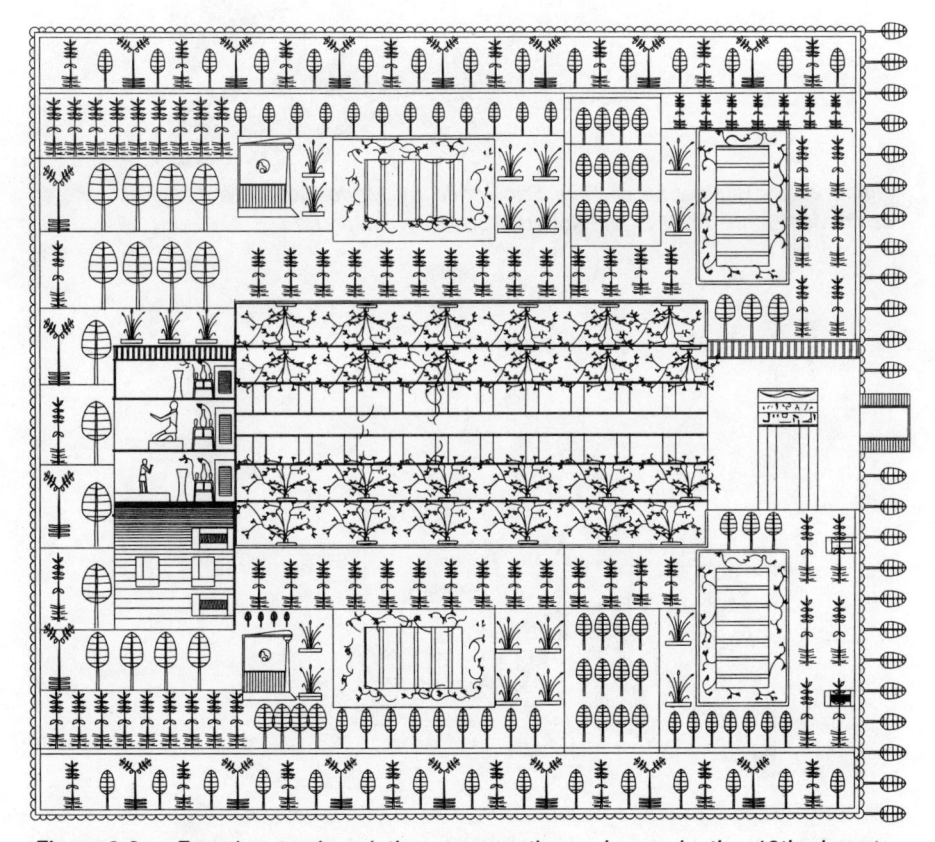

Figure 2.3a Egyptian tomb painting representing a house in the 18th dynasty. Computer sketch. Joel Murray.

Figure 2.3b Residence at Riva San Vitale by Mario Botta. A computer sketch using MacPaint. Brett Ligo. Robert Woodbury, instructor.

Figure 2.3c Saynatsalo Town Hall by Alvar Aalto. A computer sketch using MacPaint. Clemente Duran-Ballen. Robert Woodbury, instructor.

It is possible to mimic sketch drawing procedures with the computer. (see Figure 2.3a) One of the classic computer sketching and drawing programs does exactly that: create the illusion that the user was sketching on the computer screen by moving a mouse on the table [MacPaint83]. Besides the common pen, the user can select other means of drawing from a set of icons, among them completely "electronic" drawing utilities, such as rubber band and canvas sketching. Programs with such capabilities are commonly known as paint programs. They are related to manual painting as they store the resulting image two dimensionally, screen pixel by screen pixel (see Figure 2.3b and Figure 2.3c). Other computer tools to create structured graphics [MacDraw84] store drawing primitive coordinates in addition to screen pixels and consequently offer more manipulation options. Whereas manual sketches consist mainly of lines—if a pen is used—the computer is not restricted to these primitives. All serious CAD programs offer a range of utilities to facilitate sketching:

1. *Electronic Pen.* A stylus, mouse, or light pen is moved on the drawing surface and the corresponding movement appears as a line on the screen in the selected line type, thickness, and color. Depending on screen resolution and sketching accuracy, the lines will be smooth or appear stepped (see also Figure 2.1b).
2. *Rubber-band Lines.* The beginning of the line is marked on the screen. The second point of the line can be moved dynamically on the screen until it is in the appropriate location. Thus, the location and length of any line can be tested before it is finalized. The line can also be erased immediately after it has been drawn, another advantage over manual drawing.
3. *Rubber-band Rectangles.* One corner of the rectangle is marked. The opposite corner of the rectangle may be dragged across the screen until it falls into the appropriate location where it may be fixed with a click. This technique allows easy sketching of elevations and rectalinear surfaces. It is limiting, however, for perspective sketches.
4. *Moving and Copying.* Repetitive tasks such as drawing windows can be facilitated by drawing the part once and then copying and moving it to the appropriate position. Mistakes on the screen can sometimes be corrected by moving the object to the correct location.
5. *Filling in Tones.* Once an entity on the screen, such as a polygon, has been defined and closed (an absolute necessity), it can be filled with patterns. They reach from press-type patterns such as lines, stars, or crosses to entirely user-defined patterns.
6. *Painting and Spraying.* The bit mapped displays offer various

paintbrush and spraying techniques. As the cursor is moved on the screen, it leaves a trace of patterns of varying density, shape, and color.

These utilities, used creatively, can help to create similar or superior sketches than manual techniques. However, a number of new constraints must be realized:

1. *Transportability.* The traditional sketchbook and pen are universal and portable tools that can be carried anywhere. Even the smallest and most powerful lap top microcomputer with the appropriate display and input devices is too cumbersome for easy transportation. Therefore, sketching with the computer on the site will not be an option for some time to come.
2. *Monotony.* Even though filling, painting, and spraying techniques offer variety, their appearance tends to be similar. The lively character of manual sketches may therefore be lost.
3. *Freehand Drawings.* Although the computer offers techniques for freehand drawing and sketching, it will take practice and much computer memory to achieve similar results to manual sketching.

The presentation of computer-generated sketches is not limited to the computer screen. It is possible to plot the sketch on a line plotter, printer plotter, or even a laser writer. The double translation from the original to the computer and then to the plotting medium can lead to unexpected results. These effects, once understood and controlled, can add richness to the traditional sketching techniques.

3
Representation

Representation in the traditional design process falls into two main categories: the representation and recording of design ideas during the design process (normally in a quick and sketchy form) and representation of a finalized design solution. The visual stimulation provided by the representation of an idea can lead to additional design solutions and helps to detect problems with the current solution. Representation of a finalized design solution is the formalized means of communication between the different players in the design and construction process.

Traditionally, design ideas are recorded on some form of external medium, normally paper. Permanent representation makes drawings readily accessible and comparable. These visual collections of ideas can become rather extensive. It is quite common to flip through a collection of several dozen preliminary sketches, select the promising ones, and view them simultaneously. Microcomputers with the present memory and display limitations do not offer a comparable capability. Different ideas must be stored in one large file or in many different files. The viewing and comparison of these ideas requires some experience.

Microcomputers offer advantages over the traditional process in representing final design drawings and in translating from design ideas to formalized design. Once even sketchy information has been recorded on the computer, it is relatively easy to transform these sketches into a finalized design and represent it. The important difference to the traditional methods lies in the evolving design: If input as a three-dimensional object, it can constantly be viewed in orthographic, parallel, and perspective projections. This facilitates editing of design ideas and final production of plots or hard copies.

3.1 SCALE

Scale is the numerical relation between the size of an object and the size of its representation. It is a powerful tool of abstraction and allows the representation of large objects on a limited-sized medium or the representation of very small objects on a larger sized medium. Scaling aids in the understanding of objects by reduction or enlargement.

The Cartesian coordinate system is the abstract geometric vehicle to describe an object in its physical extensions. Once an object is formalized as a mathematical model, transformations may be applied to this model. Traditionally, this is accomplished with templates or physical scales that represent fractions of the real-world scale (See Figure 3.1a).

Architectural applications offer few opportunities to represent real-world objects such as buildings, in a scale of 1 to 1, although for special applications full-size models were built [Schulze85]. Plans, sections, and elevations are limited in their size by their media. This limitation applies even more so to computer screens. Most CAD programs therefore work with a different understanding of scale that might be confusing

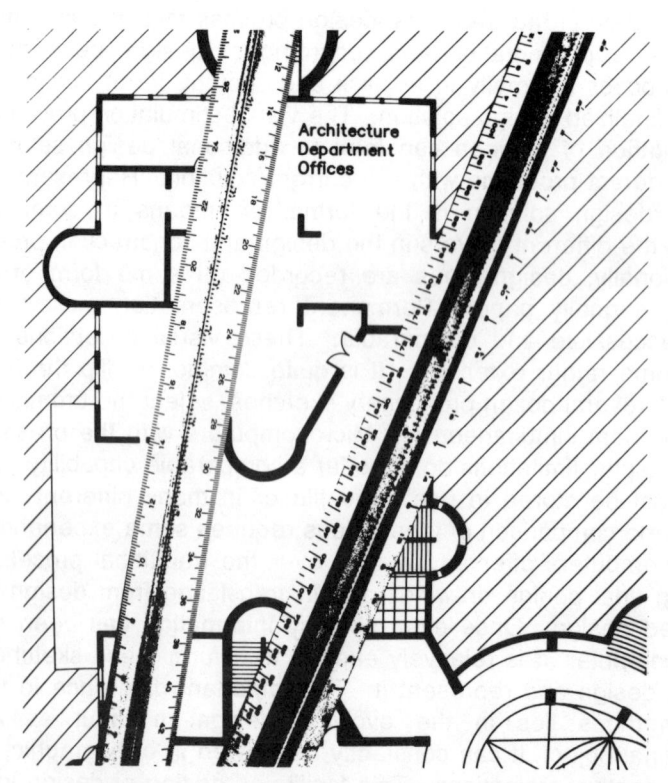

Figure 3.1a   Scales: tools unchanged over centuries.

Figure 3.1b A Henry Hornbostel window drawn to different scales.

at first, but results in a very powerful tool based on the notion of drawing units. Drawing units may be feet, inches, centimeters, meters, or another chosen increment. The physical drawing scale needs only to be dealt with and specified at the time of plotting. Thus, while the drawing is still an image on the screen, it is possible to zoom in and out to any level of detail.

Shortcomings of this approach do exist. Most architects are accustomed to drawing in a certain scale and become therefore confused in an environment without a given scale. First-time users of CAD systems tend to load all available information into one drawing. The discipline imposed by the traditional scale conventions are not supplied with computer programs and thus can lead to an information overload. The discipline to relate scale to an appropriate level of detail must be developed by the user or must be added to the system as intelligent front ends.

Figure 3.1b represents a window designed by Henry Hornbostel drawn to different scales. The viewer will notice that the proportion of the object does not change, but the character of the images changes from left to right. One reason is the line weight and thickness; they do not change for the three scales. The example demonstrates that the designer must be careful in using the same abstraction, the line, for representing objects at different scales.

Figure 3.1c shows an interesting capability of computer-aided scaling: A three-dimensional design is reduced in scale and placed inside the original design. The process of combining scaled versions of the same object has a long tradition in architecture and ornamental design.

Figure 3.1d appears similar to the previous example but is fundamen-

32 REPRESENTATION

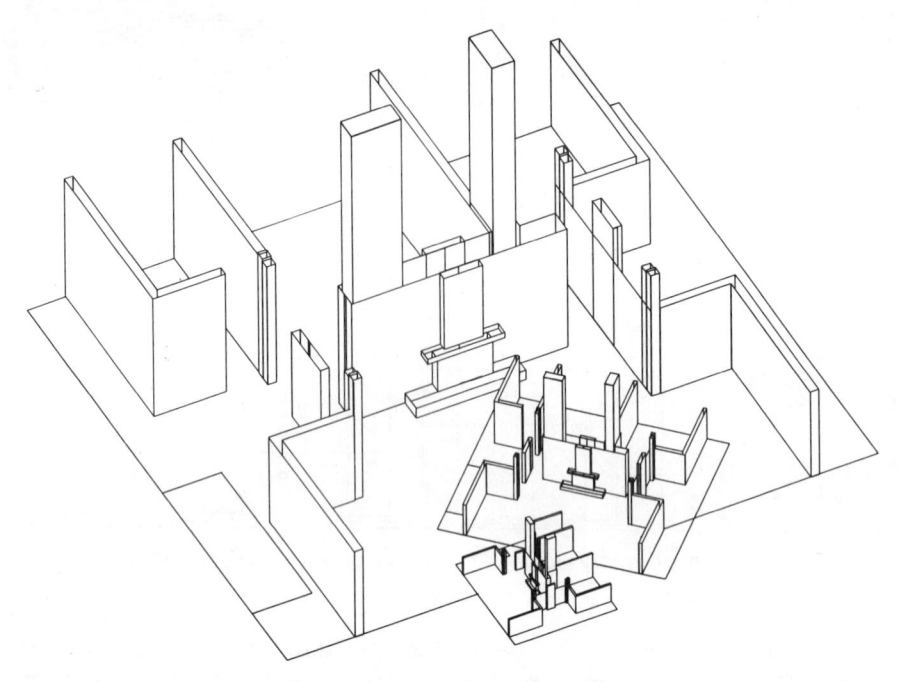

Figure 3.1c Scaling: the coordinates of the object change. An object within an object within an object—using different scaling factors to represent the same model. Fontaine residence.

tally different. The figure demonstrates the zooming capability of microcomputer programs. All three images are based on the same object, however, each one provides a different view. While in the previous example the coordinates of the scaled-down object change, zooming leaves the object coordinates unchanged. Zooming merely changes the distance of the designer's viewpoint. The viewer may detect this from examining the absolute scale placed in front of the table: The table's length or the dimensions of any object in the image do not change in relation to the absolute scale.

Figure 3.1.e is an example for an important feature that most microcomputer programs are unfortunately missing: the capability to decide which level of representation detail is appropriate for a particular scale. Experienced designers make these decisions intuitively. In a site plan it is inappropriate to display doors, windows, or furniture. Microcomputer programs do not have this decision capability, but they provide features to adjust the level of detail for each scale. The three doors in the example are composed of different "layers." Layers are the equivalent to transparent overlays that the designer may turn on or off. The outline of the doors, the outline of the frames, and the smallest ornamental frames are on three different layers. The smallest frame layer is turned off to

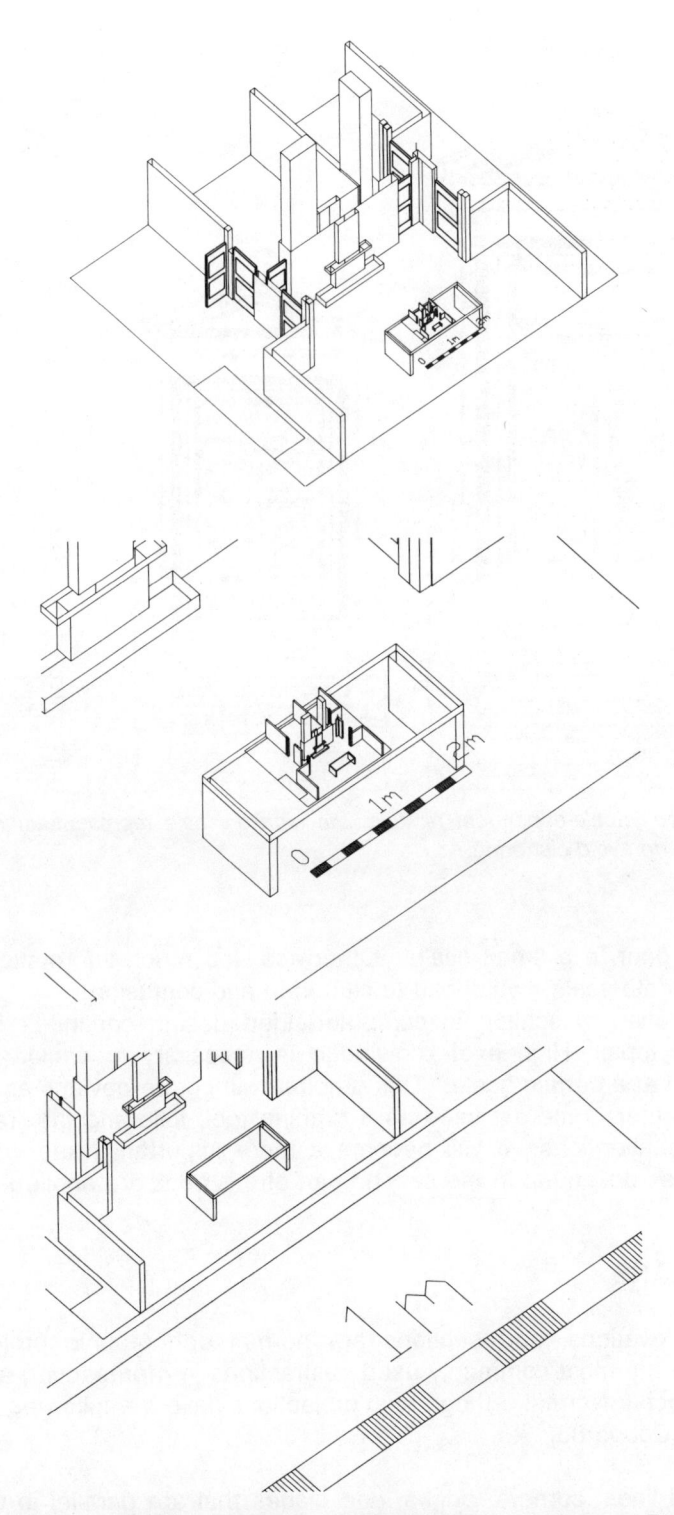

Figure 3.1d Zooming: the coordinates of the object do not change. Zooming into differently scaled representations of the same object. Fontaine residence.

Figure 3.1e Scale-dependent plotting: the smaller scale representations contain less detail to avoid cluttering.

plot the door in a small scale. Otherwise, too much information at an inappropriate scale would lead to cluttering and confusion.

The notion of scaling in computer-aided design continues to be a research topic. High-level knowledge is necessary to decide what is important at a certain scale. This problem will not be obvious as long as the computer is merely used as a drafting tool, following the traditional scaling conventions. It will become a more important issue when the techniques described in the second part of this book are applied.

3.2 PLANS

Plans, elevations, and sections are normal orthographic projections. They are the most commonly used abstractions in representing architectural objects. Normal orthographic projections have the following characteristics [Cooper83]:

1. All lines, corners, edges, and planes that are parallel in the real world object are parallel in the orthographic view.

2. All lines, corners, edges, and planes that are parallel to the picture plane can be drawn to scale.
3. All angles and planar shapes that are parallel to the picture plane can be drawn without distortion of shape.
4. All normal orthographic views represent a boundless and unlocalized visual field. They represent a direction of viewing as distinct from a position of viewing.

Plans are downward looking, normal orthographic views. Two main kinds of plans exist—site plans and floor plans. Site plans are seen from above where the picture plane is outside the object. Floor plans are sectional views with the horizontal picture plane within the object.

Advertisements for microcomputer CAD systems frequently display elaborate working drawings, most often showing plan views. From the beginning, these two-dimensional representations of a horizontal section through an object were a main target in software development based on their importance in architectural practice. Even two-dimensional microcomputer CAD systems are extremely well equipped to support the human hand for these representations.

In composing architectural plans, the use of layers or classes of objects becomes important. One should not draw all elements of a plan drawing on the same layer but group them logically: separate layers for columns, walls, windows, furniture, and dimension lines. This way it is possible to show and concentrate on selected objects. It is also possible in good drafting systems to insert the same elements in different layers and to store different elements from different layers in logical blocks.

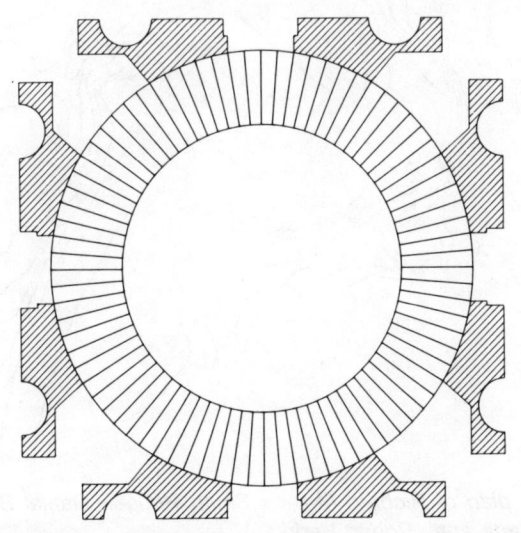

Figure 3.2a Plan view of a staircase by Andrea Palladio.

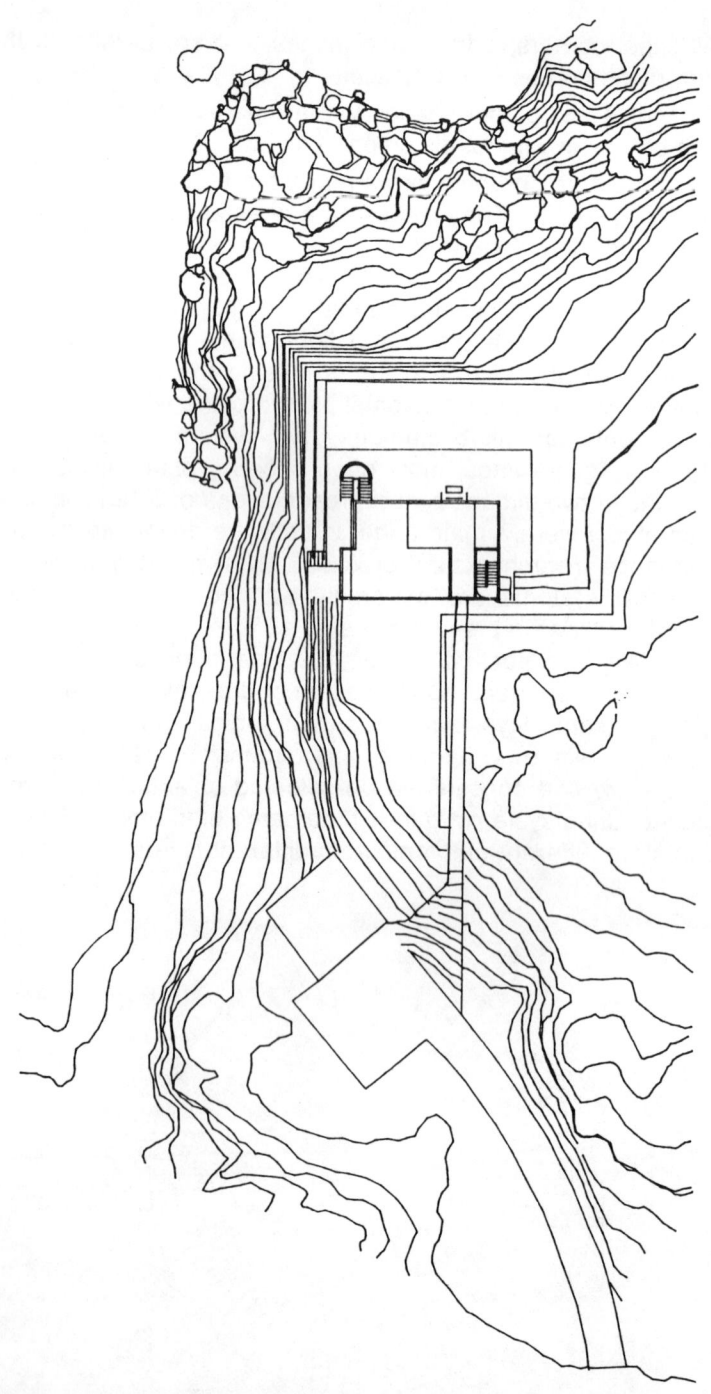

Figure 3.2b Site plan of Richard Meier's Smith House. Daniel Blander, Michael Gehr, Tassoula Hadjiyanni, Robert Hering.

This capability facilitates the easy manipulation of hierarchically organized building elements: if a wall is moved, all elements belonging to this wall will move with it.

If design is developed three dimensionally, a plan is displayed by simply viewing the object from the top. In a Cartesian coordinate system, this is equivalent to specifying the viewing direction, for example, from $(0,0,1)$ to $(0,0,0)$. Figure 3.2a is the result of such an operation. The three-dimensional object, one of the stairs described in Palladio's *Four Books of Architecture* [Placzek65], contains more information than displayed in this two-dimensional representation. Other views will be shown in the following sections.

Figure 3.2b is the site plan of Richard Meier's Smith House and the plan view of one of the floors. As in the previous case, the object represented in the drawing contains more information than shown in the plan view because all floor plans are drawn on top of each other. The program eliminated the information by "hiding" all the lines that would appear underneath. This technique does not always work due to numerical problems in hidden-line algorithms and drawing input mistakes, as some details in the example suggest. The contour lines are drawn on their appropriate elevations, which can be seen if another view of the object is chosen.

Figure 3.2c shows the simplified floor plan of the Shehzadeh mosque in Istanbul [Haider86], with the generating geometric pattern as an overlay. The example demonstrates the use of layers: The combination of the design layer (squares and circles) and the floor plan of the actual building shows information that is not obvious if only the floor plan is dis-

Figure 3.2c Floor plan of the Shehzadeh Mosque in Istanbul by Sinan. Design layer with an overlay of the generating geometric pattern (ordering layer).

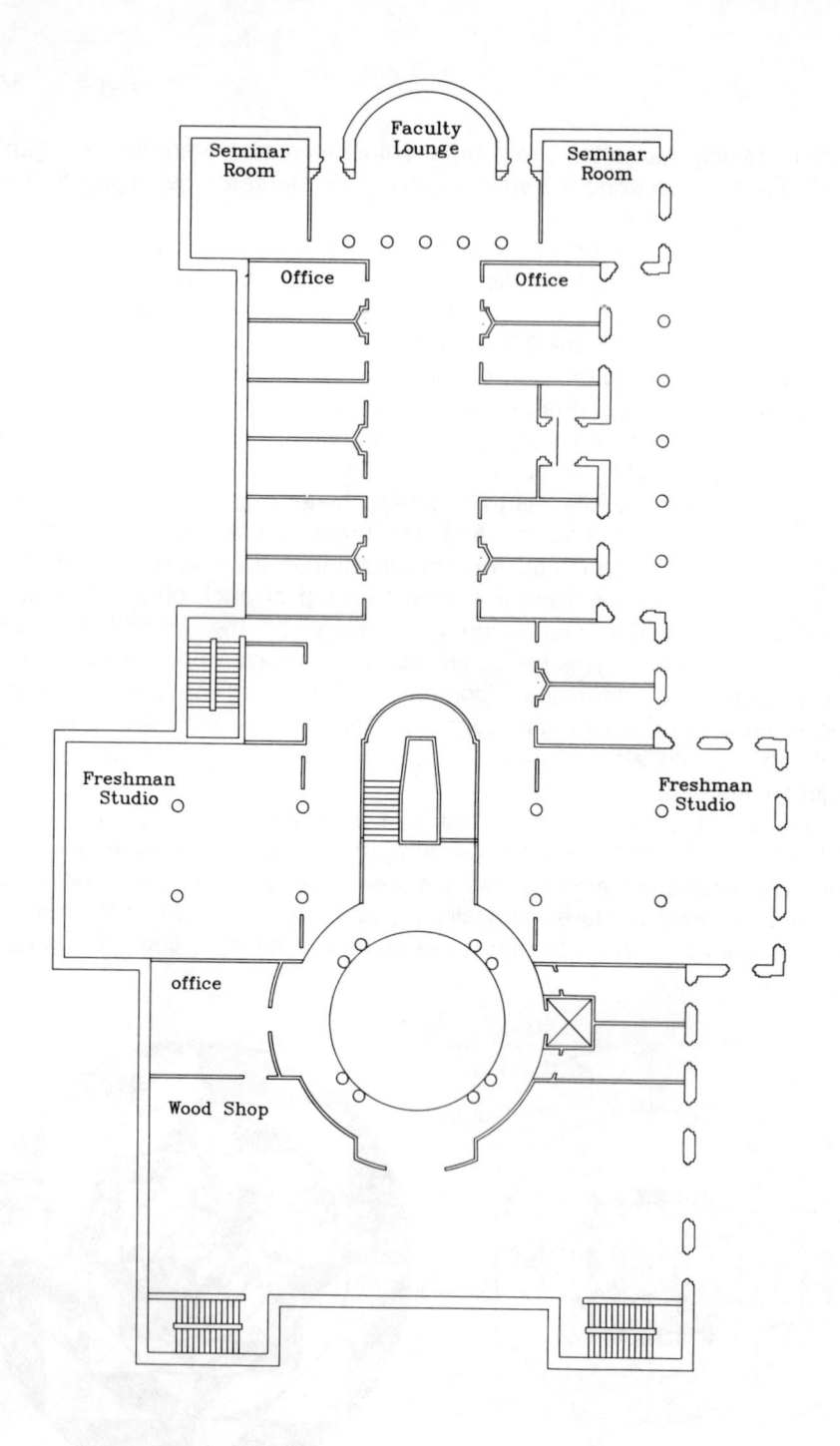

Basement Floor Plan

Figure 3.2d Plan view of a student project for a new school of architecture, containing wall information and major level changes only. Alexander Biagioli.

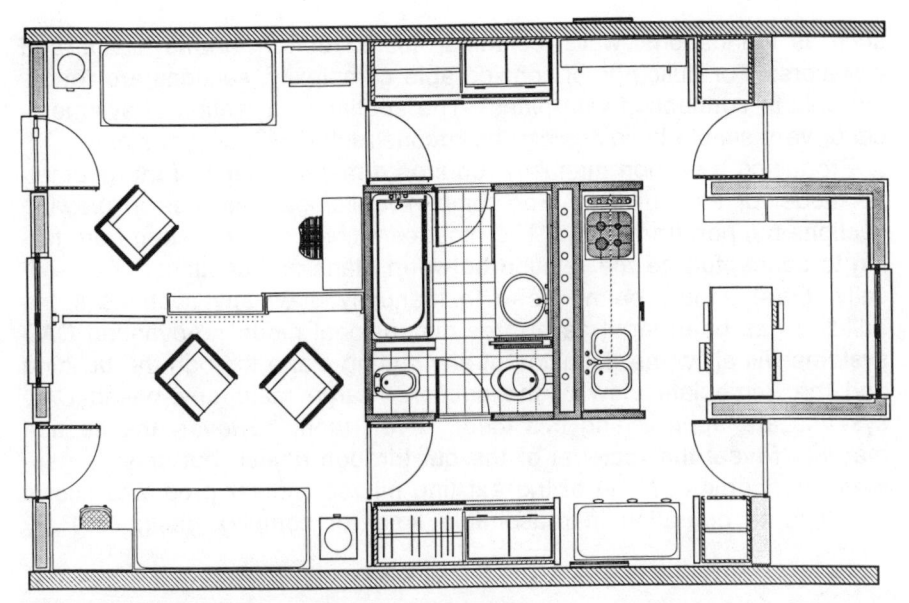

Figure 3.2e Plan view of an elderly housing unit, generated with MacDraw. Donatella Orazi, Antonino Saggio.

played. On the other hand, the additional geometric information may be unwanted and, if contained on a separate layer, is easily turned off.

Figure 3.2d represents the basement plan for a new school of architecture. In this case, the designer was interested in wall information and major level changes only. No windows, doors, or floor patterns are shown. This technique is often helpful in displaying the major structural and spatial elements of design. Figure 3.2e, a floor plan of an elderly housing unit, includes all details omitted in the previous drawing. Whereas the other floor plans were drawn with a pen plotter, this plan was produced with a laser writer.

In conclusion, plan views of design are easily created on almost all microcomputer drafting programs. The drawings produced in this manner closely resemble traditional drawings. Dimensioning, selective display of information, and lettering become almost trivial. However, the discipline required in wisely organizing layers and information contained on these layers is a foundation for the mastering of the new tools.

3.3 SECTIONS

Sections are horizontal normal orthographic projections, distinguishing between viewed material and cut through material. They are used to show geometric properties and other attributes of building components such as foundations, walls, columns, floors, roofs, windows, stairs, and elevators. For buildings of considerable complexity, sections are readable only in connection with plans. The spatial organization of symmetrical or very simple buildings can be reconstructed with sections only.

Producing a section manually requires a mental image of the geometric model of the building. For complex buildings, mistakes in drawing sections happen frequently. The most common problems stem from failing to conceptualize the relation between plans and sections. Theoretically, there should be no need to manually draw any sections if the building has been input as a three-dimensional model. Advanced CAD systems will allow the definition of any cutting plane through the building and the immediate view of the section. Large mainframe-based CAD systems are approaching this ideal. Even then, however, the section may not reveal the material of the cut through object, but only its geometric properties. None of the existing microcomputer programs allows this type of operation in reasonable time for complex designs. Fully

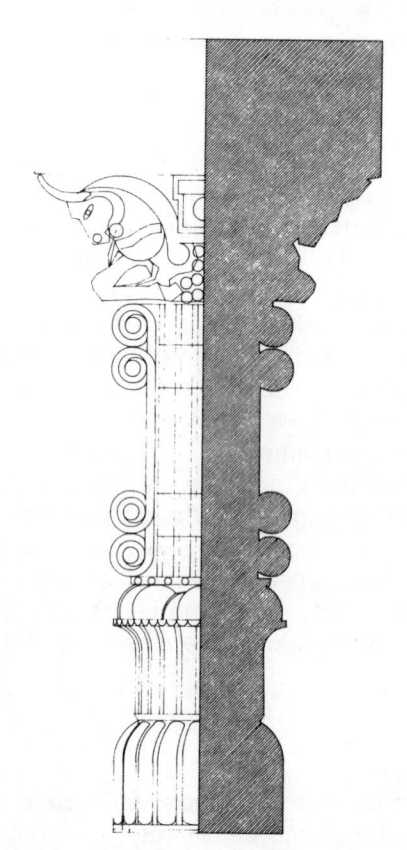

Figure 3.3a Section of a Persian column detail. Richard Cobti.

developed solids modelers with acceptable speed performance and price are not yet available for microcomputers. Consequently, the same rules that apply for the creation of plans should be used to design sections; that is, the principle of layers and blocks is recommended.

Plans can be seen as horizontal sections traditionally cut through the building at a height just above the window sills. For sections such conventions do not exist, and the location and direction of the section are therefore important user decisions. Producing sections with microcomputers involves issues similar to the ones addressed under tracing and scaling: Not all lines need to be shown, and lines further away from the cutting plane should be lighter or thinner than the ones closer to the cutting plane. The actual cut lines should be heavy to support the three-dimensional understanding of the image.

Figure 3.3a is a classical example: a section through a capital. If the capital is symmetric to its vertical axis, the entire object can be reconstructed from the section. The more complex and the less symmetric the object (as in the case here), the more plan sections and elevations are needed to describe it correctly. Otherwise, a single section could produce a number of different objects.

Figure 3.3b shows a set of sections that describe four different window types [Andersen87]. Top drawings represent sections through the

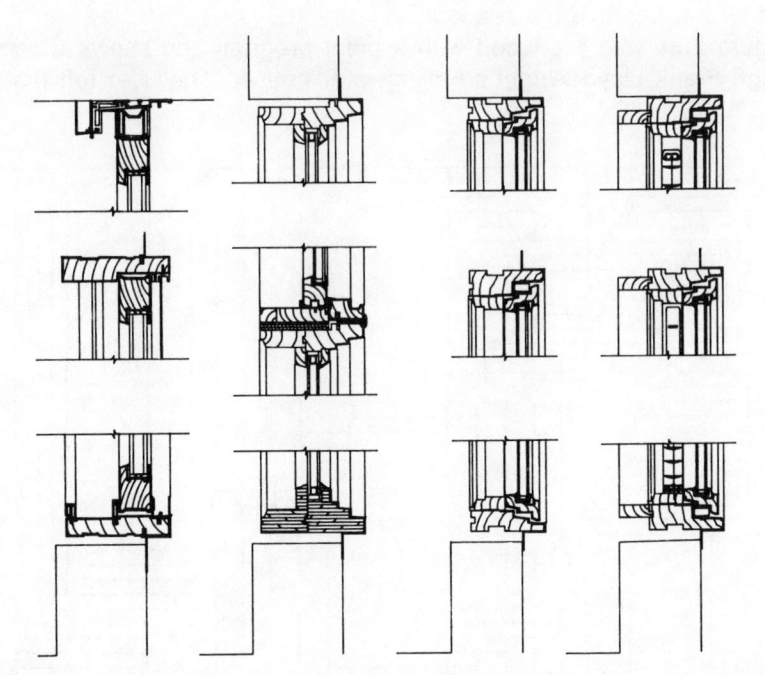

Figure 3.3b Detail sections of different window types at various frame locations. Andersen Corporation.

42   REPRESENTATION

upper part of the window. Bottom drawings show detail sections of window and sill. Middle drawings are horizontal sections through the window. Wood, glass, and metal appear in distinct colors on the screen. These sections are available in manufacturer catalogues as standard details. The interesting property of the example sections is their availability as drawing files on disks that can be used with popular drafting packages. The designer draws the opening in the wall, and then simply inserts the appropriate detail in the drawing. As the detail sections are developed in absolute units and not relative to a scale, the architect has the immediate feedback whether or not and how the detail will fit into the design. Detail sections are only appropriate in detail drawings and should not appear in larger scale sections.

The vertical section through a Palladian staircase in Figure 3.3c, which was shown before demonstrates some of the limitations mentioned above: Although mathematically correct, the drawing is difficult to read as a section because all lines have the same weight and thickness. The three-dimensional quality of the stairs is only perceived by the curved arrangement of the steps.

The section in Figure 3.3d seeks to overcome these limitations by hatching the cut parts of the wall. Different materials are on different layers: the vertical walls, horizontal ceilings, roof, and the elements that appear in the interior and exterior elevation. Manually added shades could further improve the readability.

Figure 3.3e was produced with a paint program and shows a section through Frank Lloyd Wright's Fallingwater house. The user felt that the

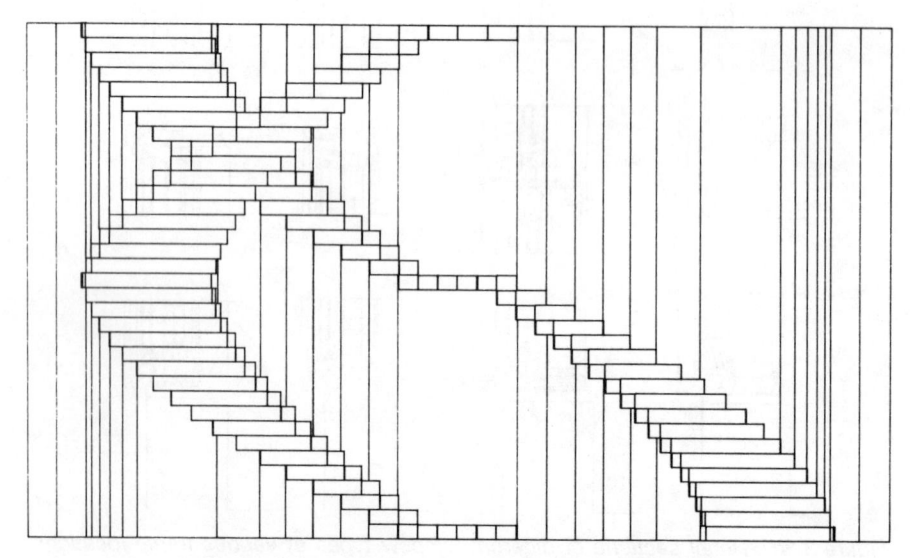

Figure 3.3c   Section of stair by Andrea Palladio.

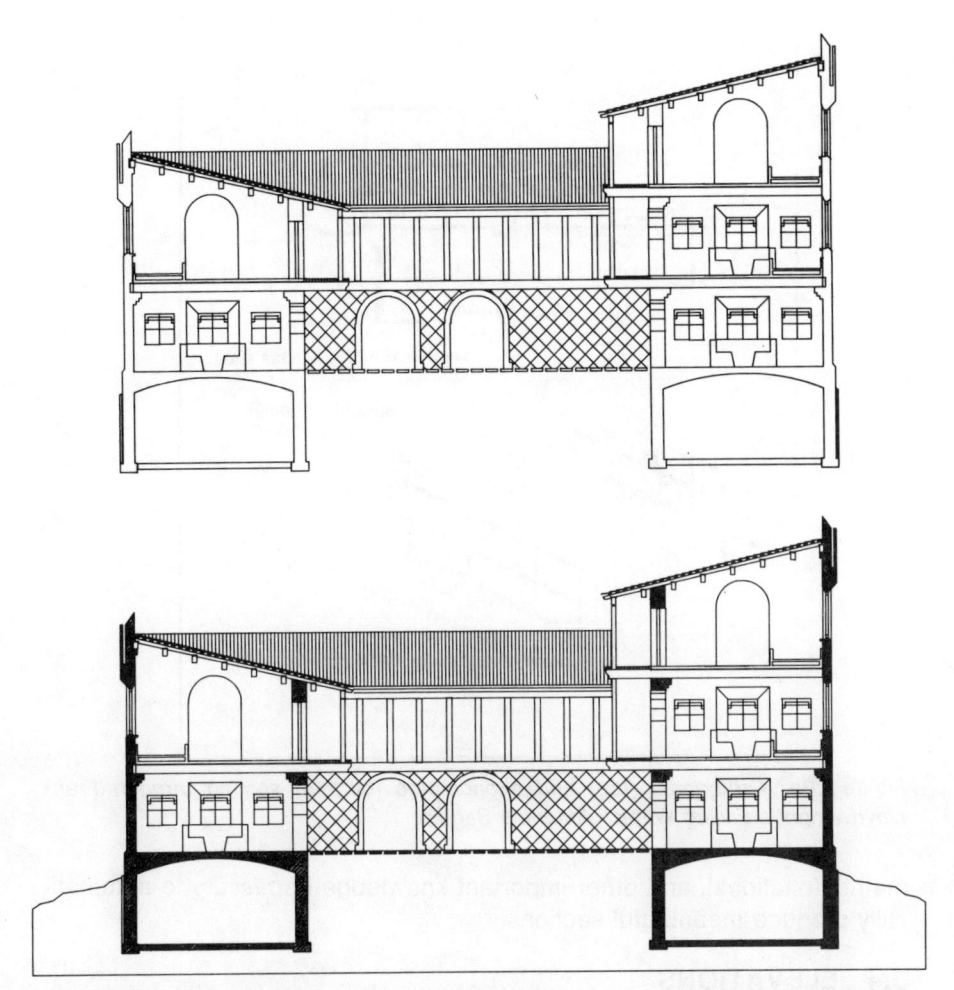

Figure 3.3d Section through a monastery design (top). Hatching of cut-through elements differentiates solids and voids (bottom).

section through the residence looking west was not descriptive enough and therefore added an axonometric section. The cut parts were then filled with black to enhance the readability. Drawing inaccuracies show that the image was generated manually.

The present software and machine limitations that become apparent in the construction of the preceding examples will not be permanent. Advances in building description methods will have a positive impact on the development of software that can execute intelligent sections through buildings. With the definition of a general building description language, it will be possible to drastically improve the handling of geo-

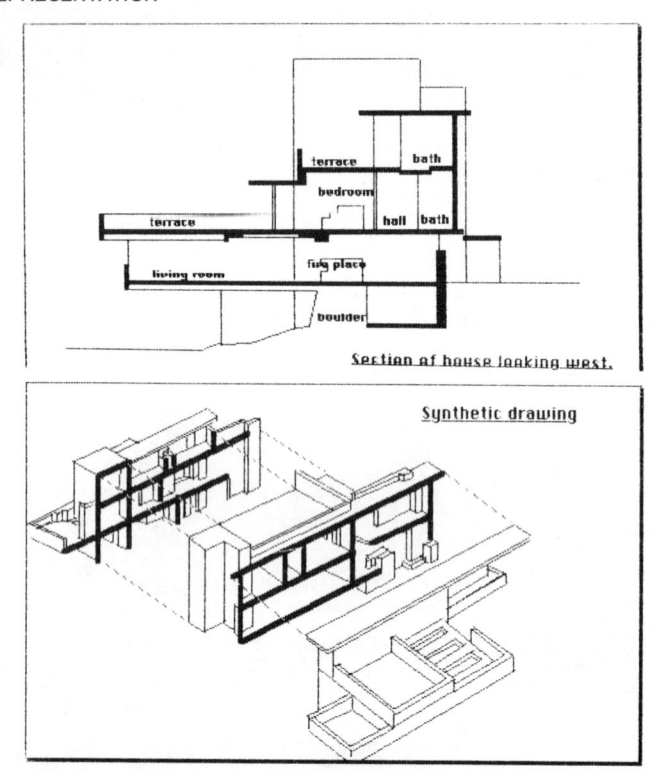

Figure 3.3e Orthogonal (top) and axonometric (bottom) section through Frank Lloyd Wright's Falling Water. Antonino Saggio.

metric, functional, and other important knowledge necessary to automatically produce meaningful sections.

3.4 ELEVATIONS

Elevations are horizontal normal orthographic projections where the picture plane lies outside the building. They are used to represent the exterior appearance of a building or parts of a building. The dimensions and proportions of walls, roofs, and openings are typically shown. Manual techniques have been developed to represent nonplanar surfaces, such as curves and cylinders, in elevation. Shading and toning are used to create the illusion of depth. As in the case of sections, missing or wrong relations between floor plans and elevations are not uncommon.

If the object is to be input two dimensionally, that is, if no three-dimensional information is attached to the plans, then the creation of elevations with the computer is not much different than manual drafting. The new aspects that advanced CAD programs offer are the automation of elevation generation from extruded plans and the opportunity to view the building not only from orthogonal projections.

Figure 3.4a East elevation of Hamerschlag Hall at Carnegie Mellon University by Henry Hornbostel (1913).

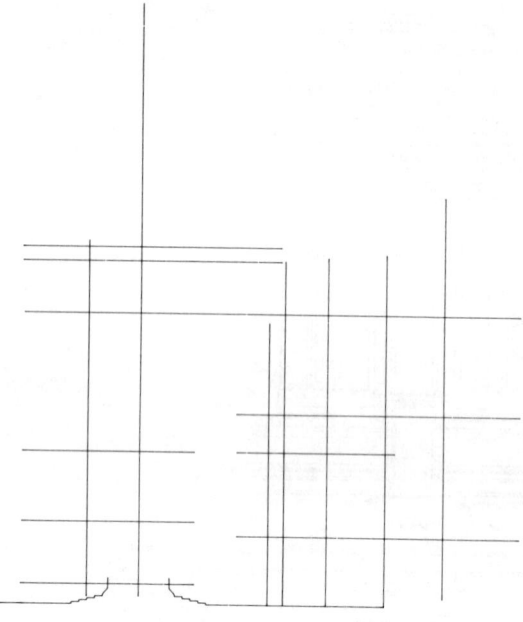

Figure 3.4b Hamerschlag Hall. Main axes and ordering lines in the elevation.

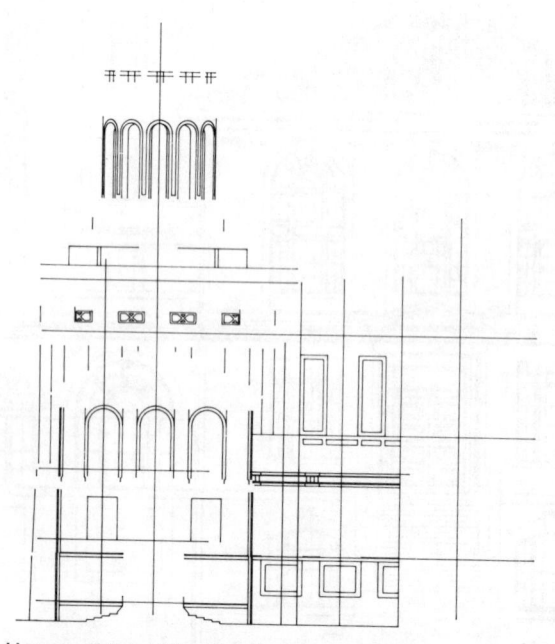

Figure 3.4c Hamerschlag Hall. Brick elements displayed on a different layer.

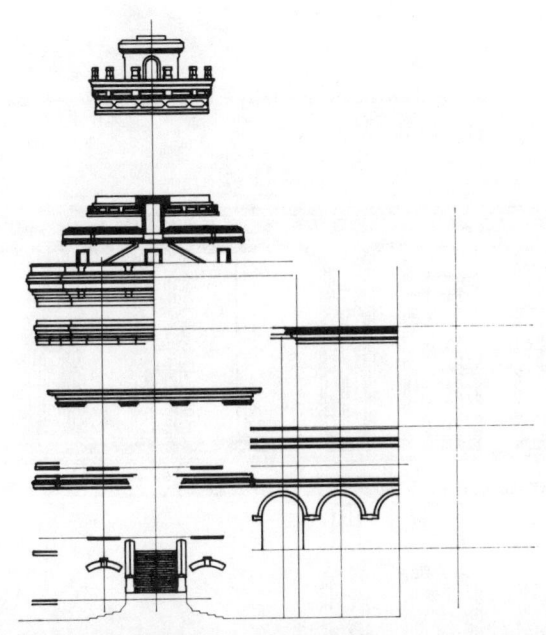

Figure 3.4d   Hamerschlag Hall.   Limestone elements displayed on a different layer.

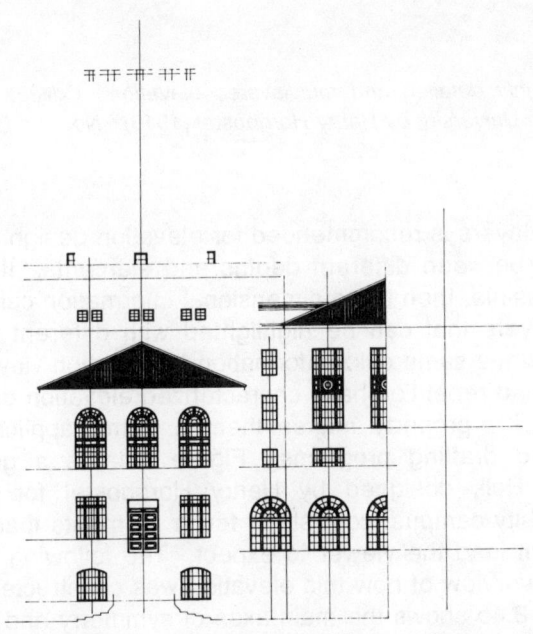

Figure 3.4e   Hamerschlag Hall.   Layers displaying roofs, windows, and major axes.

47

48   REPRESENTATION

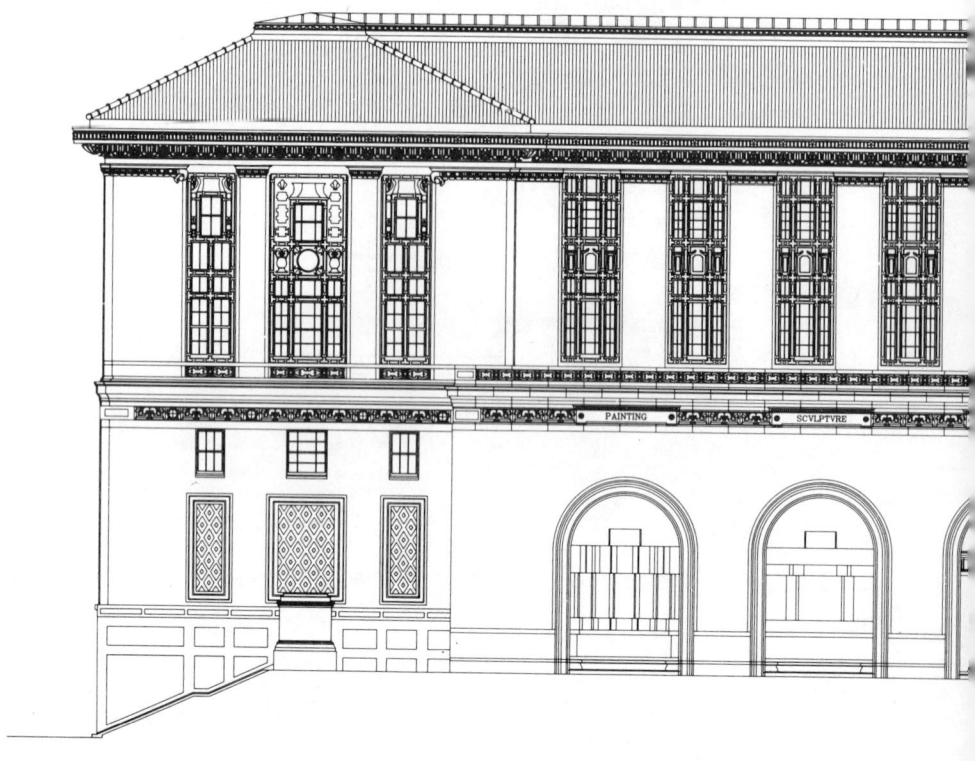

Figure 3.4f Highly detailed and multilayered elevation. College of Fine Arts at Carnegie Mellon University by Henry Hornbostel (1913). Norman Larson.

The use of layers is recommended for elevation design as a means of distinguishing between different depths and elements. If the extrusion of plans is possible, then three-dimensional information can be viewed in elevation. Layers that can be highlighted with different colors in plan view will show the same color information in elevation view.

Symmetry and repetition have characterized elevation design throughout history. This property makes them a prime application area for computer-aided drafting programs. Figure 3.4a is a good example: Hamerschlag Hall, designed by Henry Hornbostel for the Carnegie Mellon University campus, consists of fewer elements than the complex elevation might lead the viewer to expect. The following figures give a step-by-step overview of how this elevation was constructed on the computer. Figure 3.4b shows the main axes of symmetry and the horizontal window placement lines. Figure 3.4c represents, in addition, important brick elements on a separate layer. On yet another layer, Figure 3.4d shows some of the limestone elements in the elevation. Figure 3.4e displays the windows and the roofs, superimposed on the main axes. The symmetry of the elevation order and the repetitiveness of the elements becomes obvious. The combination of all layers produces Figure 3.4a.

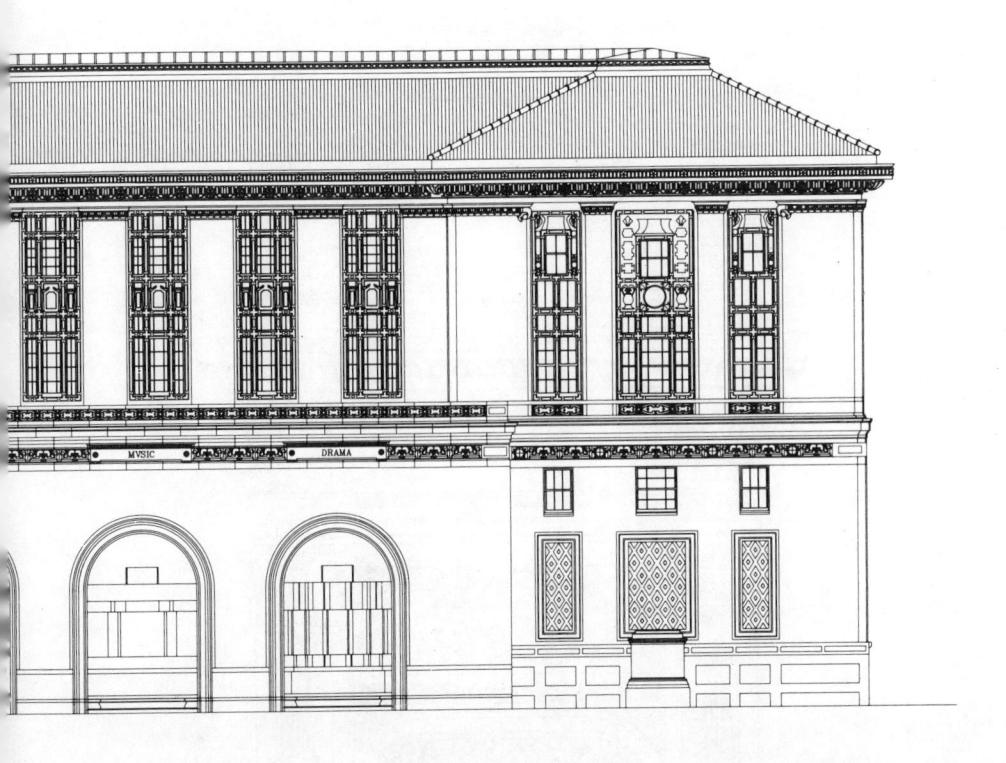

A second building by Henry Hornbostel, the College of Fine Arts on the Carnegie Mellon University campus, displays these qualities more definitively. Figure 3.4f shows the result of a student exercise to reconstruct the elevation in a similar manner to the building construction. Groups of students worked on individual windows, roof, granite elements, brick walls, and terracotta ornaments. Others designed the underlying axes of symmetry and the location for each element. In a final effort, all elevation elements were inserted as different drawing files in the master drawing.

The French Renaissance niche designed and developed after the Chateau of Chambord in Figure 3.4g appears extremely complex at first sight. Again, axes of symmetry in every part of the niche simplify its representation as a two-dimensional elevation drawing. A full three-

Figure 3.4g French Renaissance style niche elevation. A two-dimensional representation of a semicircular space in the College of Fine Arts at Carnegie Mellon University. Richard Cobti.

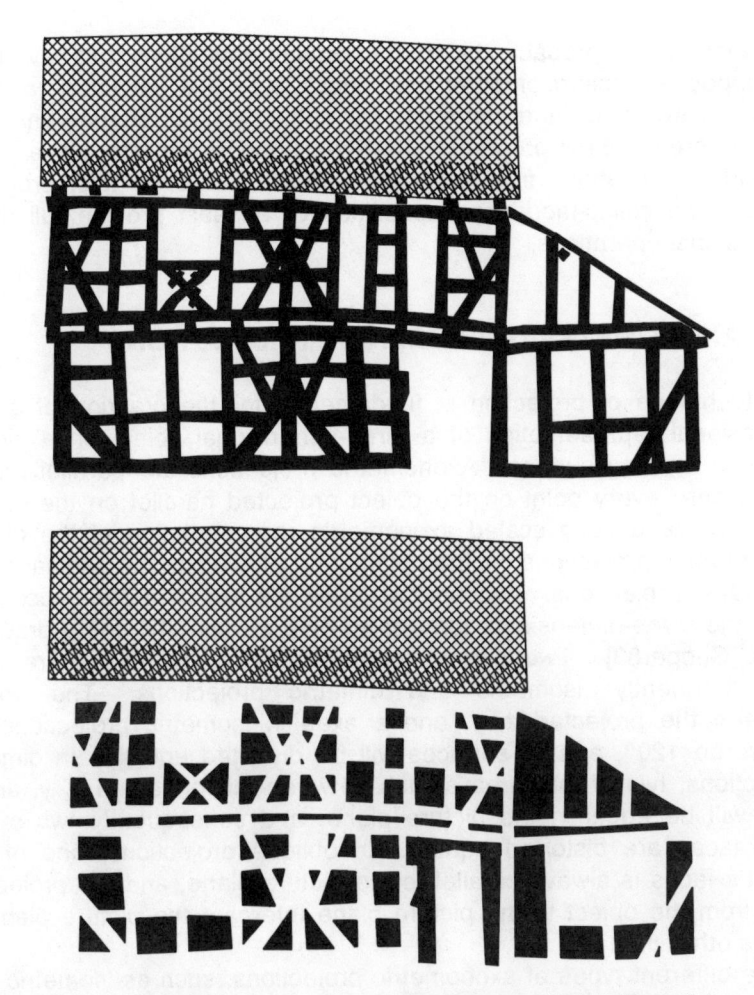

Figure 3.4h Front elevation of a 15th-century German timber frame house. Roof and wood frame (top), roof and adobe fillings (bottom).

dimensional model of an object of this geometric complexity goes beyond the capabilities of present microcomputer programs.

Figure 3.4h shows the south elevation of a sixteenth-century timber frame or "Fachwerkhaus" in Germany. As the entire building is constructed with hand-crafted materials and has settled over time, symmetry and repetitiveness are not easily discovered. Careful measurement revealed, however, that the facade is constructed of four almost identical rectangles in the proportion of the golden section. The computer allows the simple overlay of these rectangles, thus proving the point visually. The two images also show the computer's potential to demonstrate the notion of figure – ground in elevations.

Elevations are probably the most satisfying projections that have been developed with microcomputer programs. They take advantage of repetition and symmetry and can easily be enhanced with shades and color on the screen. Few programs, however, support the interactive development of elevations from plans and sections. To do this, programs would need solids-modeling capabilities or at least provide full three-dimensional operations.

3.5 AXONOMETRIC AND OBLIQUE PROJECTIONS

The technique of projection is fundamental for the creation of a two-dimensional representation of a three-dimensional object on a picture plane or drawing surface. Axonometric projections are parallel projections where every point on the object projected parallel on the picture plane will produce a scaled axonometric representation of the object. Orthographic projections such as plans and elevations are special cases of parallel projections. Axonometric drawings are useful because they show the three-dimensional form of an object while still being drawn to scale [Cooper83]. Two classes of axonometric projections are used most frequently: isometric and dimetric projections. The angles between the projected x, y, and z axes in isometric projections will always be 120°, and all surfaces will be distorted equally. In dimetric projections, two of the three angles between the projected x, y, and z axes will be equal in the picture plane, and consequently two of the three faces are distorted equally. In oblique projections, one of the object's faces is always parallel to the picture plane, and the projection lines from the object to the picture plane intercept the picture plane at angles other than 90°.

The different types of axonometric projections, such as isometric and dimetric projection, can easily be obtained by setting the appropriate viewing parameters in the computer program. As all projections follow known mathematical calculations, this manually difficult task is trivial for the microcomputer. A set of predefined viewing parameters will facilitate the creation of different views. To produce an isometric projection of an object, for example, the user would specify the viewing direction from $(1,1,1)$ to $(0,0,0)$. To produce a dimetric projection, the user would specify the viewing direction from $(1,1,2)$ to $(0,0,0)$. The generation of oblique projections follows the same technique.

CAD software that does not feature 3-dimensional or at least "2.5"-dimensional operations cannot be considered useful in producing axonometrics. The only possibility of constructing axonometric projections with 2-dimensional drafting systems is a simulated extrusion by rotating a floor plan and then placing a copy of the floor plan above it at the distance of the floor height. Some additional editing is necessary after this operation to have the drawing appear as an axonometric projection.

Axonometric projections are the real strength of evolving microcomputer CAD systems if the necessary 3-dimensional information has been introduced in the plan drawings. It is not possible to manually produce the number of axonometric views from different viewpoints in such a short period of time that can be easily achieved with an advanced 2.5-dimensional or 3-dimensional CAD program. Again, the layering system described in the plan, section, and elevation sections can be applied in axonometric drawings as well.

A feature that is new and surprising for the novice CAD user is insertion of 3-dimensional drawing elements, called blocks, from a database. Blocks are drawing files that exist within a created file or separately as an external file. In two-dimensional representations this feature appears quite natural. It takes on a new dimension when it is done within an axonometric drawing. If the elements have been stored as three-dimensional objects, the results can resemble realistic animation. A good example is to furnish a room interactively by calling the various pieces of furniture from the database and dragging them to the position in which they belong. This feature definitely adds a new quality to interactive design.

It is possible with the more sophisticated CAD systems to remove hidden lines from axonometric views. This feature, although very helpful

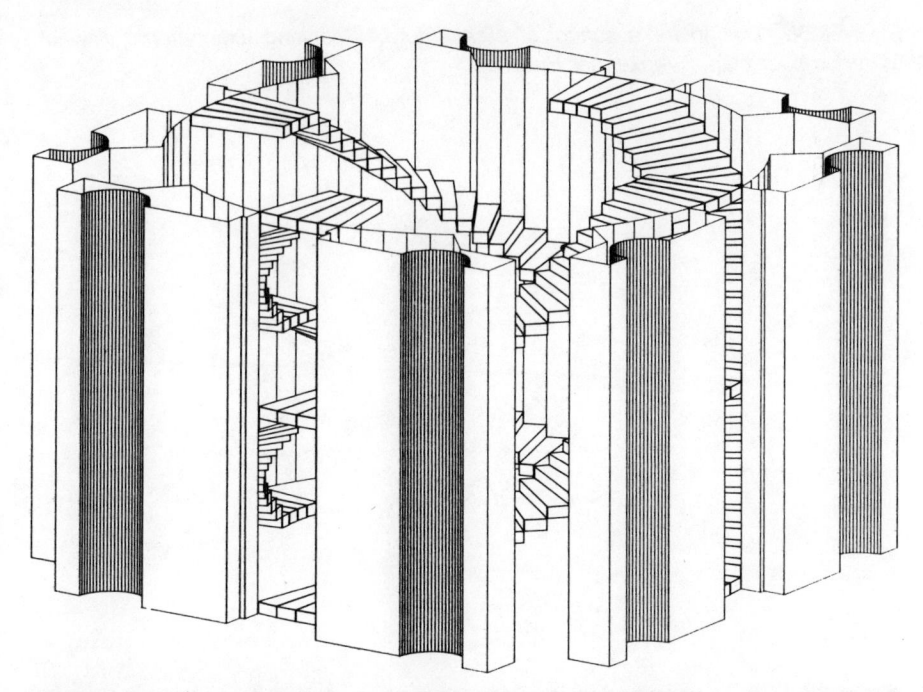

Figure 3.5a Axonometric view of a stair from Andrea Palladio's Four Books of Architecture.

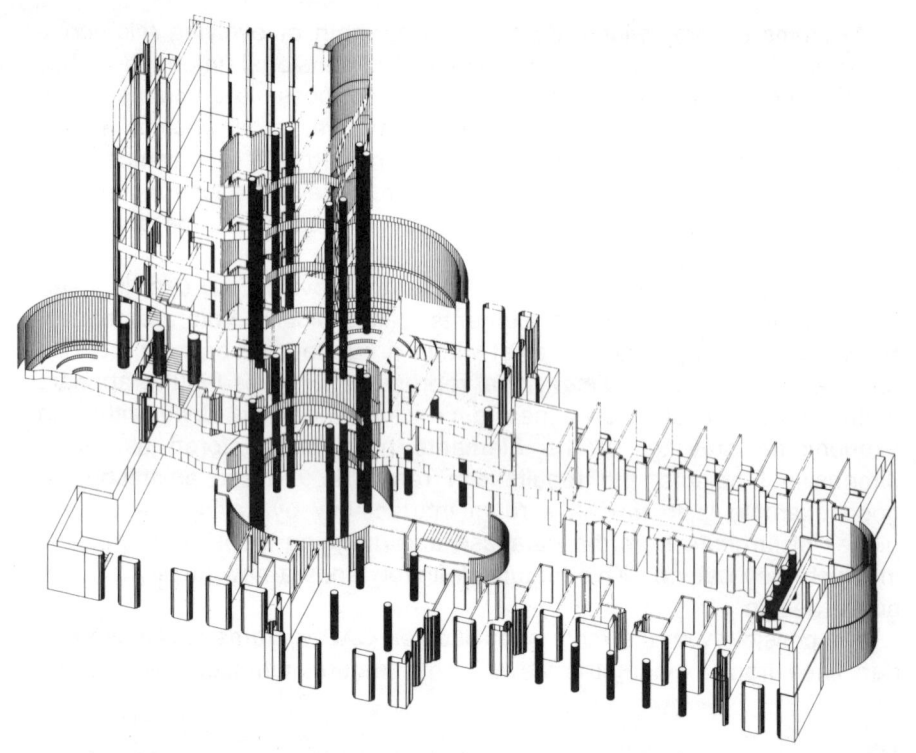

Figure 3.5b Design for a school of architecture. Resulting axonometric view of extruded floor plans. Alexander Biagioli.

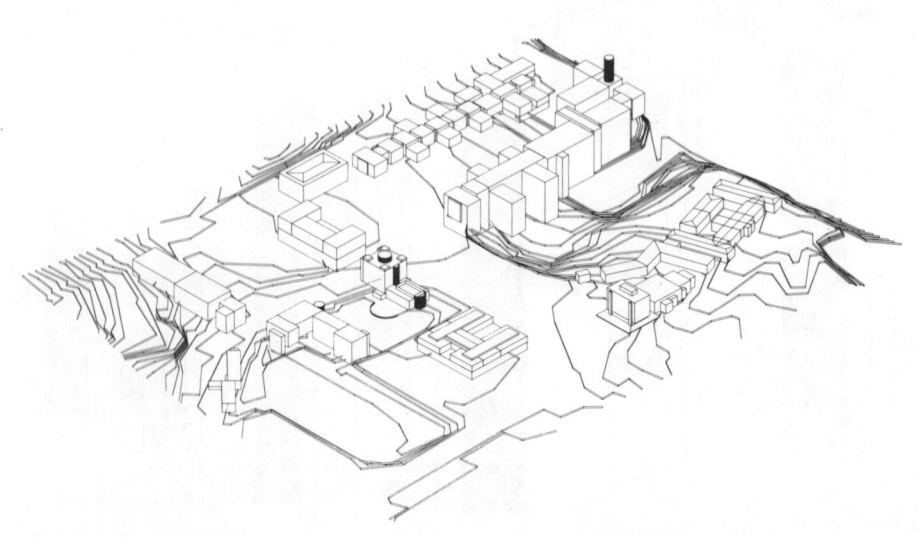

Figure 3.5c Axonometric view of Carnegie Mellon University campus. Norman Larson.

for understanding the object, is time consuming for complex buildings. Two other problems are associated with microcomputer-generated axonometrics that are less visible in manual methods: depth cues and intensity effects. Depth cues enable the viewer to differentiate between foreground and background by varying the line thickness or line intensity. Although this technique is relatively easy to implement, none of the present commercial microcomputer CAD packages offers it.

Figure 3.5a shows an axonometric view of the Palladian staircase presented earlier in plan and section views. In this view, all the 3-dimensional information is visible. The hidden lines are removed, consequently the vertical elements in the front hide the steps behind.

The apparently very complex design in Figure 3.5b is the result of simple extrusions from various floor plans and their axonometric display. The building appears as if it were made of vertical strips of paper. The impression stems from the particular program's inability to display complex extruded polygons, for example floor slabs, as one solid piece. This shortcoming causes the "see-through" quality of the entire building. Different colors are helpful to enhance the readability of the building.

The axonometric view of the Carnegie Mellon University campus in Figure 3.5c adds a new application to axonometric views. The ease of

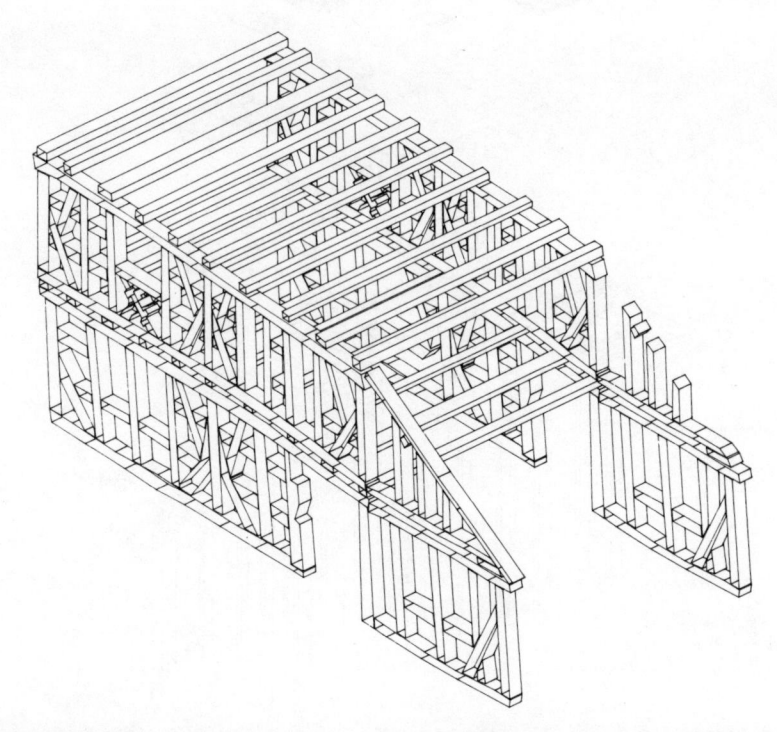

Figure 3.5d Axonometric view of the structural system of a 15th-century German timber frame house.

defining viewing directions makes insulation studies possible. The position of the sun at a given time, in the direction of the site, defines the viewing direction. A simple program allows the machine to calculate the position of the sun at any time of the day throughout the year at any location on earth. For critical time periods of the day and the year, it is possible to determine if certain parts of the campus will receive sunlight or not: If the viewing direction for the axonometric projection is that of the sun, then the places hidden after a hidden line removal operation are in shade, and all other places receive direct sunlight. This answers the question whether or not certain outdoor areas receive sunlight in critical hours of the day. In effect, this has helped to design outdoor areas according to insulation needs.

The axonometric view in Figure 3.5d shows the sixteenth-century German Fachwerkhaus that appeared before in elevation view. The viewer can see the actual depth and three-dimensional quality of the house. As

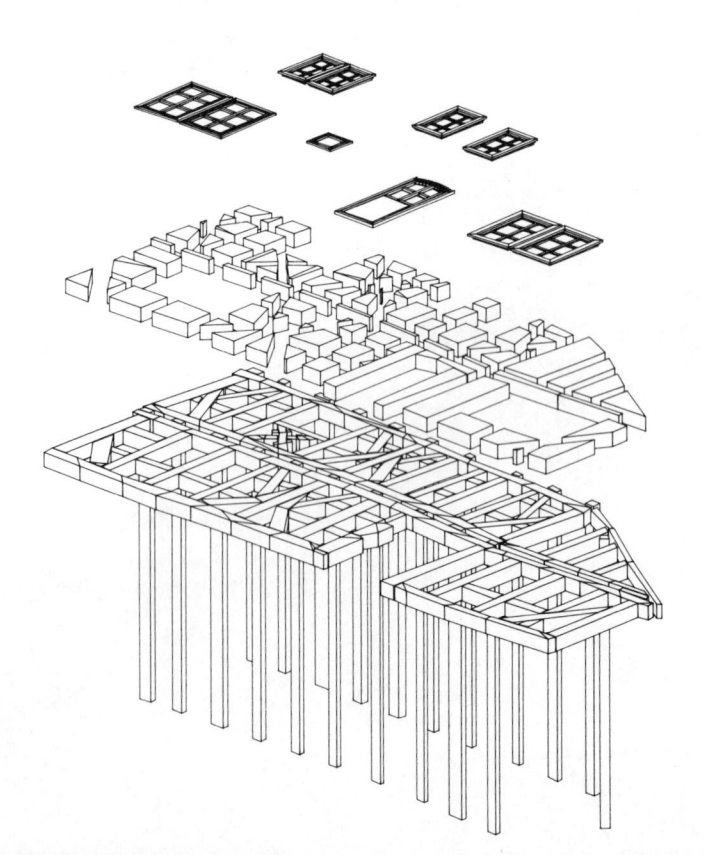

Figure 3.5e Exploded axonometric view of the structural system, adobe fillings, and the door and windows of a 15th-century German timber frame house.

in the previous examples, the wooden beams appear somewhat confusing as they resemble folded paper strips. Without the hidden lines removed, the image would be completely unreadable.

The same building is shown in Figure 3.5e, but in a different manner. The figure represents an exploded view of the building's south elevation seen from a worm's eye view. The elevation was studied for its passive solar qualities. This time, the wooden beams are represented as solids but, due to another program restriction, must be composed of small solid polygons with a maximum of four vertices. The adobe infill between the beams is "pulled out" of the elevation and can be seen as the thermal mass of the building. The door and window openings with appropriate frames are extracted even further. They represent the areas available for passive solar gain but are also a source of heat loss.

The axonometric view in Figure 3.5f helps to visualize the application of the golden section proportion in the same building. The four main

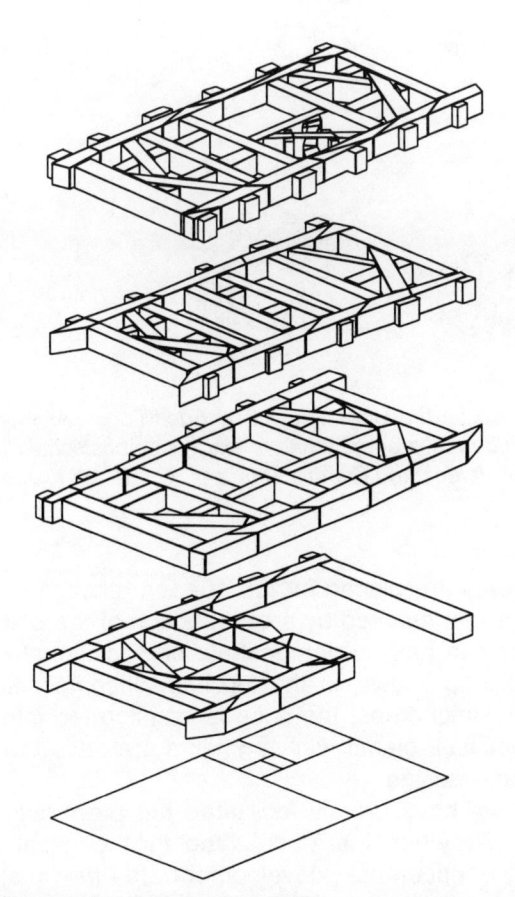

Figure 3.5f Exploded view of the four sections of the timber frame house elevation to demonstrate the use of the golden section.

58   REPRESENTATION

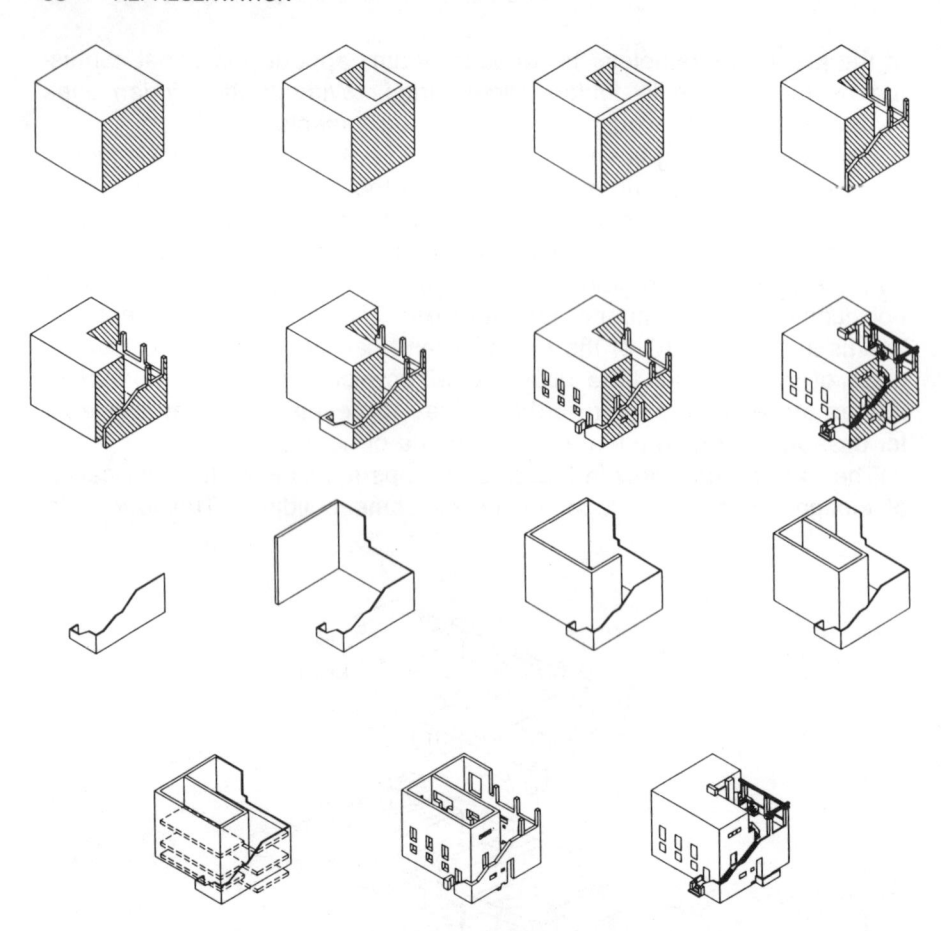

Figure 3.5g House on the Lido. Project by Adolf Loos. Axonometric projections of additive and subtractive approaches to clarify compositional design rules. Analysis by Anastasia Haidos and Cynthia Massagli with Ulrich Flemming, instructor.

elevation elements are placed on top of each other in an exploded axonometric view, superimposed by a construction of the golden section.

Axonometrics can help to demonstrate compositional rules in building design. Figure 3.5g shows, in the top half, decomposition applied to a cube: In eight distinct steps, the cube is transformed into the final building. In the lower half, planar wall segments are added in seven steps to produce the same design.

Microcomputers have greatly facilitated the preparation of axonometric projections. They become a useful tool for the visualization of design from its early conceptual development to its final presentation. Computer-generated axonometric views also find growing applications in the analysis or reconstruction of historic buildings or simply for the spatial explanation of existing buildings. With increasingly powerful hardware available, axonometric and oblique projections could subsume hand-made projections almost completely.

3.6 PERSPECTIVE PROJECTION

Perspective projections provide a view from a single position in space [Cooper83]. Images formed by photographic lenses or the human eye are perspective projections that capture the object from the viewer's point in space, whereas axonometric and oblique projections show the object from a defined direction. Thus, in axonometric projection the distance from viewer to object is of no consequence. For the construction of perspectives, the picture plane is always perpendicular to the viewer's direction, and the object's boundaries are projected on the picture plane with sight lines that converge in the viewer's eye. The representation of depth, a common problem in axonometric and oblique projections, is facilitated in perspective projection by representing distant objects at a smaller scale than closer ones. Ambiguities are still possible if the object has little depth variation. Extensive mathematical foundations are available to calculate a variety of perspectives, such as rectilinear and curvilinear perspectives [Mauldin85]. The key to computer-generated perspectives is the perspective transformation matrix.

Manually drawn and computer-generated perspectives expose some fundamental differences in appearance. Some commercial microcomputer CAD programs can produce wire frame perspectives, showing all edges of the object. They are, however, not very helpful in evaluating complex designs. Highlighting, varying line weight and intensity, and fading distant objects are well-known and often used manual means. Computer-generated perspectives will be mathematically perfect but difficult to read. Removing the hidden lines in the computer generated perspectives helps to increase the clarity and reduce ambiguities, but it is still a time-consuming process. Not enough effort has been spent on developing fast and efficient hidden-line removal algorithms for microcomputers.

Perspectives are the ideal means to create reality in presentation. Numerous books on this subject elaborate on the different techniques to manually construct perspectives. Though freehand sketches are used extensively during design development, constructed perspectives are normally the final step in the design process and primarily meant for presentation purposes. It would be helpful, however, to see higher quality perspectives of a design at an earlier stage. This is the obvious advantage of being able to produce computer-generated perspectives. For the mathematical calculations, computer-generated perspectives

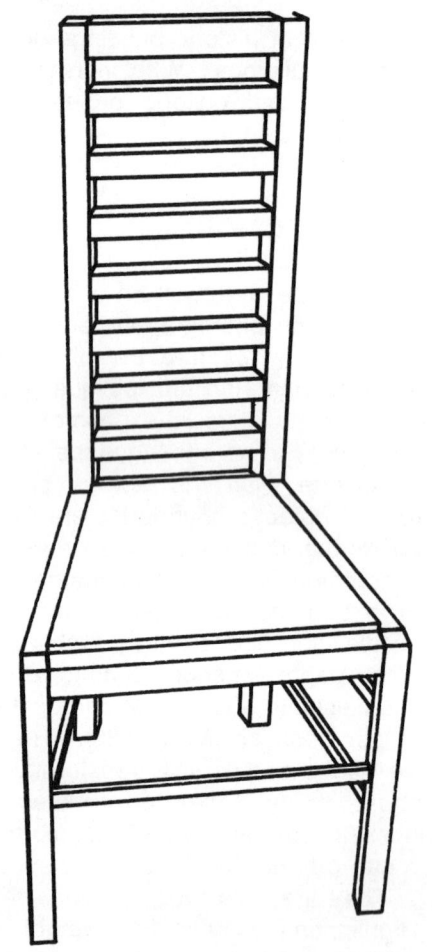

Figure 3.6a Willow II chair by Charles Rennie Mackintosh. Perspective view. Laura Lee.

require the same amount of information as axonometrics—the difference lies in the fact that for one-point perspectives a viewing point and a vanishing point and not a viewing direction must be defined. Two- or three-point perspectives are calculated accordingly with two or three vanishing points.

Figure 3.6a shows a perspective view of the Willow II chair by Charles Rennie Mackintosh. The three-dimensional information necessary to assemble the chair was taken from the two-dimensional representations described in Section 2.2. This chair is seen from the viewpoint of an adult approaching the chair from the front.

The location of the viewpoint is extremely important for the visual impact of a perspective, as the following figures demonstrate. Figure 3.6b looks at an assembly of two Willow II chairs and a table from an

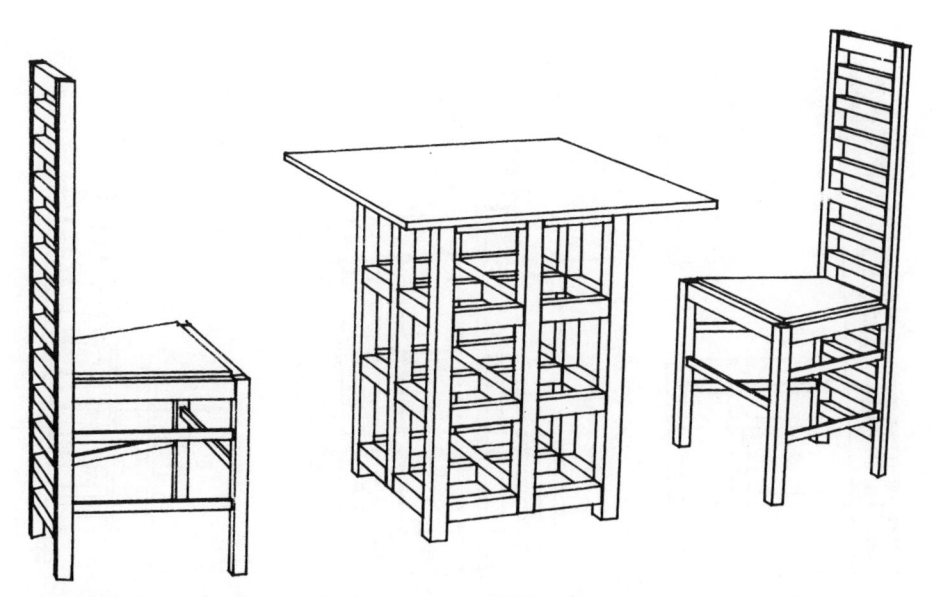

Figure 3.6b   Chairs and table by Charles Rennie Mackintosh seen from an adult's eye level.   Laura Lee.

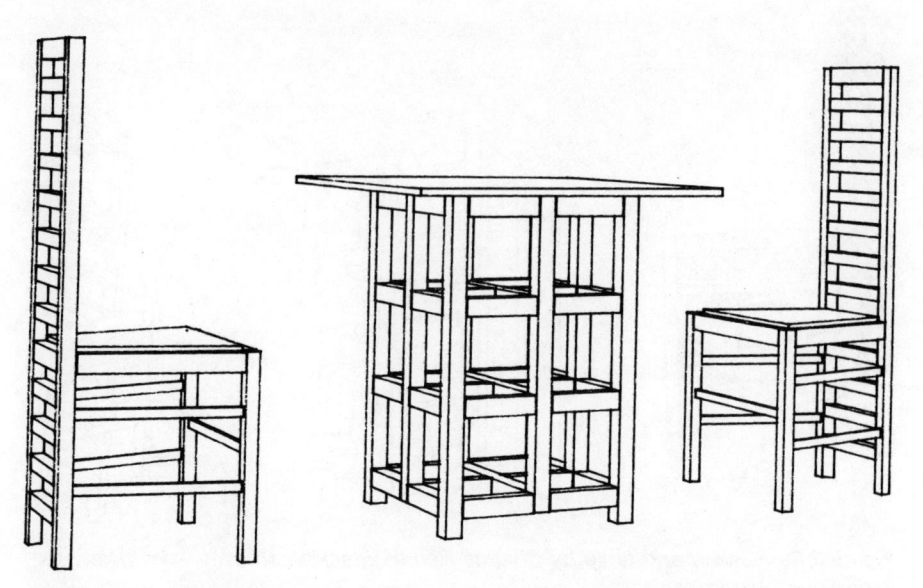

Figure 3.6c   Chairs and table by Charles Rennie Mackintosh seen from a child's eye level.   Laura Lee.

Figure 3.6d Chairs and table by Charles Rennie Mackintosh seen from a worm's eye level. Laura Lee.

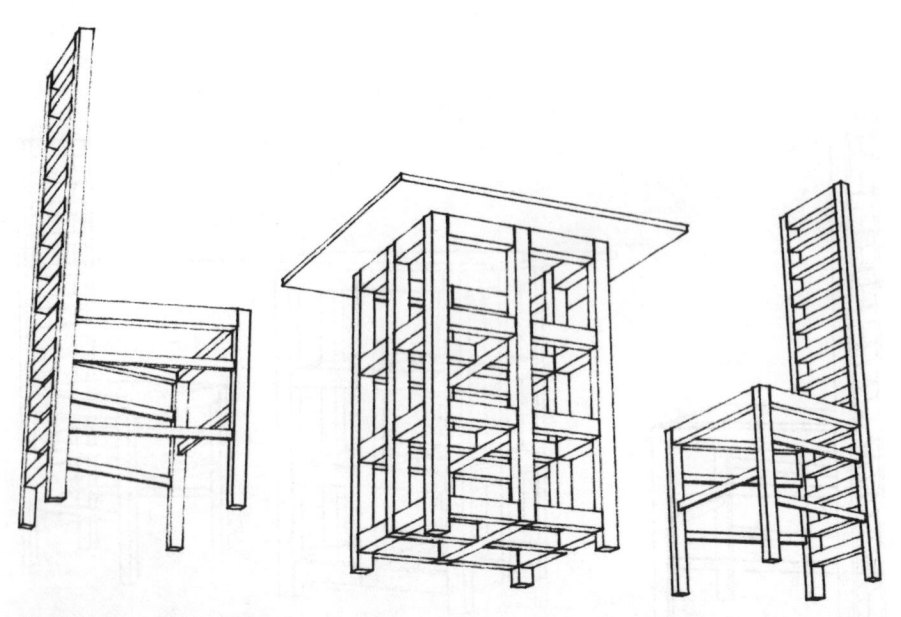

Figure 3.6e Chairs and table by Charles Rennie Mackintosh seen from below the floor plane. Laura Lee.

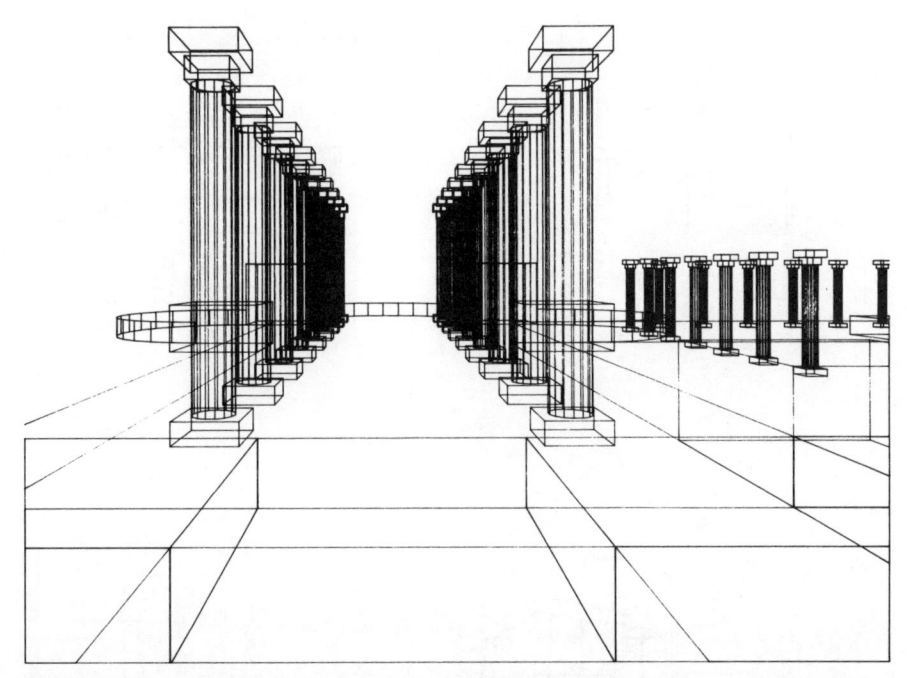

Figure 3.6f One-point perspective view of the central nave of a medieval monastery church using DRAW. Hidden lines are not removed. Jean Christophe Robert.

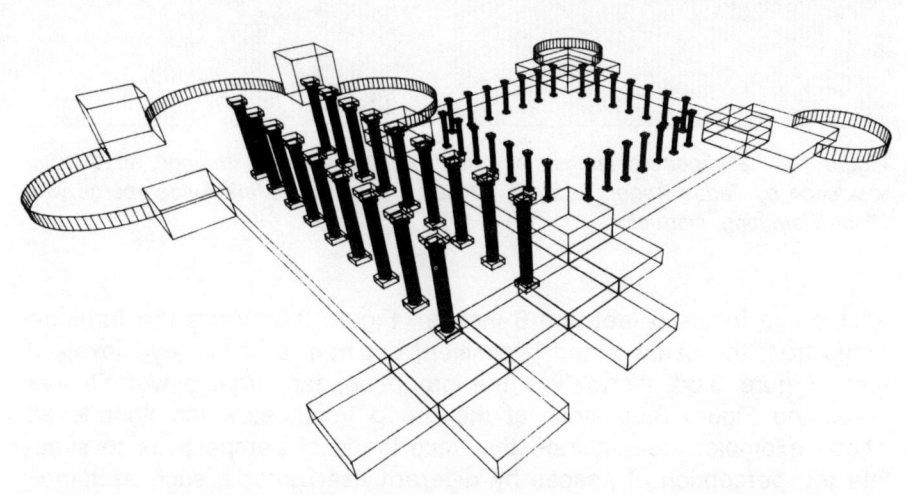

Figure 3.6g Three-point perspective bird's eye view of a schematic medieval monastery using DRAW. Jean Christophe Robert.

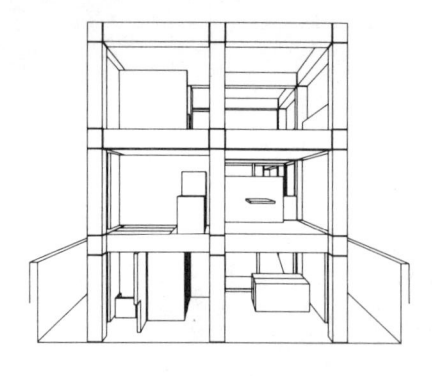

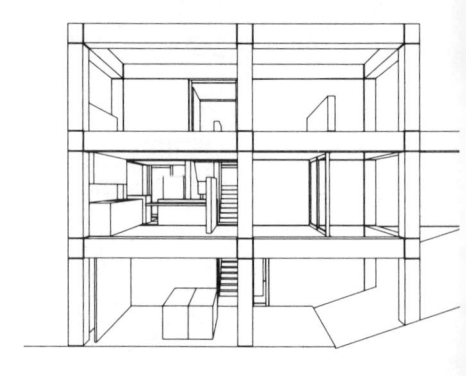

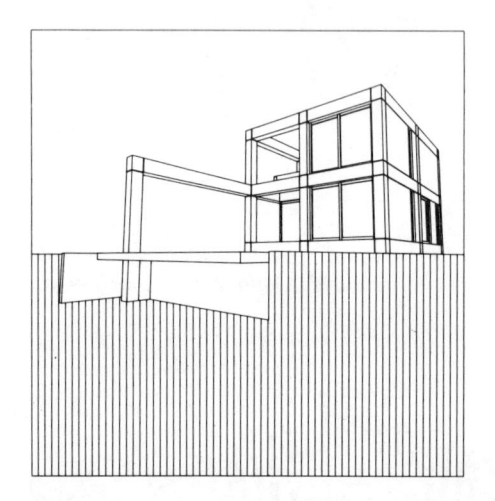

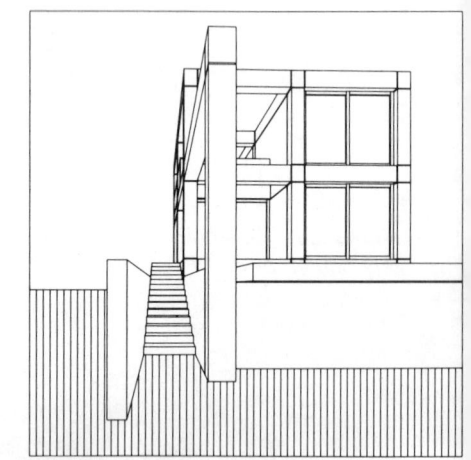

Figure 3.6h Perspective images approaching and traveling through an existing residence by Tadao Ando. Analysis by Aaron Levin and Mark Aufdemberge with Ulrich Flemming, instructor.

adult's eye level—5 feet and 6 inches. Figure 3.6c views the furniture group from the same *x* and *y* position, but from a child's eye level—3 feet. Figure 3.6d shows how the group appears from a worm's eye view, and Figure 3.6e looks at the group from below the floor level. These examples demonstrate the importance of perspectives to simulate the perception of spaces by different user groups, such as handicapped people, adults, or children.

Figure 3.6f represents a view looking into the nave of a reconstructed medieval monastery church. The hidden lines are not removed, therefore, all lines are displayed. Depth illusion in this one-point perspective is created by the increasing density of the lines toward the end of the church. The columns appearing on the right belong to the adjacent monastery and seem less important due to the focused viewing direction. Figure 3.6g shows a perspective view of the same building from a bird's eye view.

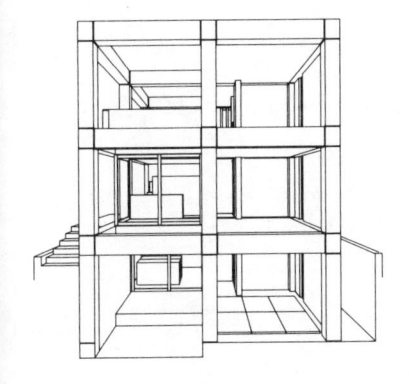

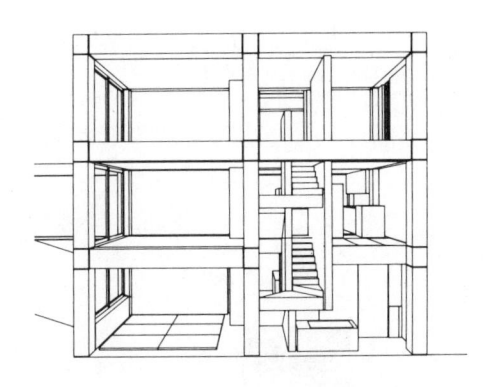

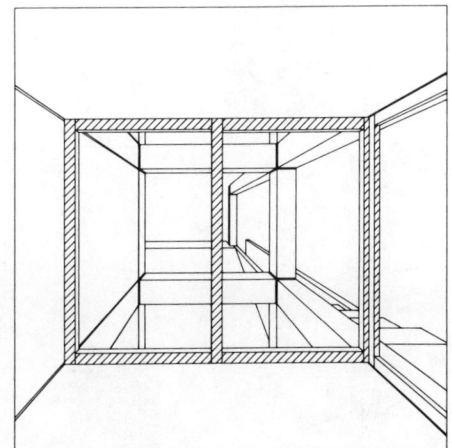

Figure 3.6h is a perspective tour through an existing residential building by Tadao Ando. With two exceptions, all images are one-point perspectives. The building is designed on a square grid, external walls and windows are infill. External and internal stairs are necessary orientation clues in otherwise difficult to distinguish perspective views.

Figure 3.6i is a perspective tour through a student design project using the panel architecture language. The problem statement was for

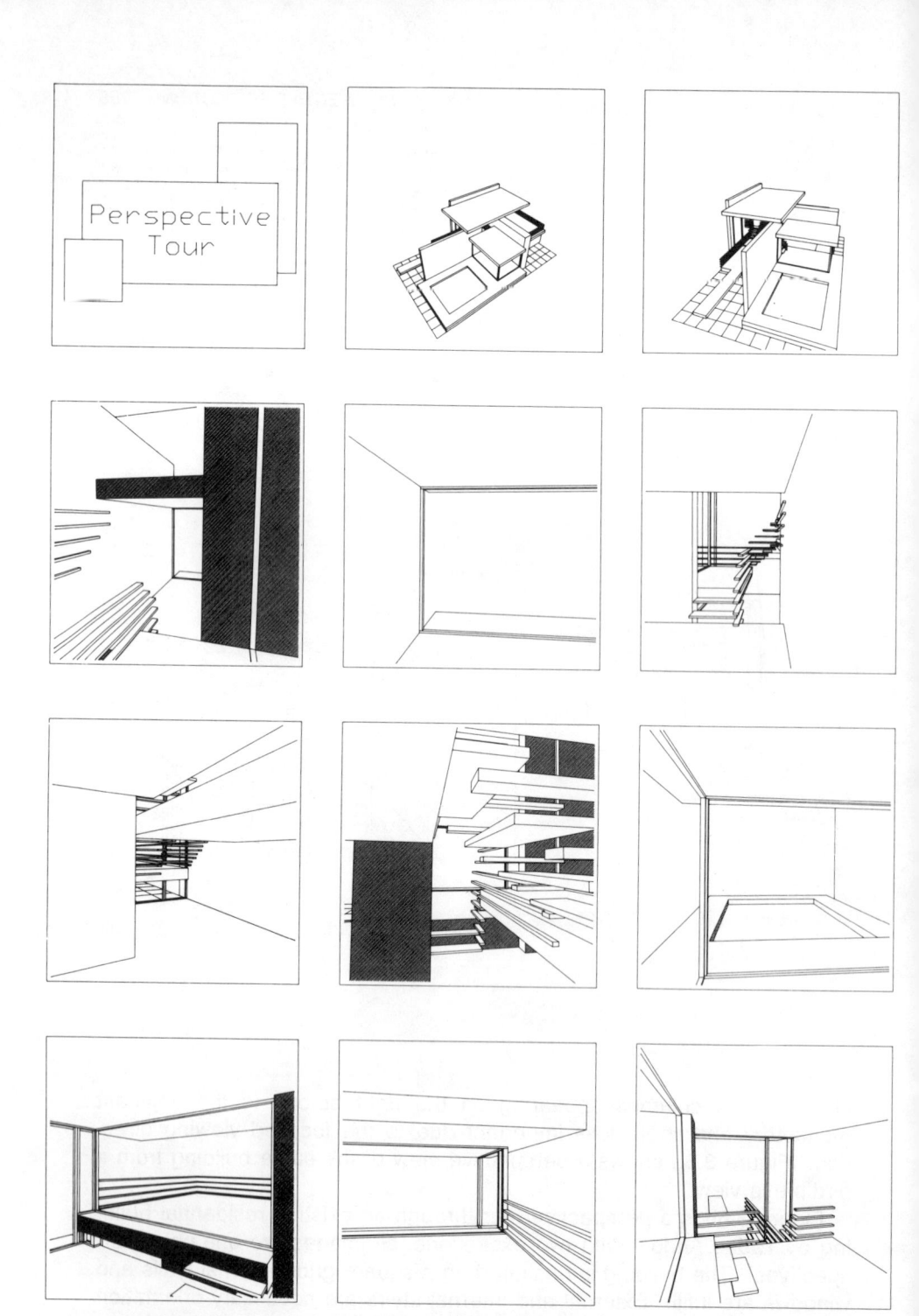

Figure 3.6i A perspective tour through the design of a writer's pavilion. Norman Larson with Ulrich Flemming, instructor.

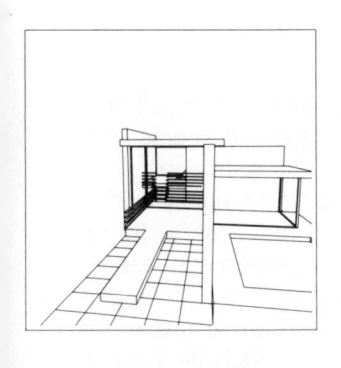

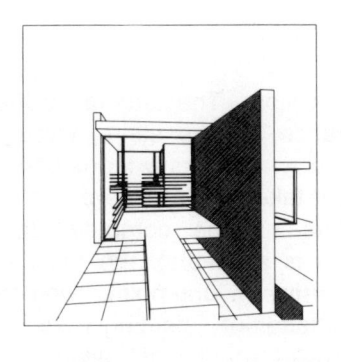

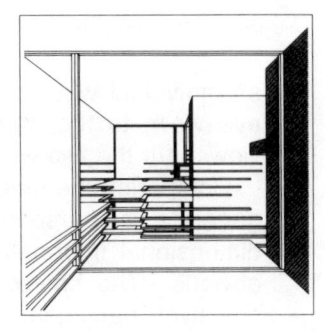

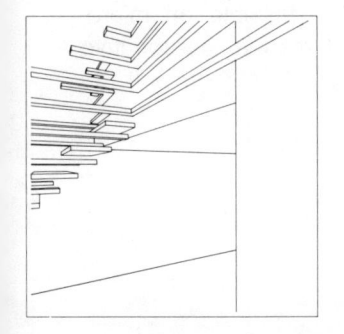

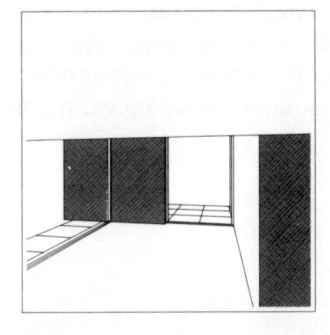

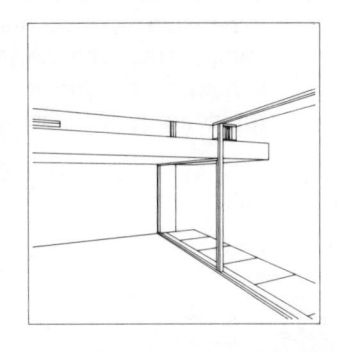

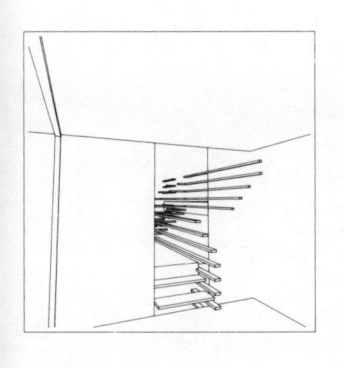

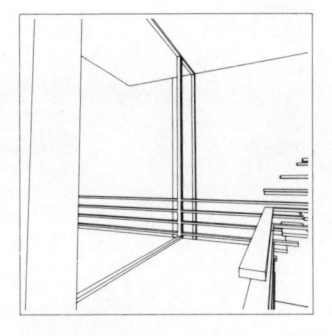

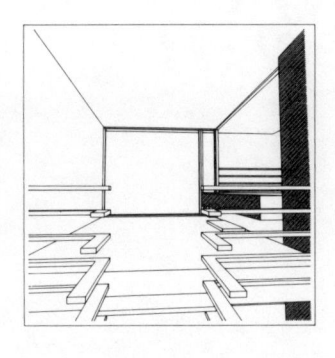

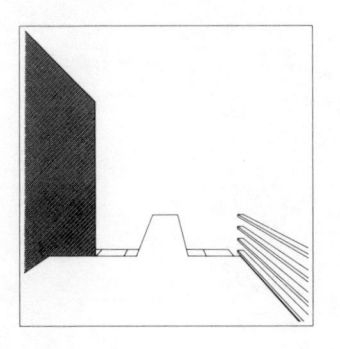

Panel Architecture

Writing Pavilion

Norman E. Larson

an individual writer's pavilion. The tour takes the viewer from a bird's eye view, to the entrance, up the stairs, through the two rooms with views, out the two windows, and finally leads back to the entrance.

Comparing the time it takes to produce a perspective manually and to generate a perspective on the computer (if all necessary three-dimensional information is available), the machine's advantage seems obvious. The choice between one-point, two-point, or three-point perspectives becomes a matter of selecting parameters from a menu. In the future, real-time walk-throughs of buildings, now available only in expensive special hardware configurations, will be possible on microcomputers. The sense of abstraction, inherent in manual perspective construction and in early computer-generated perspectives, will be replaced by realistic, animated perspective images.

4

Manipulation

Manipulation in traditional design allows a designer to transform a shape or an object into different positions, scales, and proportions as an individual entity or as part of a series. Manipulation of objects is different from manipulation of views of the object: Reducing its actual size by a factor of 2 is an object manipulation (called scaling in many CAD programs), whereas the display of the object at one half of its original size is a viewing manipulation (called zooming out in many CAD programs). Each of the manipulations and, even more so the combination of them, can increase our understanding of the design. Generally, manipulation is "skillful handling or operation; artful management or control" [Heritage70]. The number of manual manipulation techniques that have developed over time is extensive. Hanks lists 39 typical manipulative verbs [Hanks77]:

Multiply, subdue, transpose, delay, flatten, submerge, weigh, fluff-up, subtract, thicken, relate, protect, symbolize, divide, invert, unify, distort, squeeze, freeze, destroy, by-pass, lighten, stretch, extrude, segregate, abstract, eliminate, separate, search, rotate, complement, soften, concentrate, add, repeat, adapt, repel, integrate, dissect.

These verbs and the associated nouns are frequently used in design studio critiques and reviews. Although some are difficult to define properly without a given design context, they show the richness of manual tools that has developed to manipulate a design or its parts. The importance of manipulation for the design process must not be underestimated. The manipulative capabilities of most microcomputer programs are limited; which explains to an extent why they are respected as capable drafting aids but seldom as real design aids. In areas of manipulation that lend themselves to mathematical formalization easily, microcomputers offer excellent design support. In particular, transformation, repetition, and extrusion will be described in depth in the following sections, which concentrate on what object manipulations can achieve rather than how the computer executes them. Readers interested in the underlying mathematical principles and computer algorithms are referred to the appropriate literature [Newman79], [Harrington83], [Foley82], [Hearn86], [McGregor86], [Mitchell87] and to the programming appendix of this book. Many of the above verbs are combinations of the aforementioned three basic classes of operations. Within the near future, all manipulative verbs that entail quantifiable operations only could be formalized and made available for microcomputer programs, thus significantly expanding the manipulative vocabulary of the new machines.

4.1 TRANSFORMATION

Architects commonly use the three transformations of translation, rotation, and scaling in the design process. Different transformations applied to one object can create a variety of images that only vaguely resemble the original object. Standard mathematical techniques such as coordinate geometry, trigonometry, and matrix methods are used to accomplish transformations on the computer. Most microcomputer CAD programs allow the following transformations to manipulate an object:

1. *Translation.* The commonly used command for this transformation is MOVE. To move an object results in a change of its location in relation to the origin of the coordinate system. A variation is the COPY command that allows the object to remain in its original location and to move a copy of it to a new location.
2. *Rotation.* The commonly used command is ROTATE. Rotating an object results in a change of its vertices in relation to the origin of the coordinate system. Some programs allow the rotation of a copy of an object while the original remains in its place.
3. *Scaling.* The commonly used command is SCALE. Scaling of an object is a change of one or more of its vertices in relation to the origin of the coordinate system, that is, shrinking or expanding it. Some programs allow a uniform scaling only; others allow the scaling in x, y, and z direction. Scaling must not be confused with zooming, which means the temporary change of the viewing window. A scaling factor will scale the object permanently in relation to its original size.

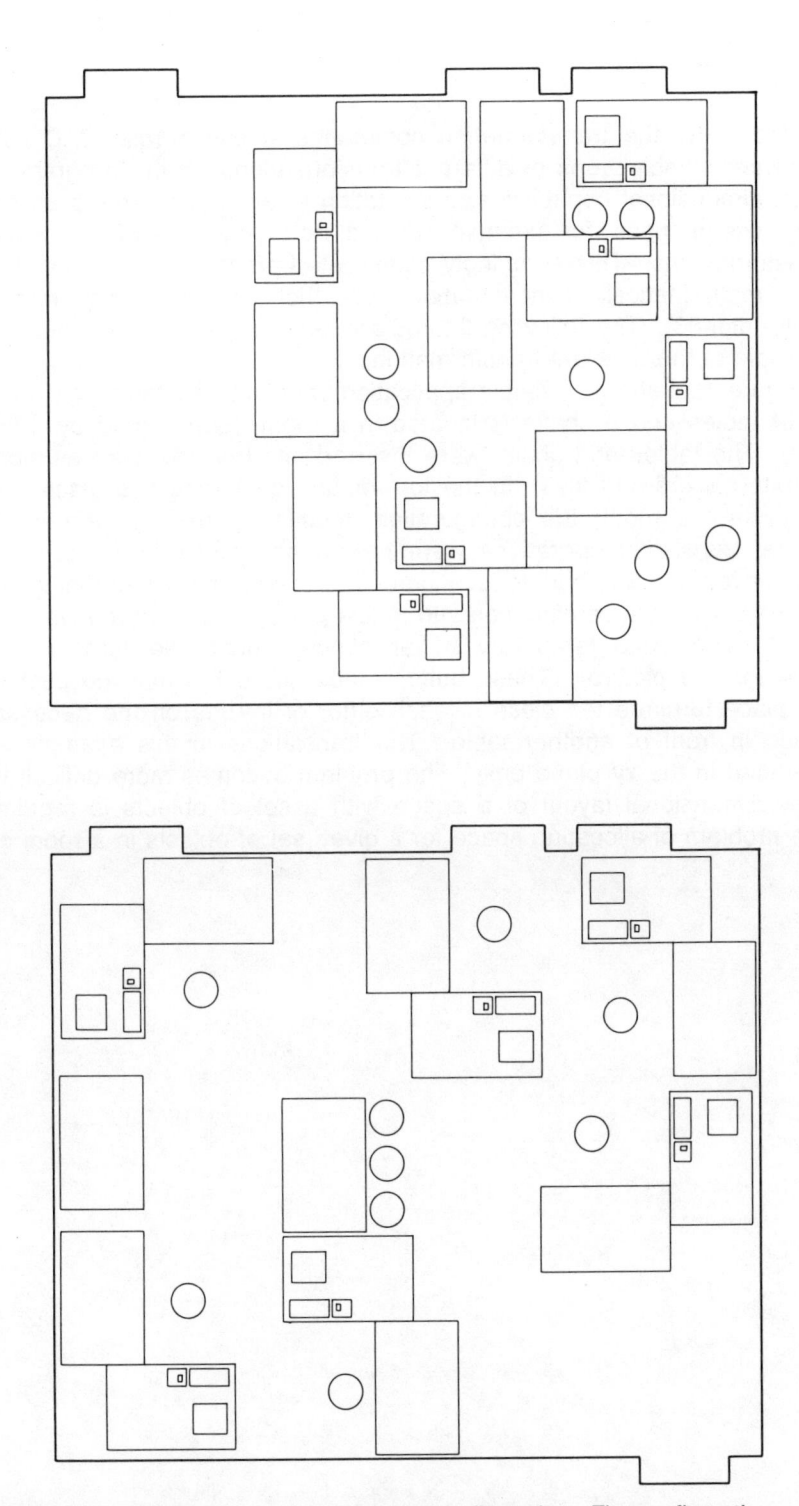

Figure 4.1a Translation: moving furniture in a floor plan. The configuration on the top is unfit for use; the configuration on the bottom is the final layout.

72   MANIPULATION

Underlying the transformation commands in commercial CAD packages are combinations of different transformations. If the program has three-dimensional capabilities, the rotation of an object around an arbitrary axis in space, for example, will require a sequence of six different transformations. This seemingly complicated procedure is facilitated by the mathematical concatenation of the matrix transformations [Harrington83]. The following figures are kept very simple to explain the principle of the different transformations.

Figure 4.1a shows a simple application of object transformation. A set of 14 tables and 9 chairs is located in a room, represented by a floor plan. The tables and chairs were inserted into the floor plan as blocks or external drawing files. In the top image, the furniture is placed randomly in the room; the configuration is unfit for use. In the bottom image, translation operations were performed on the furniture, and it was moved into appropriate locations. This happened by "dragging" the pieces alone or in combination into a new place. The ordering was facilitated by drawing temporary buffer zones around the furniture (not shown in the picture). These buffer zones guarantee that the user will not place furniture too close to each other or intrude on the necessary space in front of another table. The translations in this example are executed in the *xy* plane only. The problem becomes more difficult if a three-dimensional layout of a space with a set of objects is required. The problem of allocating space for a given set of objects in a room can

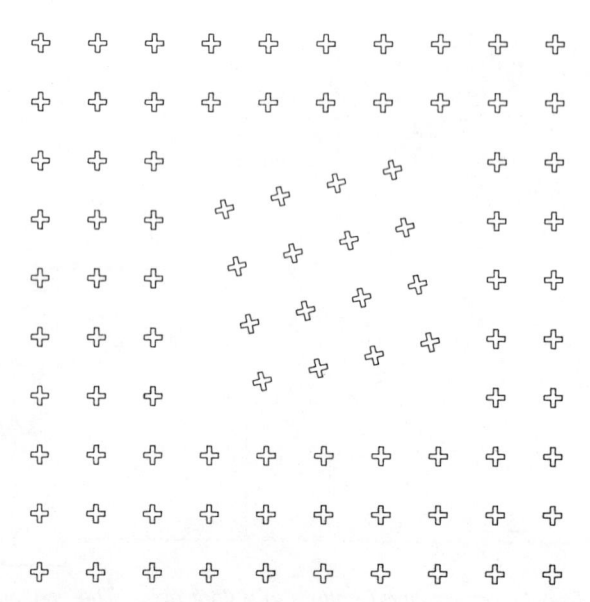

Figure 4.1b   Rotation: the grid in the center is rotated by a specified angle.

be automated and has become an area of architectural research [Flemming86b].

Figure 4.1b was constructed using the rotation option in a CAD program. The operation started with establishing a grid of 10 columns in the x direction and 10 columns in the y direction. Each column is specified by its location; for example (1, 1) is the lower left and (10,10) is the upper right column. In a second step, columns (4, 4) – (4, 8) and columns (5, 8) – (8, 8) are removed. After this, columns (5, 4) – (8, 7) are selected for rotation. The base point of the rotation is defined close to the center point of column (5, 4). The rotation angle is specified, and the entire set is rotated. The designer can then study the visual impact of this transformation in other projections, such as axonometrics or per-

Figure 4.1c Scaling: in an elevation with equally sized windows, one stands out through its scale.

74   MANIPULATION

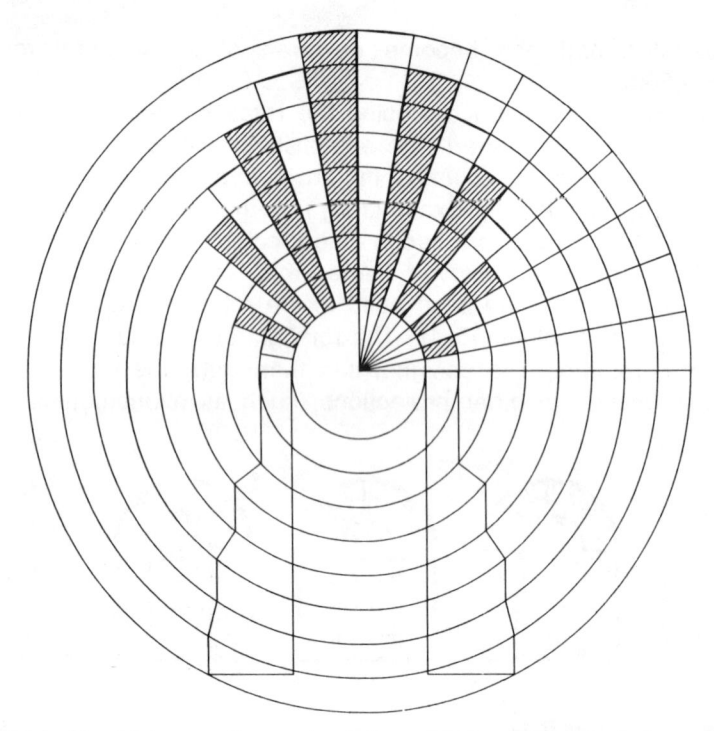

Figure 4.1d Combining scaling and rotation of two primitives, circle and line, to construct an ornamental arch.

spectives, and rotate the objects again, if necessary. The designer selects objects for transformation by drawing a rubber-band rectangle around them or by picking them directly on the screen.

The notion of scale was addressed in Section 3.1, but in a different context. Scaling as a transformation operation can help to increase or diminish the importance of architectural elements. Figure 4.1c represents a hypothetical four-story elevation with five columns of windows. One window has been scaled up significantly. The viewer will expect something special to happen behind this window because it stands out in size. The scaling operation was performed in three steps: first, the designer selects the window; second, the base point of the scaling is established (in this case, the lower left corner of the window); third, the scaling factors in the x and z directions are supplied (in this case, the same x and y scaling factors were chosen to maintain the proportion of the scaled-up window). Many architectural examples use scale transformations to demonstrate the importance of particular building parts or axes.

Figure 4.1d displays the result of a concatenation of transformations. The starting figure is a circle. Through scaling, eight larger instances of the circle with the same center point are created. A horizontal line is drawn from the center to the largest circle. This line is selected, copied, and rotated around the center nine times, increasing the rotation angle each time by 10°. A stepped line is drawn from the intersection of the vertical line and the largest circle to the intersection of the horizontal line and the smallest circle. This outline is mirrored around the vertical line, and corresponding fields are hatched in. Thus, the entire figure was created through transformations of a line and a circle.

The manipulative capabilities of transformations are limitless. The main task in applying transformations using the computer is to retain control over meaningful alternatives. Once the architect fully understands the transformational capabilities of the computer, they become powerful tools for the development of new design ideas. There is, of course, also an element of surprise and discovery in applying transformations, which is treated in depth in Part Two of this book.

4.2 REPETITION

Repetition is one of the oldest manipulative techniques in architecture. During the design process, it is powerful and economical. Applied excessively though, it becomes boring and can degenerate into a predictable pattern. When computers first entered architecture, it was generally expected that the repetitive character of computer-generated buildings would be dominant. Experiences with the new medium reveal the opposite. In fact, studies of historical buildings, especially floor plans, show that the use of repetition in plan, section, and elevation was a strong design characteristic throughout history. Repetition is applied to the following different parts of a building:

1. *Structural System.* The repetition of walls or columns at equal distances has the advantages of economy and predictability. Structural experiments or calculations need only be performed once and can then be applied repeatedly. This approach leads to a modular, additive design with few elements.
2. *Floor Plans.* The regular repetition of rooms is particularly evident in Greek, Roman, and Renaissance architecture. The modern office layout often pushes this principle to an extreme. It seems that over time the complexity of the repeated object decreased, resulting in a higher predictability of the design.
3. *Sections.* Until the advent of the high-rise office and apartment buildings, sections of buildings were rarely repetitive. Forced by gravity and material limitations, they followed special rules. This changed with the use of steel and concrete, materials that allow almost as much design freedom vertically as horizontally.

76   MANIPULATION

4. *Elevations.* Since the beginning of architecture, repetition has been a fundamental technique in elevation design. Sometimes, but not necessarily, repetition in elevations is related to repetition in the structural system and floor plans. In baroque times, however, repetition and symmetry in elevation became overpowering, regardless of the rooms behind the elevation.
5. *Furniture.* The repetition of furniture in buildings is an economic necessity. The existence of templates with prototype standard furniture confirms this observation. The repetition of furniture is particularly obvious in large public spaces such as auditoria and concert halls.
6. *Urban Planning.* Whereas the repetition of furniture as one of the smaller building elements is readily used, the repetition of entire buildings in site plans is less common. There seems to be a reverse relation between repeatability and size. Examples for large-scale repetition in urban planning projects are evident in schemes such as Le Corbusier's Ville Radieuse or Garnier's Cite Industrielle. Repetition in urban planning is a sometimes depressing reality in modern industrial cities.

Figure 4.2a shows a brick wall with three I-beams placed on top. Bricks are one of the smallest repetitive modules in building construction. Their proportion, adjusted to human scale, has had considerable

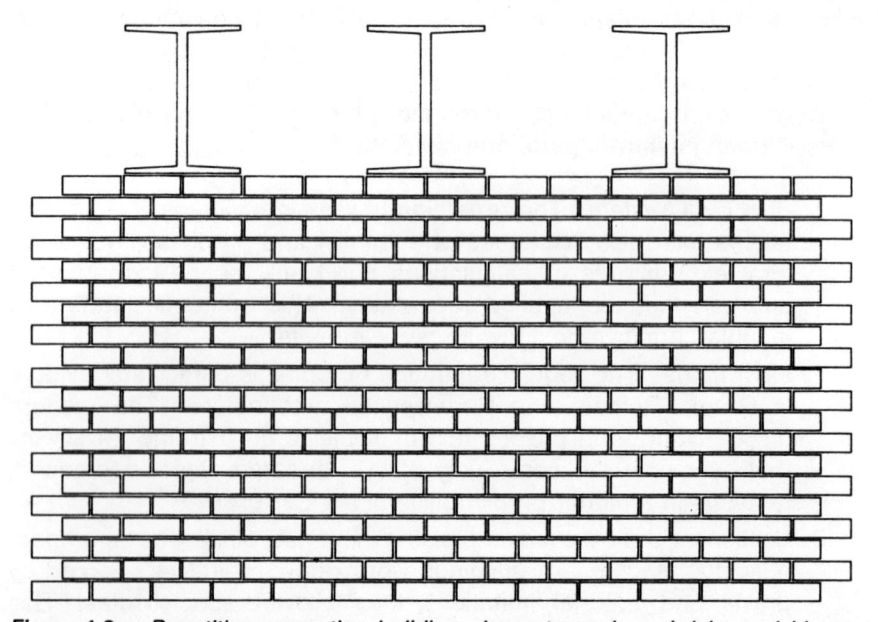

Figure 4.2a   Repetition: repeating building elements such as bricks and I-beams to form walls and ceiling.

impact in architectural history. The art of bricklaying was one of the most important building skills from the Roman Empire to the nineteenth century. Microcomputers allow the user to design brick elevations with ease: All possible brick formats can be stored as blocks or small external files and inserted and repeated in the appropriate locations. Small-scale structures can be "built" on the computer almost stone by stone, thus simulating the traditional construction process. The development of details, floor patterns, and corner solutions is greatly facilitated.

The same is true to an extent for other repetitive elements in design, for example, the two-by-fours in residential construction. The standard length wooden members are inserted in the appropriate locations in the floor plan. If the members are supplied with attributes, such as cost, weight, and dimensions, material lists and other quantities can be directly extracted from the drawing. Figure 4.2b gives a simple example.

Figure 4.2c displays eight instances of the same composite element, repeated and placed at an angle. The composite element itself consists of only two distinct pieces: one column and one half arch mirrored about the center line of the arch. Simple repetition creates a quite complex spatial object. The appendix contains a program that constructs a similar object with a short LISP routine.

On a smaller scale, Figure 4.2d demonstrates the application of repetition and mirroring in a facade design by Henry Hornbostel. The figure

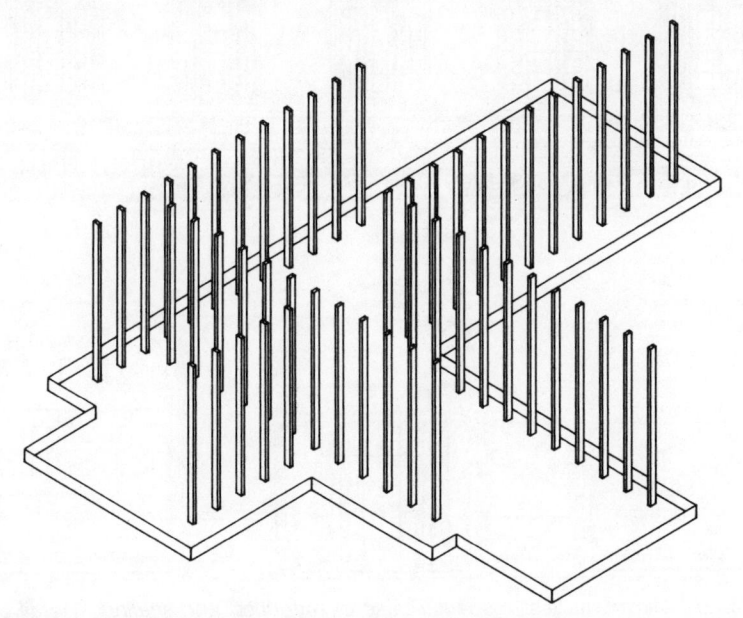

Figure 4.2b Repetition: repeating wooden studs in residential wall construction.

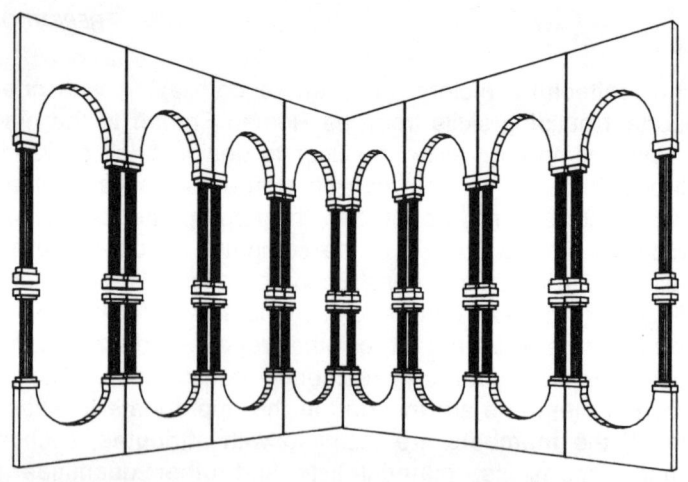

Figure 4.2c Repetition: repeating and mirroring elements consisting of columns and arches to form a space.

Figure 4.2d Mirror images: a special case of repetition and scaling. Detail of the east elevation of the College of Fine Arts at Carnegie Mellon University. Norman Larson.

also shows that repetition is not necessarily boring. A relatively small number of repetitive elements placed in an ordered framework can produce quite exciting architectural expressions.

The manual repetition of buildings or building elements requires a conscious decision and extensive drawing effort. Present microcomputer programs accomplish repetition of any element with very little effort. It is not surprising that repetition as a manipulative technique is often employed in the elevations of large buildings.

4.3 EXTRUSION

Extrusion is the conversion of a point into a line, of a line into a surface, or of a two-dimensional shape into a volume by extruding the shape by a given increment, perpendicular to its plane of origin. This plane may have any orientation in space. Most microcomputer CAD systems, however, only allow extrusions from the *xy*, *xz*, or *yz* plane. Examples in architecture are cylinders as extrusions of circles and beams as extrusions of rectangles. Columns with an entarsis cannot be constructed by extrusion but rather by revolution around the center line.

Although the limitations of the extrusion technique are obvious, it is used quite frequently as a manipulative tool. Extruding a shape by different increments will create volumes of different proportions. If the proportion of an object is to be maintained, the original shape must be scaled appropriately. Many elements in a building or parts of a building can be obtained by extrusion of plans or sections. Office buildings by Mies van der Rohe often appear as extrusions of plans [Schulze85]. An example for a building apparently derived from extruding a section is the Pacific Design Center in Los Angeles by Caesar Pelli. Extrusions can also serve as an abstraction of real shapes.

Figure 4.3a shows a circle and the plan of a more complex object. The objects on the left and the right of the circle show extrusion of these two-dimensional shapes. Different extrusion heights will create objects of different proportions. If the proportion of the once extruded object is to be maintained, every change in size must consist of a scaling and a related extrusion operation.

Figure 4.3b demonstrates the effects of extrusion combined with translation. First the building was drawn in plan. The building elements were then extruded and lifted to the appropriate elevation. The resulting figure appears as a three-dimensional object. The creation of tilted roofs is not possible with this technique. Instead, the tilt of the roof would have to be simulated with a number of horizontal "contour lines."

Figure 4.3c is an example of the creation of a building by extruding a section or elevation. The elevation is drawn once and then extruded to the length of the building. In architecture, this approach has much fewer precedents than the vertical extrusion of building plans.

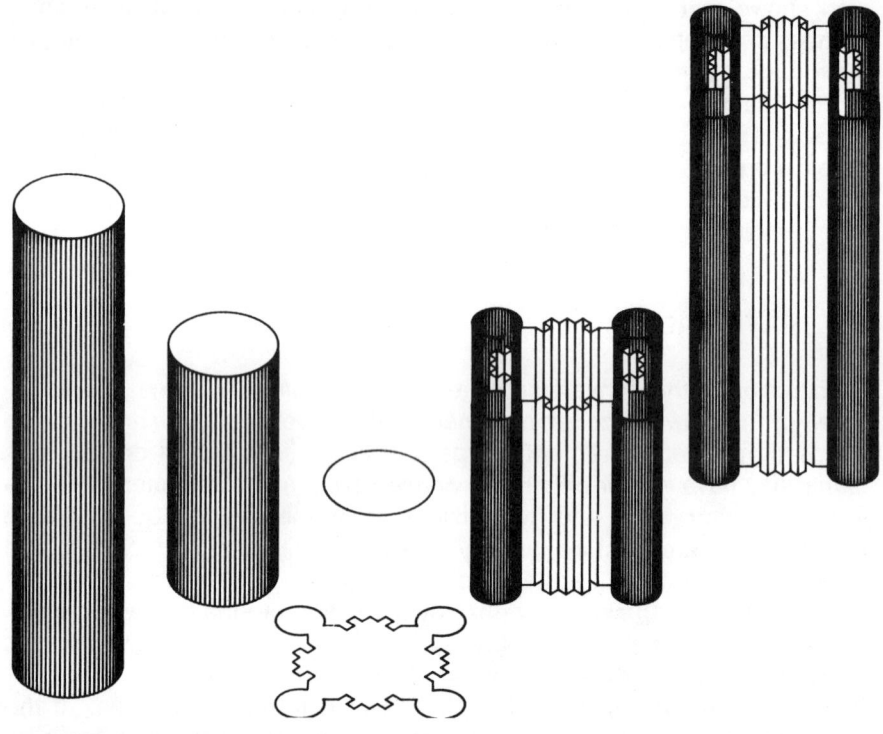

Figure 4.3a   Extrusion of a circle and a more complex shape: the extrusion factor determines the height.

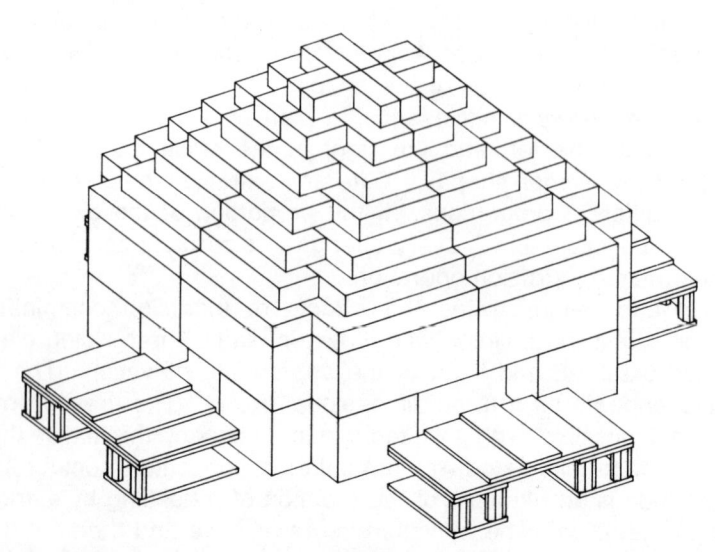

Figure 4.3b   Vertical extrusions and translations: building elements are raised to the appropriate elevation and then extruded.

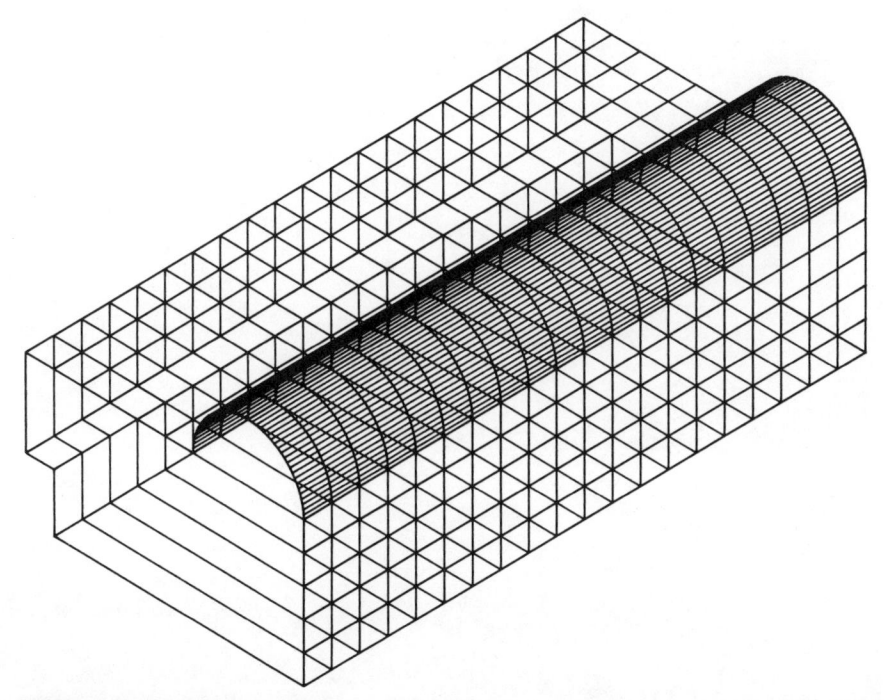

Figure 4.3c Horizontal extrusion: the section of a building is constructed once and then extruded horizontally.

Extrusions are the first three-dimensional features offered by most microcomputer CAD programs. They are conceptually and computationally simple, as they require only one z coordinate for all points in the xy plane. Extrusions are sufficient for many simple design tasks. They do, however, restrict design options. Advanced microcomputer-aided design programs therefore must support full three-dimensional operations that allow the construction of tilted roofs, spheres, and other complex forms that cannot be achieved with extrusions only.

PART TWO
Innovative Design Approaches

5

A New Design Approach

Part One described the use of computers in the traditional design process emphasizing integration of the new tool in a design process that has not fundamentally changed in the last 200 years. Part Two presents ideas and strategies for using machines for a fundamentally different approach to design.

Chapter 5 is an introduction and establishes major differences between the traditional and a new computer-assisted architectural design.

Chapter 6 describes architectural abstraction as it relates to computing and the powerful concept behind it. Similarities between architectural and natural language will be explored and used for forming architectural words and sentences.

Chapter 7 addresses the process of discovery. By describing architectural discovery as a process of directed and informed search for a solution, one possible definition of the architectural discovery process is given.

Chapter 8 explores the related area of architectural creativity. Although most designers use the computer as a productivity and not as a creativity tool, there is evidence that microcomputers can increase our creativity significantly. Presently, this happens through creativity support utilities, which include algorithmic and rule-based programs.

Chapter 9 is dedicated to the growing role of the microcomputer as evaluation tools. Evaluation is performed of manual as well as of computer-aided design. Evaluation areas of visual appearance, energy, structures, and cost will be described as examples. Although not complete, this list indicates the important feedback role that microcomputer evaluation programs can have on the design of the building.

5.1 COMPUTER-ASSISTED ARCHITECTURAL DESIGN

A short description of a traditional design process is included in Part One. The use of microcomputers in this process began with the automation of mechanical and manual labor intensive activities. The computer thus functioned as a mapping device and expedited mechanical processes. Office automation and computer-aided drafting are typical examples.

Computer-assisted architectural design is the next step in the integration of the new machines into the design process. It is different from the present use of microcomputers as it begins to employ the machine's special capacities to assist the designer's decision making. It allows the user to automate a growing percentage of the design process and to transfer information easily from one design stage to the next. Computer-assisted design will eventually allow a high-level dialogue between machine and designer.

In the general-purpose commercial software market, the integration of computers into the decision-making processes is slowly gaining ground. In architecture and design, it seems, too many factors must be considered from the very beginning to guarantee the successful implementation of computers as decision support systems. Architectural problems are often ill-defined, and there seems to be no limit to the set of possible solutions. However, if the architect has long-lasting practical design experience, the solution set is drastically reduced. These observations are true not only for architecture but for all disciplines involved in design.

A number of conceptual frameworks and application languages exist that provide a structure to record and make use of these observations. Thus, the new computer assisted design process will take advantage of these utilities. How, then, will the computer assisted design process be different from the present one?

The first difference will be the amount of information that is available to the designer. Information will be stored in databases of different kind and size, on personal and networked workstations. Extracting and managing information will become a major organization problem due to the size of the databases. In particular, visual information such as site plans and building documentation will require major database search and maintenance support. During and after the acquisition and ordering of information, the actual design process starts. The existence of the documentation, design sketches, and final design on the same machine environment will have consequences that are difficult to predict. There is no reason, however, why this information could not be inferred by the machine to produce design suggestions. The entire process will become much more interactive. The designer will allow the machine to address and solve limited aspects of the design process based on pre-

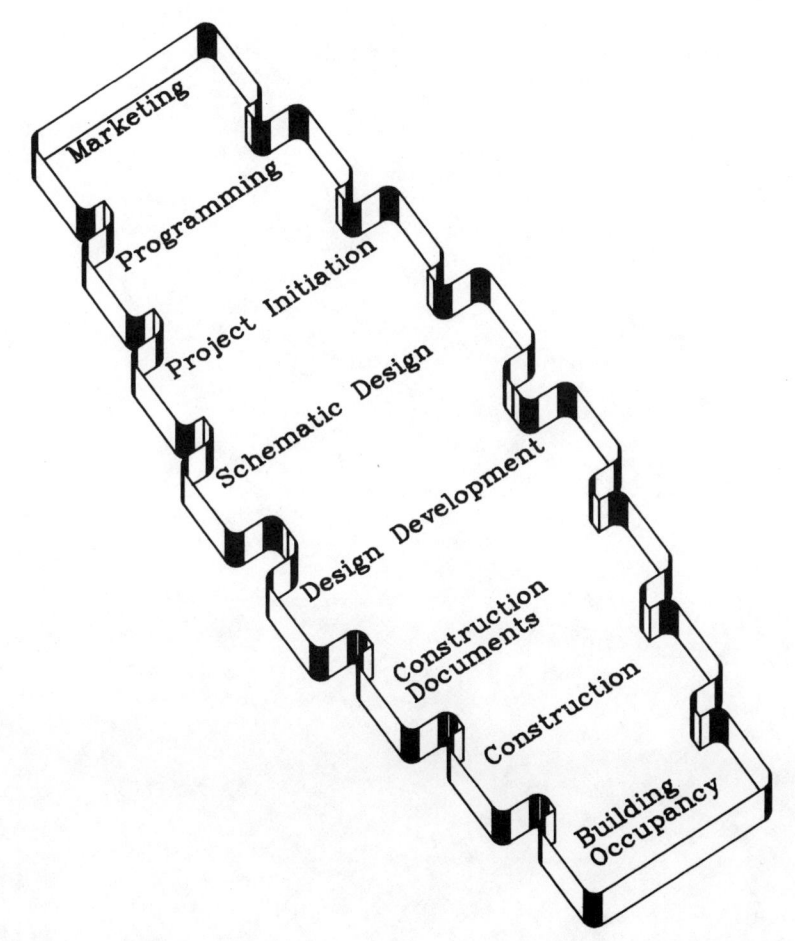

Figure 5.1a Stages to be integrated in a computer-assisted architectural design process.

vious idiosyncratic design solutions. Eventually, it is perceivable that the designer acts as a critique to the design generated by the computer.

How far and how fast these possibilities will change the way we design and build depends on several factors. Hardware improvements in speed and capacity will definitively influence the time frame. Significant changes will take place with the introduction of software tools that allow the encoding, representation, and application of architectural knowledge. These software tools will be based on algorithmic, sequential programming approaches, as well as on rule-based, frame-based, logic-based and object-oriented programming techniques. The next chapters describe these techniques as they pertain to architectural design and further explore their potential.

6

Abstraction

Every attempt to represent reality is a form of abstraction. The only true representation of reality is reality itself. Abstraction requires an agreement on certain conventions. The higher the level of abstraction, the more conventions that must be agreed on. One form of abstraction consistently used in architecture is the model. This includes not only physical models, such as working models and final presentation models, but also geometric or mathematical models. These mathematical models are most important for the use of microcomputers in the design process because they allow communication between the physical world and the computer.

The use of models in architectural design has a long history. In fact, no successful design process is possible without a model that is common to all participants. Representations of traditional architectural models are plans, sections, elevations, axonometrics, and perspectives. The three-dimensional model with all relevant attribute, object, and functional information is only mentally recorded by the designer. Drawing the projections of the model, that is, its representation, requires coordination and the knowledge of the laws of projection. The real power of computers will only become obvious once a similar body of knowledge and experience resides in the computer.

The use of computer-based models as an abstraction of reality offers some distinct advantages over the use of traditional models. As a primary advantage, the often tedious process of representing projections of the model is facilitated through the automatic generation of plans in a two-dimensional CAD system. If the program allows a three-dimensional definition of the model, then the automatic generation of elevations, axonometrics, and in some cases perspectives is possible.

This chapter will introduce forms of architectural abstraction that are important for the effective use of microcomputers in the design process. The forms of abstraction presented have analogies in natural and other languages. The objective is to explain the advantages of abstraction by building on the similarity of ordering principles governing both architectural and natural-language abstraction. Microcomputers are extremely well equipped to function according to these ordering principles.

The sequence of the sections in this chapter begins with the description of the highest level abstraction—the architectural language—and continues through to the lower order elements such as vocabulary, relations, rules, and grammar. If the reader prefers the top-down over the bottom-up explanation approach, the sections should be read in reverse order.

6.1 ARCHITECTURAL LANGUAGE

Language is a high-level means of abstraction to describe and represent reality. According to McKim, "a language consists of a set of rules by which symbols can be related to represent larger meanings" [McKim80]. Winograd further describes the main elements of a language as vocabulary, syntax, semantics, context, and style [Winograd83]. Several researchers have pointed out the fact that there may be strong parallels between portions of the architectural design process and the linguistic paradigm [Coyne86], [Schmitt86b]. If this assessment can be proven, then an entirely new field of architectural theory and tools will result. In fact, one could imagine the emergence of design processors that could influence architectural design to the extent that word processors influenced the creation and distribution of written documents.

The most commonly used language is natural language. It characterizes people and varies with time and location. Different languages have different capabilities to express complex facts and relations; they can describe, hint, and suggest. Technical languages have been developed for the expression of well-defined areas. They are more specific than natural language and can achieve more specific tasks in a defined area of interest. Procedural computer languages, an invention of the last 40 years, are highly formalized and specified languages to solve a particular class of deterministic problems. These procedural languages are able to achieve and to execute tasks in a very short time—if the problem has been well defined and is deterministic. Most of them do not allow syntactical errors and still require the definition of all the variables and constants to be used.

Whereas natural languages are often quite ambiguous in their use of words to express or describe a problem, computer languages require precision. Attempts are underway in Artificial Intelligence and architectural research to integrate some of the advantages of natural language and apply them to "architectural language processing." Although the problems may seem overwhelming at first, a number of successful attempts have been made with knowledge-based and expert systems to capture and use human expertise and apply it to a specific problem domain in design.

Graphic language is an abstraction of particular interest for architecture. Laseau describes its main elements as grammar, vocabulary, relationships, and modifiers [Laseau80]. It is interesting to compare these elements to the ones identified by Winograd earlier in this section. Graphic language has some definite advantages over natural or computer languages. It can be understood by a larger group of people, even by people of different natural languages. In its simplest form, it consists of lines, points, and arrows. A typical example is the quick directional sketch drawn by a native for a traveler in a foreign country. The sketch does not usually need any associated words or explanations; its symbolic content, supplemented by the traveler's previous experience, suffices to guide the person to the destination. Graphic language is at the same time highly general and idiosyncratic. Only in the case of final architectural drawings for buildings or equipment does it reach a level of formalization comparable to computer or technical languages.

An important advantage of graphic language is both its procedural and simultaneous or parallel character. Graphic language information must be presented on some medium. In the past, stone, canvas, or paper was used; now the medium is the computer screen. It can be read in a predefined sequence or supplemented by numbers and words on the same medium; but more importantly, it can be related to other parts of the drawing simultaneously. This unique ability of the human senses is known as graphic composition. Musical compositions, a well-known and studied phenomenon, are subject to the relativity of time. Graphic compositions are not. They can be loaded with information, hints, suggestions—just as natural languages—but presented on the appropriate medium, they represent a constant over time. They reflect the thoughts and feelings of the graphic composer at his or her time.

Computer languages and programs written in these languages still cannot capture and express the entire spectrum of graphic or even natural language. Perfect natural language processors or interfaces that, based on their domain knowledge, can detect and resolve all ambiguities, still do not exist. Much less do they exist for the processing of graphic language. The capability of drafting and painting programs to visually express symbols and their relations should not hide the fact that

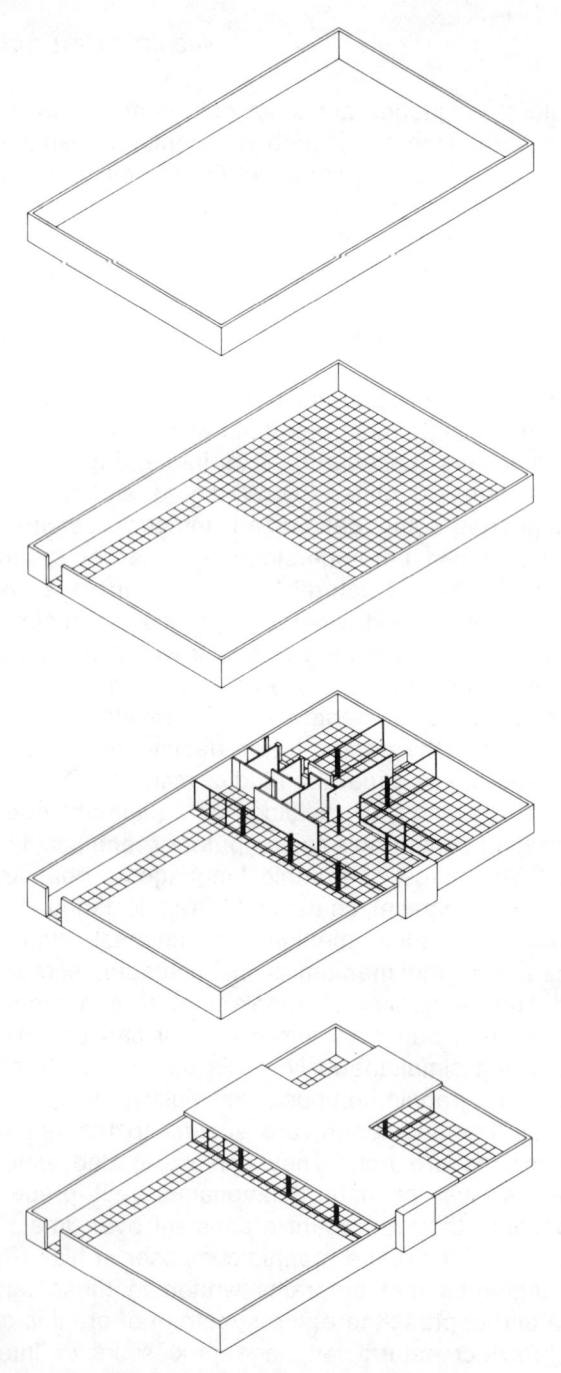

Figure 6.1a Court house projects by Mies van der Rohe. A system to arrange panels in different configurations determines the architectural language. Analysis by Norman Larson and George Zaglakas with Ulrich Flemming, instructor.

93

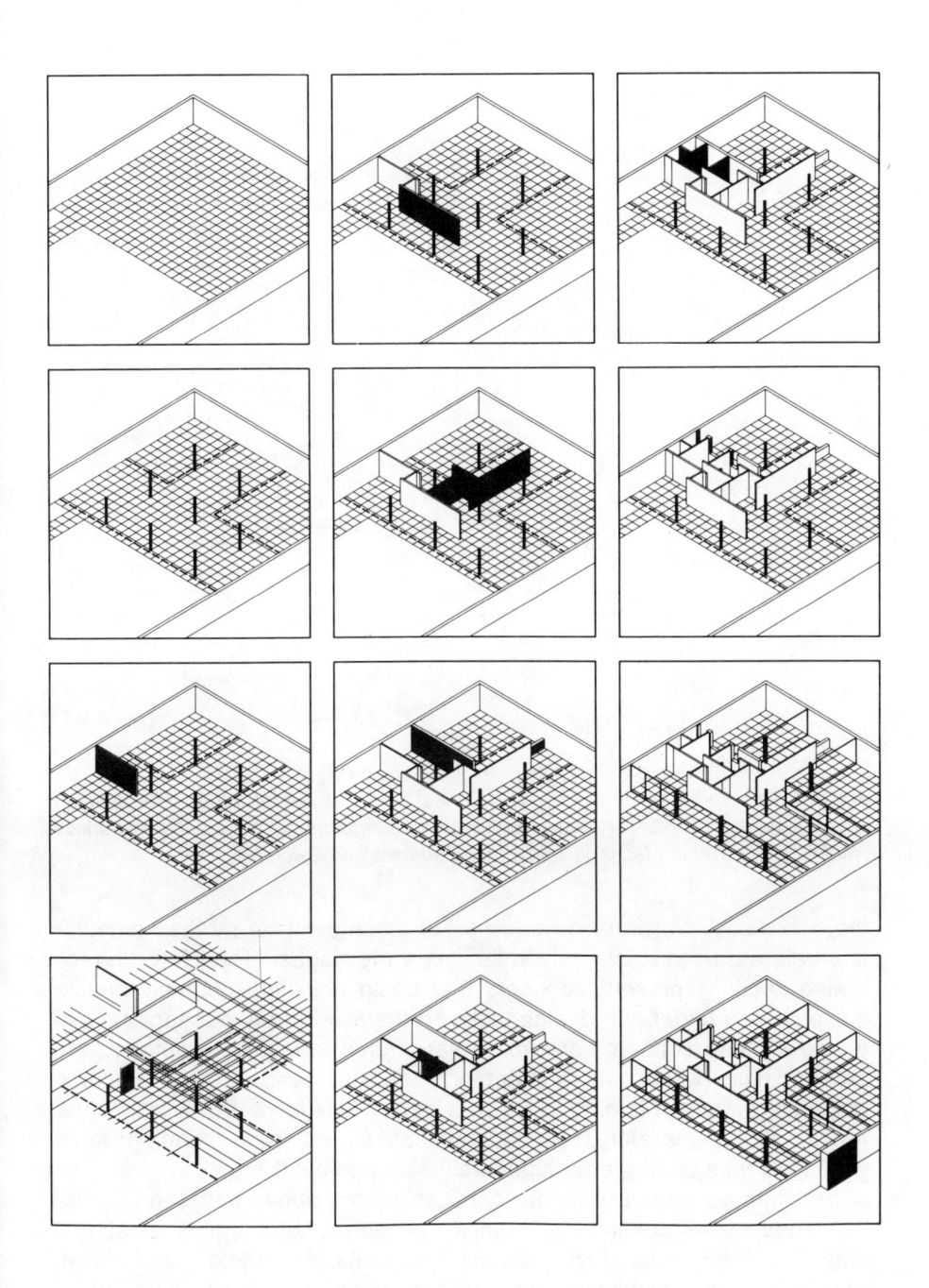

94   ABSTRACTION

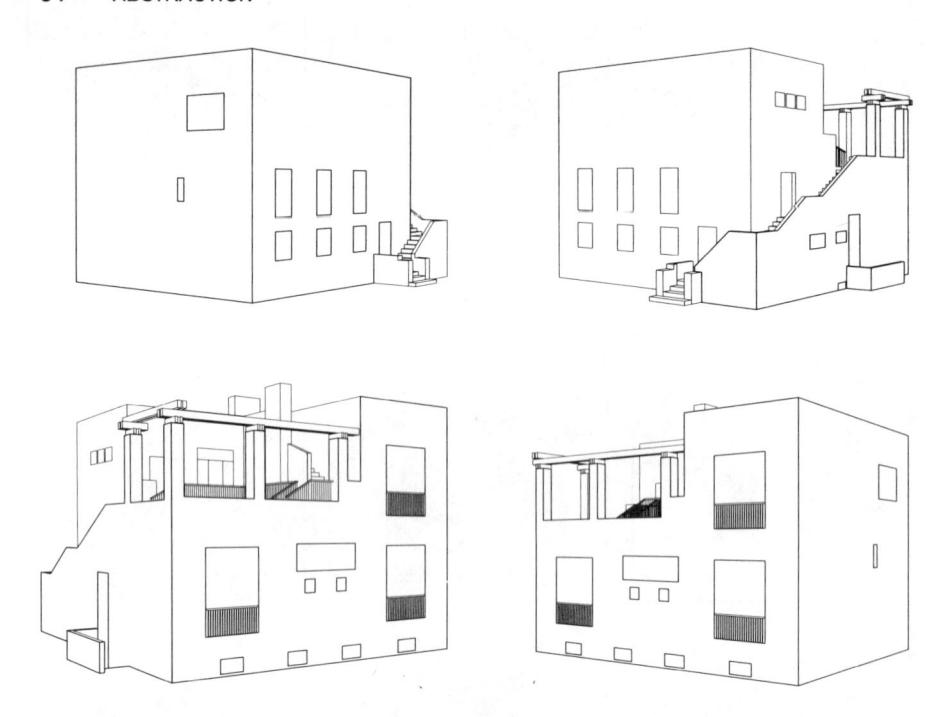

Figure 6.1b House on the Lido. Residential project by Adof Loos. The building is an example of wall or mass architectural language. Analysis by Anastasia Haidos, and Cynthia Massagli with Ulrich Flemming, instructor.

the necessary interpretation and use of these symbols by the computer to create a design exists only in its very early stages. Therefore, the following sections present concepts that could help to eventually enable computers to undertake design tasks on the level of an architectural language. These concepts are vocabulary, rules, relations, grammar, and programming within an architectural design context. The natural-language paradigm is only to be considered as a loose framework. The reader should therefore not be confused by the new meaning some words will take on in the architectural design context.

Architectural language is distinct from all the above and can best be examined in built examples. Similar to natural language, architectural language has vocabulary, syntax, semantics, context, and style. Although many buildings are not designed and built in a pure, identifiable architectural language (which is not to be confused with architectural style), there are a few exceptions. Figure 6.1a illustrates a court house project by Mies van der Rohe in the "panel" architectural language. Figure 6.1b displays a project by Adolf Loos, using "wall" or "mass" architectural language. Figure 6.1c is an example of the expressive ornamental character of Islamic architectural language.

Figure 6.1c Islamic niche design. The ornaments follow strict grammatical rules to form an architectural language. Richard Cobti.

While these figures show the finished product in a particular language, the next sections will concentrate on the definition of the vocabulary, syntax, and context of architectural language and the composition of buildings in a defined language.

6.2 VOCABULARY

Words form the vocabulary of natural languages. Although dictionaries contain more than 350,000 different words, the average person does not use more than a few hundred of them regularly. The number of new words that can be invented or developed from fractions of existing words is virtually limitless. However, words only make sense to the person who knows the language and its structure, and even more critically, they are only meaningful when used in the proper context by speakers and listeners with a common understanding of this context.

The intent of this chapter will be to explore architecture on the level of a language that bears similarities with natural language. This is followed by a study of the notion of graphic or architectural symbols as

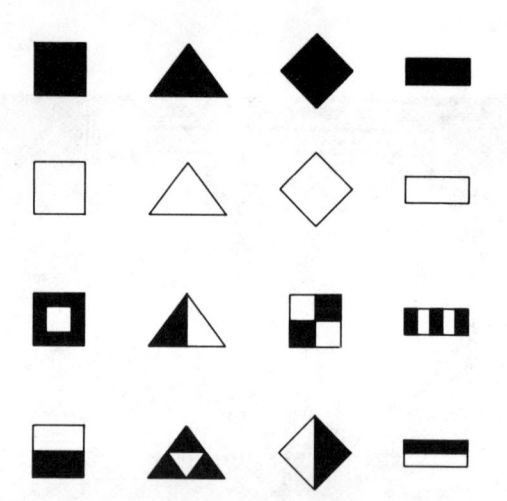

Figure 6.2a Basic graphic vocabulary consisting of square, triangle, rotated square, rectangle, and a selection of subdivisions.

Figure 6.2b Henry Hornbostel's opening vocabulary for Hamerschlag Hall: one door and five different window types.

"words" in a graphic language. It will become obvious that, particularly on the level of vocabulary, the natural-language paradigm has equivalents in the architectural design paradigm, but the similarities are limited [Coyne86].

Beginning with the similarities between the paradigms, we should agree that architectural words or symbols are the smallest units in a design language. In order to be meaningful, they must occur in the appropriate context. As a first example, Figure 6.2a shows a set of primitive graphic symbols that, depending on their specific domain, take on different meanings. The interpretation of the symbols or graphic words can range anywhere from navigation signs to architectural concept outlines. The message these words contain for the viewer will change with the domain. The second example, Figure 6.2b, is more refined. The message of the symbols is less abstract or context neutral. In addition, these "words" (in this case, windows) usually require a higher level context for their meaningful existence, in this case a wall or elevation. Figure 6.2c shows the combination of graphic words into simple graphic "sentences" in Palladio's Villa Rotonda. A third example introduces a conflict: A window detail in scale 1"=1", placed in a floor plan in scale 1"=16', will confuse the reader of the drawing, although the detail and the floor plan may be drawn correctly. A symbol of a bed appearing in an apartment kitchen plan will surprise the viewer because

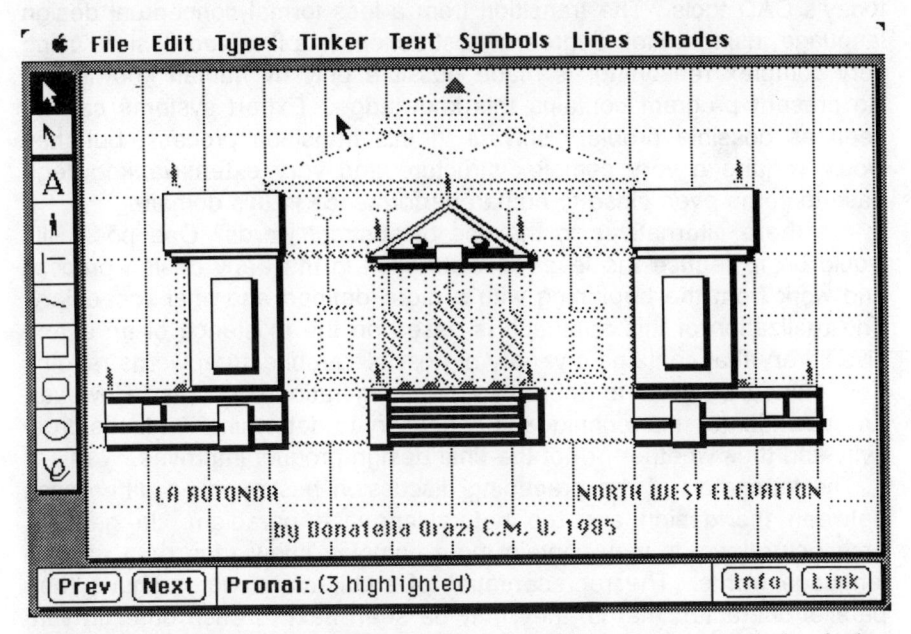

Figure 6.2c Complex vocabulary: sets of columns and pronai in Andrea Palladio's Villa Rotonda drawn with FileVision. Donatella Orazi.

a bed is not expected in the kitchen; the architectural word appears in the wrong context. A baroque window placed in a romanesque palace will cause curiosity because the symbol has changed its form but not its meaning over time. These examples show that architectural symbols, although we place them at the bottom of the language hierarchy, do carry meaning. They are not neutral and cannot be used in a context-free manner.

In manual drawing and traditional design methods the objective is to reduce the complexity of symbols in the abstraction stage to a minimum, that is, load the maximum amount of information into the vocabulary, trying to express as much as possible with a minimum of drawing effort. This can be achieved by applying different weights, colors, size, and other attributes to the graphic or architectural symbols. Otherwise, an excessive amount of drawing would be necessary, possibly resulting in an overly complex vocabulary or set of symbols thus detracting from the level of abstraction intended. In the design process it is often necessary in an early stage to consciously exclude certain complex representations to avoid being locked into premature decisions.

In this stage it is more important to show, for example, that a corridor is connecting two rooms than drawing the corridor itself immediately in its final dimensions. The designer can then in a later stage make the transition from the graphic "word" corridor to the actual corridor represented in a more formalized way. Here lies a basic problem with today's CAD tools. The transition from a less formal conceptual design language, using a high degree of abstraction, to a finalized design, using very complex reasoning, is made possible only by human knowledge. No present program contains this knowledge. Expert systems can be seen as possible problem solvers in this transition process, but they would require a very complex structure and very extensive knowlege base to come even close to human performance in this domain.

Are there alternatives to the use of abstract words? One possibility would be to reduce the level of abstraction in the early design process and work from the beginning with a more defined and final vocabulary. The realization of this approach is based on the existence of an extensive library that contains a variety of possible architectural words ranging from standard details to entire design configuration concepts. However, an evaluation of this technique is necessary to determine if it limits creativity and thus whether or not the final design product improves.

The latter part of the preceding discussion has exposed differences between the design and the natural-language paradigm. In general, architectural words may contain more complex knowledge than natural-language words. The representation of architectural words shows their parallel character, that is, they may be seen next to each other in various dimensions. Natural-language words, in contrast, are expected to appear in a certain sequence.

6.3 RELATIONS

The previous discussion of vocabulary has shown that architectural words need context to be meaningful. The following chapters are concerned with combining words into entities, called sentences, to form a composition. The application of three concepts is necessary to achieve this goal: relations, rules, and grammar. The dual character of architectural language—being both procedural and simultaneous—allows the explicit, static representation of relations between parts. The graphic representation of relations in an architectural drawing is the abstraction of implicit relations expected in a building. The graphic representation of relations can be formalized by way of rules to form a grammar. The grammar is then used to form the language.

Using graphical language in the traditional way means being accustomed to expressing relations with a set of different line types, arrows, blocks, or other similar elements. Lines that connect circles in a bubble diagram have a definitive meaning, both practically and symbolically. Graphical language allows the designer to make relations explicit in the stages of design where this information is necessary for clarification.

Whereas the same line types and other symbols can easily be produced by computer, the knowledge embedded in a manually drawn line is only graphically reflected on the computer screen. The machine has no knowledge whatsoever of the meaning of the line expressing the relation. An example will help to explain this dilemma: A bubble diagram consisting of five rooms labeled entrance, kitchen, bedroom, living room, bathroom and the appropriate relations expressed by lines will enable an architect to convert this diagram into a floor plan of a simple residential building. If the same drawing is transferred to the computer for interpretation as a basis for a residential design, it will not be able to interpret it and suggest a building layout, even if it could scan and vectorize the diagram and its relations (see Section 2.3). In order to design the building layout, the computer needs the relational information in a different format, for example, in the form of an adjacency matrix. Microcomputer programs that design layouts based on such matrices and other relevant information are possible and within reach. A second possibility to have the computer understand and interpret the relations expressed in the bubble diagram is the use of sketch recognition or intelligent computer vision. The example leads to the conclusion that microcomputers are presently not well enough equipped to perform the tasks of recognizing and applying graphically expressed relations in the design process.

Microcomputers, however, outperform humans in two other aspects of the interpretation and handling of relations. The first area is that of relational database management systems (DBMS) for a wide variety of microcomputers [dBASEIII84]. These databases store relational infor-

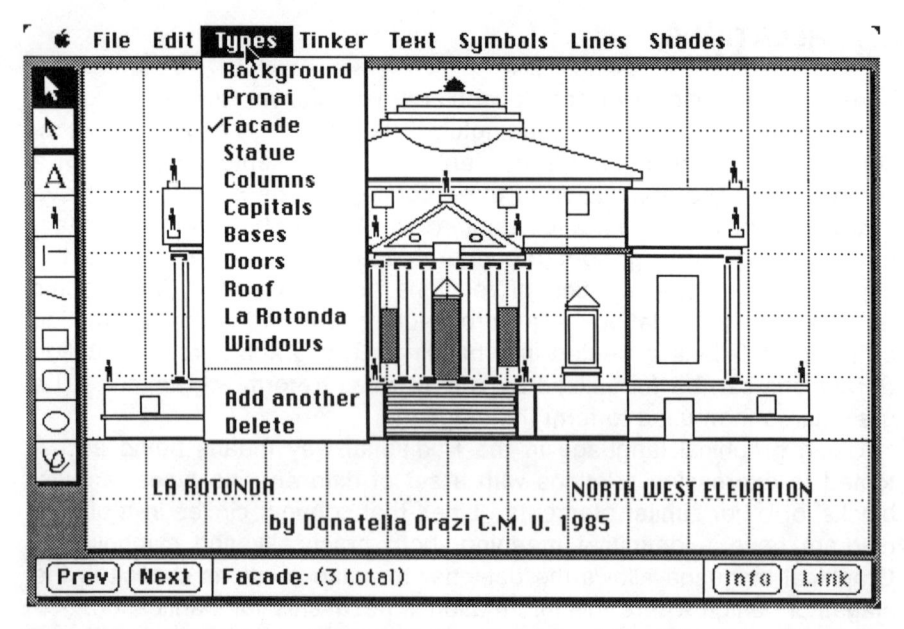

Figure 6.3a Establishing relations in the elevation of the Villa Rotonda. Using FileVision to express hierarchical relationships: the facade shows statues that are linked to files with text information. Jonatella Orazi.

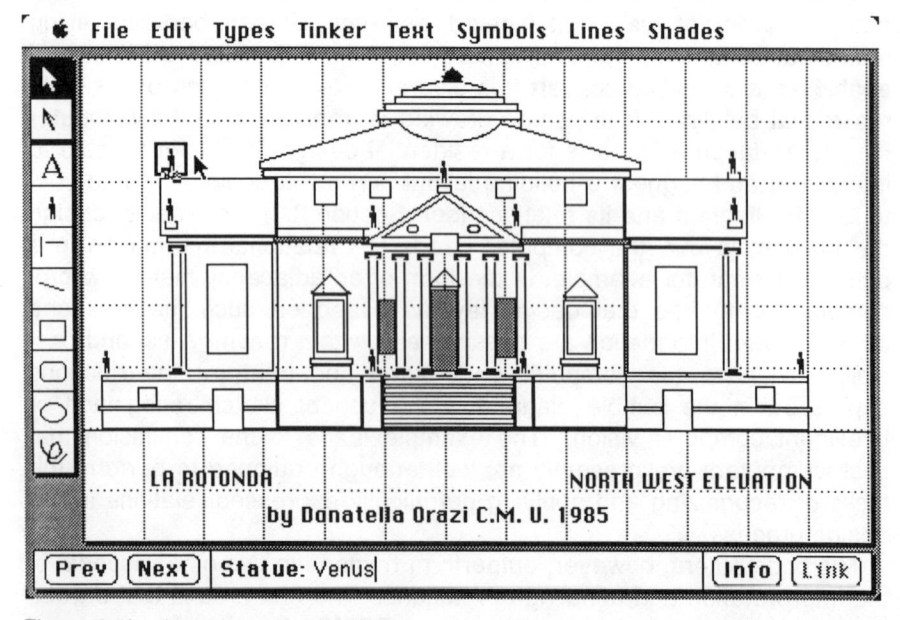

Figure 6.3b Inquiring about relations: requesting textual information about the statue by highlighting, using FileVision. Donatella Orazi.

100

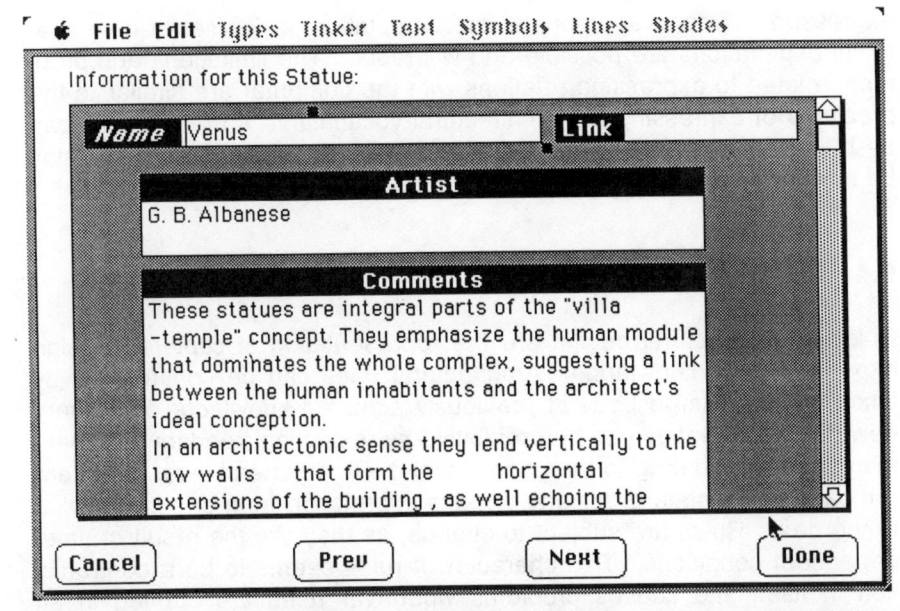

Figure 6.3c Explaining relations: text information about the statue of Venus on the northwest facade of Palladios's Villa Rotonda can be related to other FileVision text files containing, for example, information about the artist. Donatella Orazi.

mation and the attached data in two-dimensional tables or relations. If relations between different parts of a building or between functions of a building design can be translated into these tables, a customized DBMS will readily create reports and query results, as well as possible building configurations in table format. For the user to understand this format, it is often necessary to translate it back into graphical form. A special form of DBMS are visual databases [Filevision84] These programs allow the user to attach descriptions and relational information as attributes to manually created or scanned-in objects (see Figure 6.3a). If information is supplied for particular objects, the user can display it by clicking to the appropriate object (see Figure 6.3b) and it will be displayed in text form (see Figure 6.3c). In this way, relations are normally hidden from the user, but are made visible upon request. The second area in which computers excel is the mathematical representation of spatial relations. A set of techniques was developed and described in the literature [Flemming77], [Mitchell77]. Once these relations are encoded, the microcomputer will produce layouts according to these relations in a number and precision that go far beyond traditional design explorations. The next sections will describe some of these methods.

Microcomputers are weak in imitating the traditional, graphical method of describing relations. However, if the relations are defined and expressed in a form appropriate for computation, a rich set of new relational explorations are possible and will result. The limitations and problems related to expressing relations with the computer are similar to the problems of expressing the architectural vocabulary. If the relations can be built in as grammar of a particular architectural language, there may be a reduced need for expressing relations explicitly.

6.4 RULES

Rules in architectural design are the representation of captured design experience and knowledge. Architectural rules can be constructive by incorporating a large body of previously acquired knowledge into every new design, and they can be prohibitive by restricting freedom of experimentation by adhering to them too closely. On a general level, rules are a means to maintain order and to pass information from one generation to the next. Rules are subject to change, as they are the result of time-dependent conditions. This character of rules seems to be a contradiction in itself and causes problems whenever rules are applied in an absolute sense.

Two particular applications of rules in the architectural design process are presented: production rules and design rules. The first one leads to production systems, and the second to shape grammars, a specialized kind of production system [Waterman78].

Production rules in their simplest form consist of a left hand side (LHS), which contains a condition, and a right hand side (RHS), which contains the associated action. The rule is "fired" or executed if the program finds the conditions on the LHS to be true. The program will not execute the RHS if the conditions on the LHS are false. Figure 6.4a shows an example of a simple production rule. The rule is first formulated in English (top) and then translated into a particular computer language (OPS5), making it possible for the machine to process it [Forgy81]. Rules are important elements in the development of expert systems, that is, computer programs that capture human experience and knowledge and, when applied to specific problem domains, can achieve a performance that is similar or superior to human performance. Figure 6.4b gives an indication where rule-based systems could be applied in the design process. Although there are serious limitations to the relevance and application of if-then rules in design, they are powerful constructs that may potentially aid in the following areas:

1. *Preliminary Layout.* Traditional computer programs allow the composition of layouts by selecting program elements from a library and placing them on the screen or by algorithmic automated lay-

```
; All comments start with a semicolon

; IF      the office building is located in a cold climatic region
;         and the building size is small
;         and the building has one floor
;         and the building has 10% exterior glazing
; THEN    assign data from case number 101 to the building

(p case-101
       (goal ^level 2     ^status p)
       (office ^region cold  ^size small    ^story 1    ^glazing 10)
    -->
       (make case   ^num 101      ^HVAC PTAC       ^fuel elect
                    ^gas 0.000    ^elec 18.4       ^demand 0.06165
                    ^option1 3    ^s1 0.09         ^g1 0.00
                                  ^e1 17.5         ^d1 0.06165
                                  ^s2a 0.21        ^g2a 0.00
                    ^option2a 5   ^e2a 16.7        ^d2a 0.05776
                    ^option2b 24  ^s2b -0.04       ^g2b 0.00
                                  ^e2b 16.7        ^d2b 0.05776
                    ^option3 14   ^s3 1.52         ^g3 0.00
                                  ^e3 15.6         ^d3 0.05688)
```

Figure 6.4a   A simple production rule in both natural language (top) and computer language OPS5. Chen Cheng Chen.

out generators. Rule-based expert systems [Flemming86b] allow a much more complete and responsive design of architectural floor plans.

2. *Cost Estimation.* Traditional cost estimation programs operate on algorithms. Rule-based cost estimation programs can take into account personal experiences of the estimator, as well as local conditions.

3. *Energy Consumption Prediction.* Existing algorithmic programs require excessive amounts of input in order to make exact predictions. Rule-based energy consumption prediction can achieve the same level of accuracy with less, but sensitive input [Schmitt85].

4. *Structural Safety.* The existing procedural programs may be supplemented by rule-based expert systems to make high-level decisions and to provide expert front-end knowledge [Maher84].

5. *Building Code Checking.* Existing drawings, once recognized by the machine, can be checked for code compliance using rule-based expert systems. The rules are a translation of the regulations found in the building code.

Rule-based expert systems in architecture are in their infancy, and systems that perform reliably under realistic office conditions are small in number [Rehak87]. However, the approach to formulate experience,

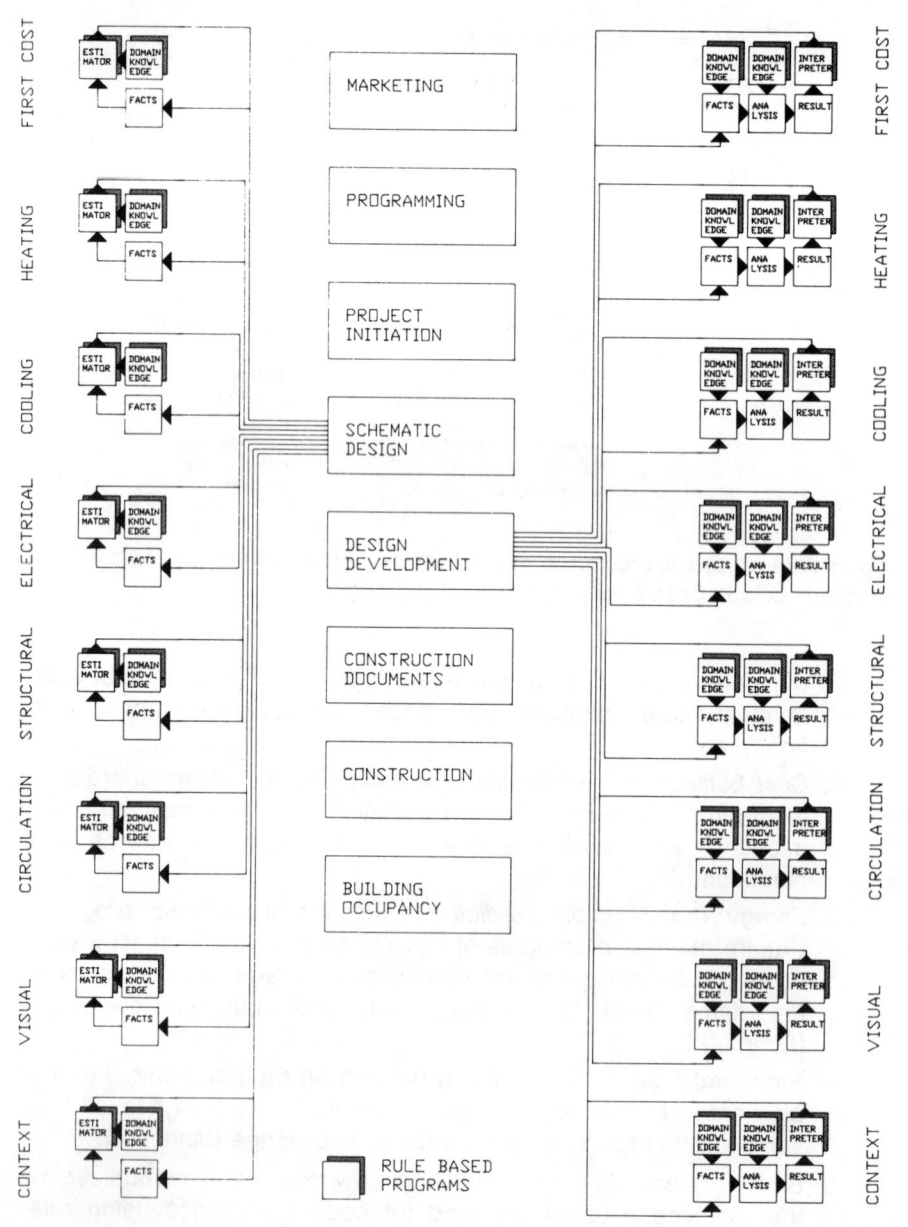

Figure 6.4b Possible applications of rule-based systems in the design process.

rules of thumb, and design knowledge is appealing and facilitated by a growing number of programs available for microcomputers.

The second, more specialized application of rules in the design process are those that, when supplied with the appropriate relational information, can lead to the development of shape grammars. Because a separate section will be dedicated to grammars, the description of design rules will suffice here. The definition of a design or transformation rule is similar to our general definition of a production rule: A LHS describes the facts or configuration of a design state, the RHS describes the facts or configurations to replace the LHS facts. Design rules are often represented graphically. An excellent example for the application of design rules to build a practical building pattern grammar is shown in Figure 6.4c representing a set of six transformation rules to allocate public space around the entrance hall of Victorian residences in Shadyside, a neighborhood in Pittsburgh [Flemming86a]. Notice the use of primitive shapes and labels to clarify the effect of the transformation. The left side of the graphic rule corresponds to the LHS in a rule-based production system, the right side of the graphic rule corresponds to the RHS. Similar to production systems, and in contrast to algorithmic programs, the order in which the rules are executed is not predetermined. The results of the application of these rules in a shape grammar are outlined in Section 6.5.

Whereas Figure 6.4c deals with entire spaces and their possible arrangements, Figure 6.4d presents more detailed graphic rules, which

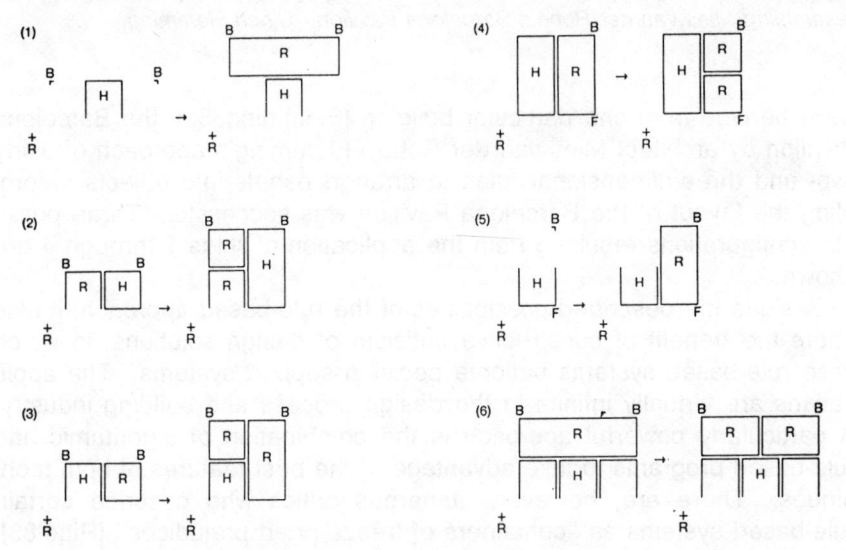

Figure 6.4c Six graphical rules to allocate public spaces in Victorian houses, using the shape grammar paradigm. Ulrich Flemming.

106   ABSTRACTION

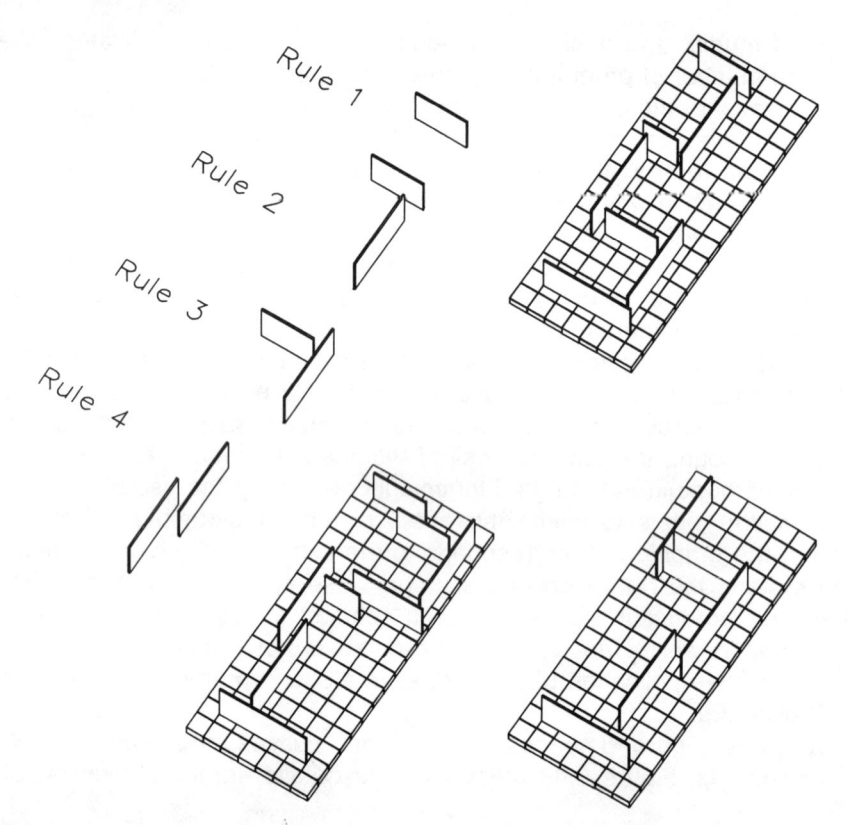

Figure 6.4d Using two-dimensional rules to arrange panels producing layouts resembling Mies van der Rohe's Barcelona Pavilion. Ulrich Flemming.

were derived from one particular building [Flemming86b], the Barcelona Pavilion by architect Mies van der Rohe. Flemming's approach of using two- and three-dimensional rules to arrange panels into objects resembling the layout of the Barcelona Pavilion was successful. Three possible configurations resulting from the application of rules 1 through 4 are shown.

Besides the described possibilities of the rule-based approach, it also offers the benefit of constructive criticism of design solutions, in which case rule-based systems become decision support systems. The applications are virtually infinite in the design process and building industry. A particularly powerful approach is the combination of algorithmic and rule-based programs to take advantage of the best features of both techniques. There are, however, numerous critics who describe certain rule-based systems as "containers of freeze-dried prejudices" [Rittel85]. This points out one of the weaknesses of present rule-based systems, which lies in the confinement of results to the limits established by the rules.

6.5 GRAMMAR

This section addresses the notion of grammar as it pertains to graphic language. Grammar in natural languages uses rules to define how words may be combined to form sentences. The definition of design grammars takes into account the analogy between natural language and design. Accordingly, relations are defined by rules that govern how design elements can be combined to design. We already explored relations and rules. Of particular interest are shape grammars [Stiny80], which form an important subset of the design grammar idea. A word of warning at the beginning is appropriate: Similar to the use of natural-language grammars to construct grammatically or syntactically correct sentences that are semantically incorrect or do not make sense in a larger context, it is possible to use syntactically correct shape grammars to create semantically wrong design. In other words, the use of complex and syntactically correct shape grammars does not guarantee good design. Sometimes, however, the misuse of shape grammars can lead to interesting and unexpected designs.

Laseau proposes a graphic language that has grammatical rules comparable to those of verbal language [Laseau80]. He relates the basic parts of natural-language sentences—nouns, verbs, modifiers such as adjectives, adverbs, and phrases—to identities, relationships, and modifiers that qualify or quantify the relationships between identities. In his graphic language Laseau shows the identities as circles, the relationships as bidirectional arrows, and the modifiers as changes of line weight in the circles or lines. This approach does not guarantee successful design either, but it is an important conceptual step toward understanding the role of design grammars in architecture.

To explain the concept of shape grammars in more detail, we shall begin with two simple examples that use primitive shapes to create a complex two-dimensional pattern. It is possible then to examine existing works of architecture and attempt to extract the design rules that may have led to the particular design solution, generalize these rules, and formalize them into a shape grammar. These will re-create the building under consideration in addition to many other buildings that the grammar can generate.

The first example has three rules. Rule 1 transforms the initial shape into a square with a label. Rule 2 inserts a square into the previous square with one edge on the label, removes the first label, and puts a new label in the corresponding location of the inserted square. Rule 3 removes the label from the square. Figure 6.5a shows the application of rules 1, 2, and 3 in sequence at the bottom. The figure also shows the different geometric configurations that result if we change the position of the label. If the label appears in the midpoint of one of the square's edges, the resulting figure characterizes regular floor patterns found in classical and Renaissance buildings. If the labeled point moves closer

108   ABSTRACTION

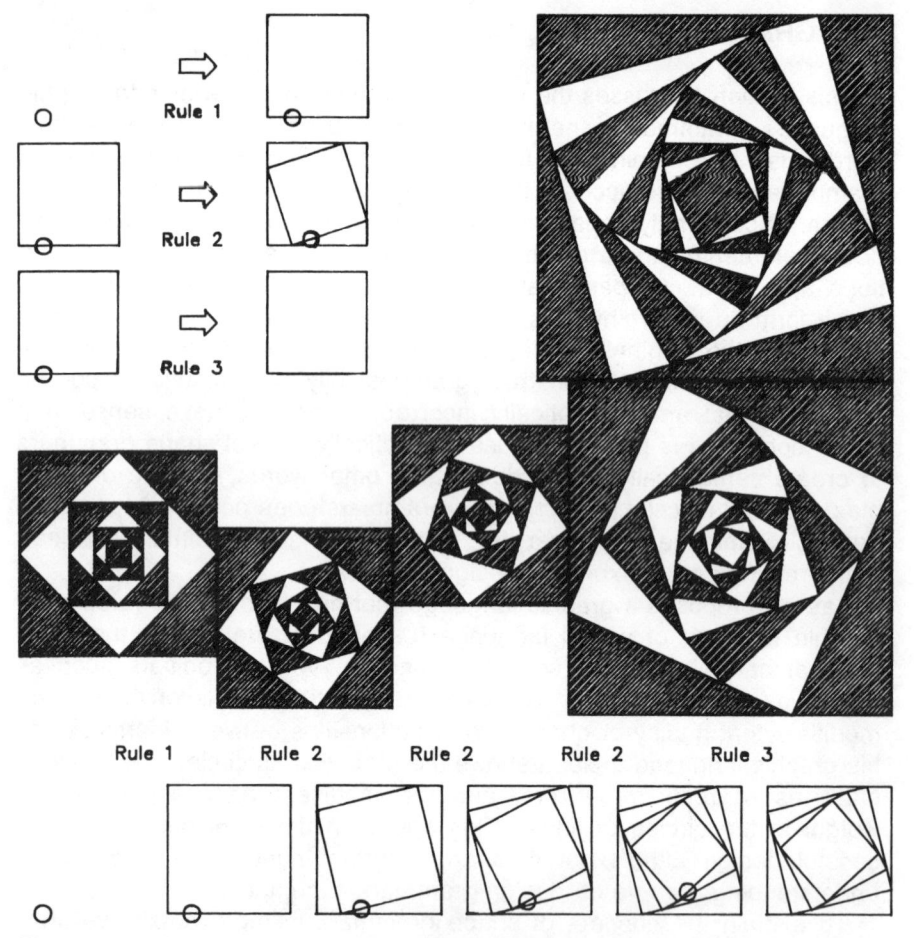

Figure 6.5a Shape grammars: three generating rules (top left), application of rule 1, three times rule 2, rule 3 (bottom), and derivations (center).

to one of the vertices, the figure resembles a spiral. A listing of the program that allows the user to execute and experiment with the shape grammar is included in the appendix.

The second example is a generalization of the first one. Stiny refers to this as a parametric shape grammar [Stiny85]. Again, three transformation rules create complex two-dimensional objects from simple shapes. Rule 1 transforms the initial shape into a polygon with four vertices and places a labeled point on one of the edges. Rule 2 divides each of the three remaining edges proportionally to the first edge and connects the newly created points. It removes the label from the first point and puts a new labeled point on the corresponding edge of the newly created polygon. Rule 3 removes the label. Figure 6.5b shows the application of the three rules at the bottom. It also lists some of the

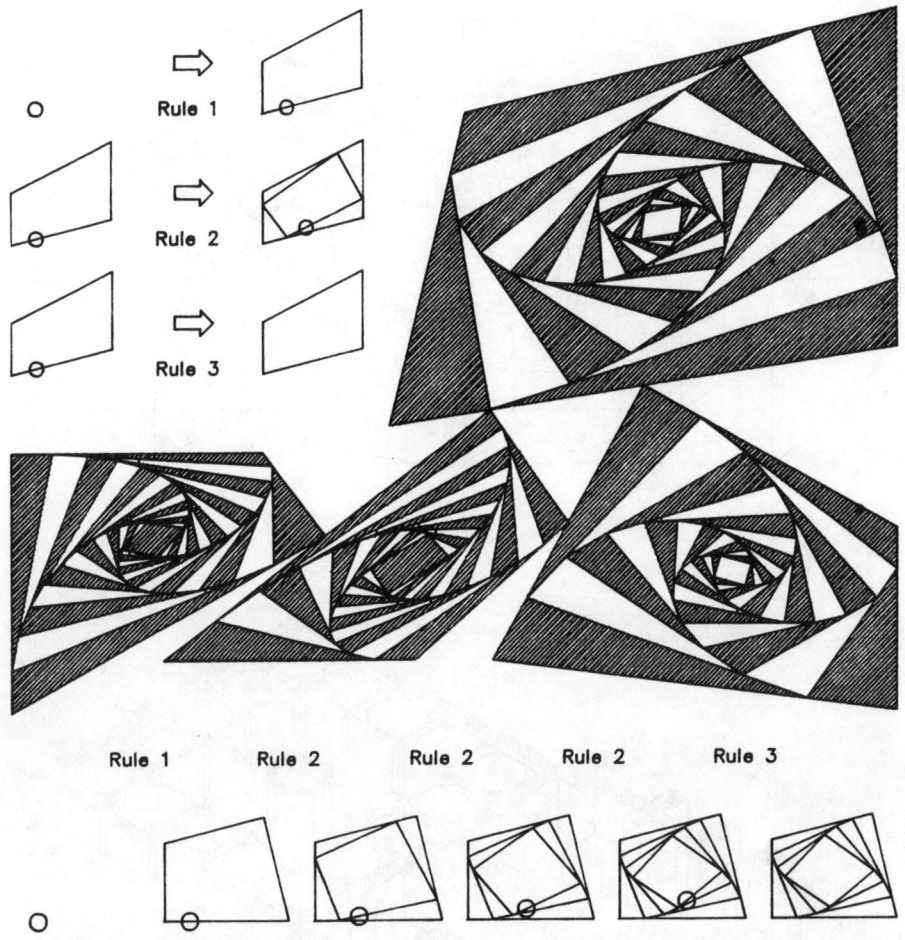

Figure 6.5b Parametric shape grammars: three generating rules (top left), application of rule 1, three times rule 2, rule 3 (bottom), and derivations (center).

shapes derived by applying the rules to a different set of initial polygons. A listing of the program that allows the user to execute this parameterized shape grammar is included in the appendix.

Whereas the previously described shape grammars are extremely simple, the third example is more applicable to an architectural context. The basic shape grammar used to create the underlying framework, shown as circles and inscribed squares, is similar to the first example. The building, then, generated by a different set of rules, is placed in this framework (see Figure 6.5c). Gulzar Haider's research on Ottoman architecture proposed the idea of re-creating the Shehzadeh Mosque in Istanbul in this manner [Haider86]. The root two proportions and the incongruent grids are found in plan, sections, and elevations of this building complex (as representations of the major architectural elements

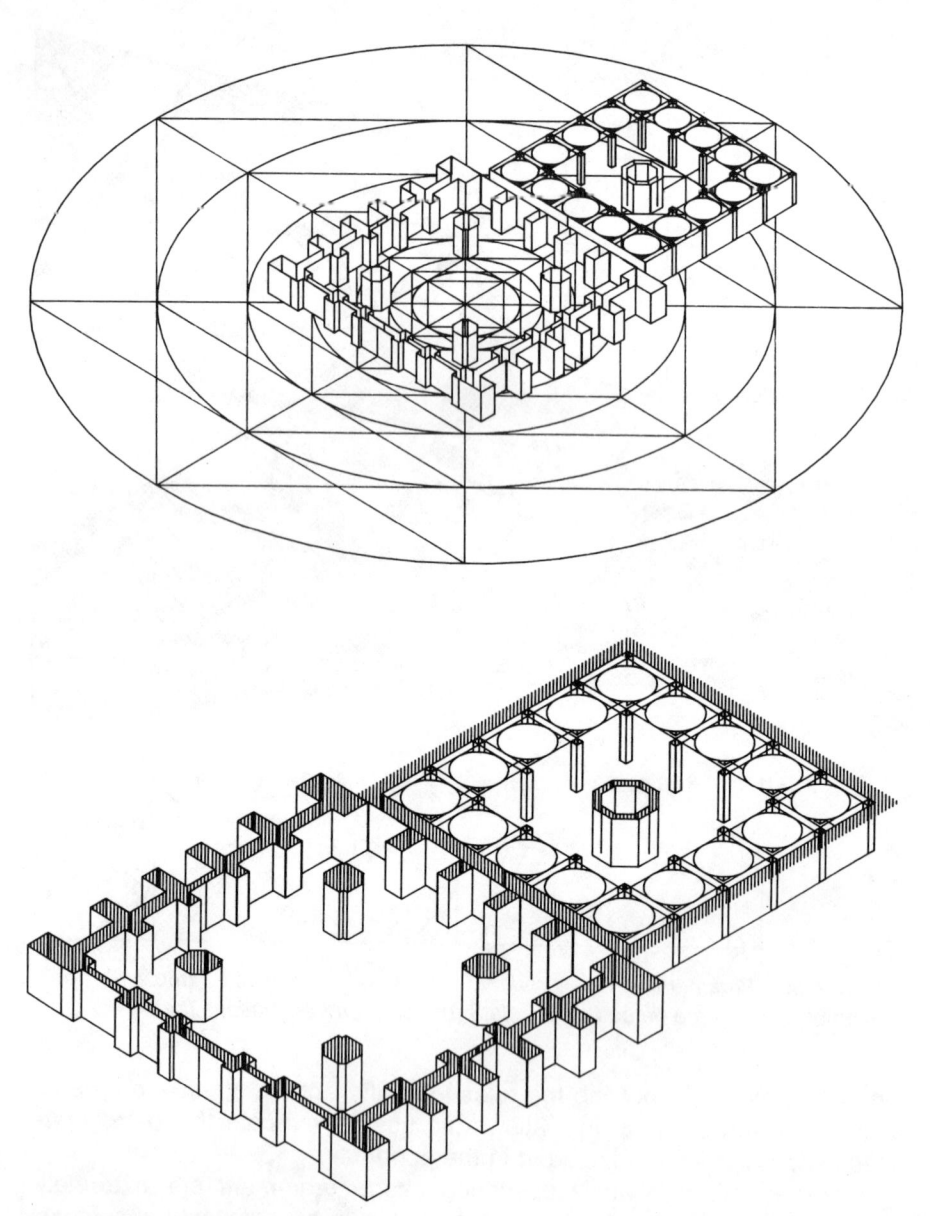

Figure 6.5c Shape grammars: creating the underlying construction framework for the Shehzadeh Mosque in Istanbul.

110

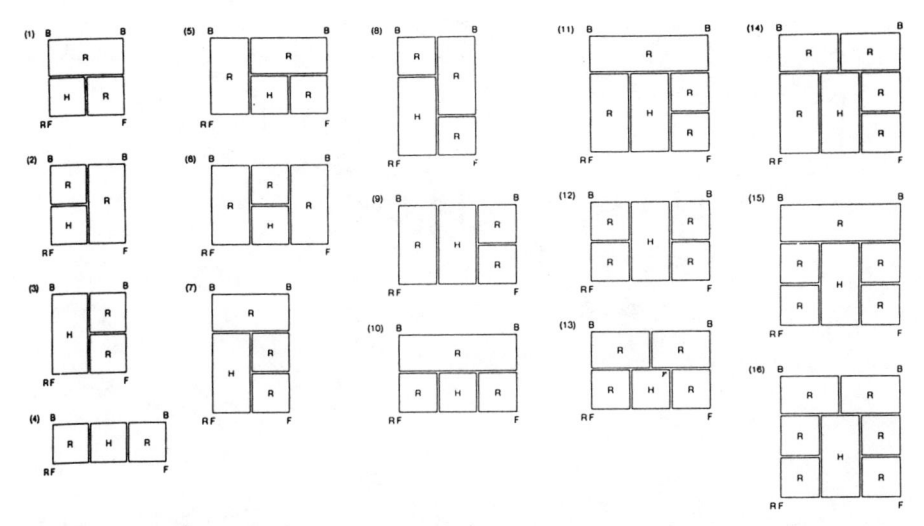

Figure 6.5d Shape grammars for layout generation. The schematic floor plans are created by applying rules shown in Figure 6.4c. Ulrich Flemming.

only). Obviously, it is possible to generate or re-create a particular instance of architectural representation in many other ways, but shape grammars are one possible technique, and are well suited for computer implementation when applied in this context.

Figure 6.5d is the result of applying rules for Victorian houses presented in the previous section to produce layouts [Flemming86a]. The last example deals with more recent architecture and is based on Flemming's work on design grammars [Flemming86a]. Similar implementations of shape grammars were also instrumental in the generation of Frank Lloyd Wright Prairie houses and Palladian villas [Stiny85]. Figure 6.5e displays one possible result of applying the design rules presented in Figure 6.4d—a building with distinctly Miesian character. The windows are added manually. Figure 6.5f illustrates the result of three different applications for Richard Meier design rules. The generating grammar is controlled manually as opposed to the Miesian grammar, which is executed automatically according to high-level design rules [Schmitt86b].

Shape grammars provide a conceptual framework for the construction of "design sentences." For the re-creation of existing architecture, the main development effort lies in the analysis of buildings and the formulation of a workable shape grammar. The quality of the grammar is related to the similarity of the original and re-created object.

At this point, another important difference between traditional and computer-generated designs becomes apparent. Mathematically, there is no difference between the representation of a simple symbol or a very

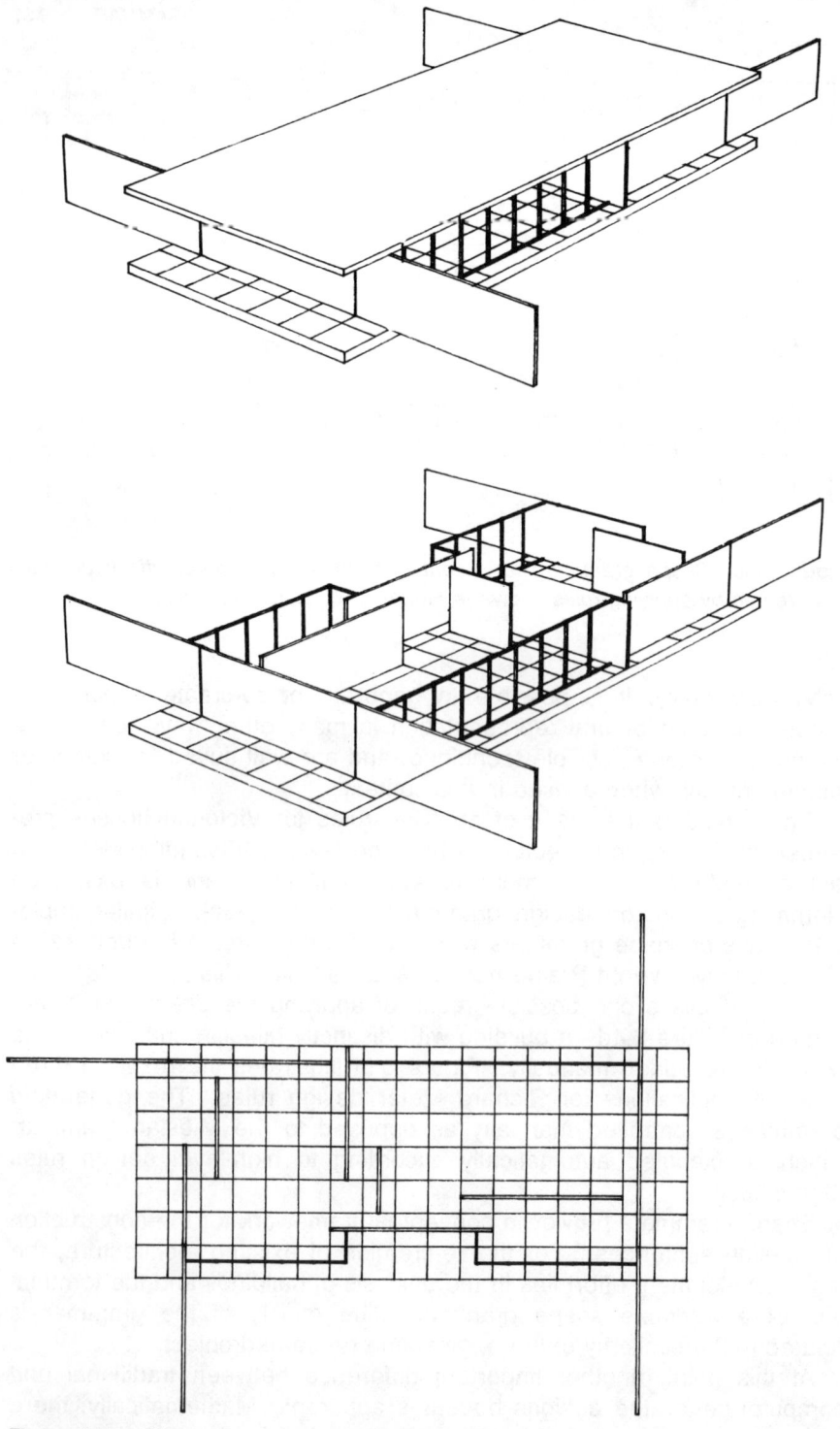

Figure 6.5e   Shape grammar to design according to panel architecture rules. The resulting building has Miesian character.

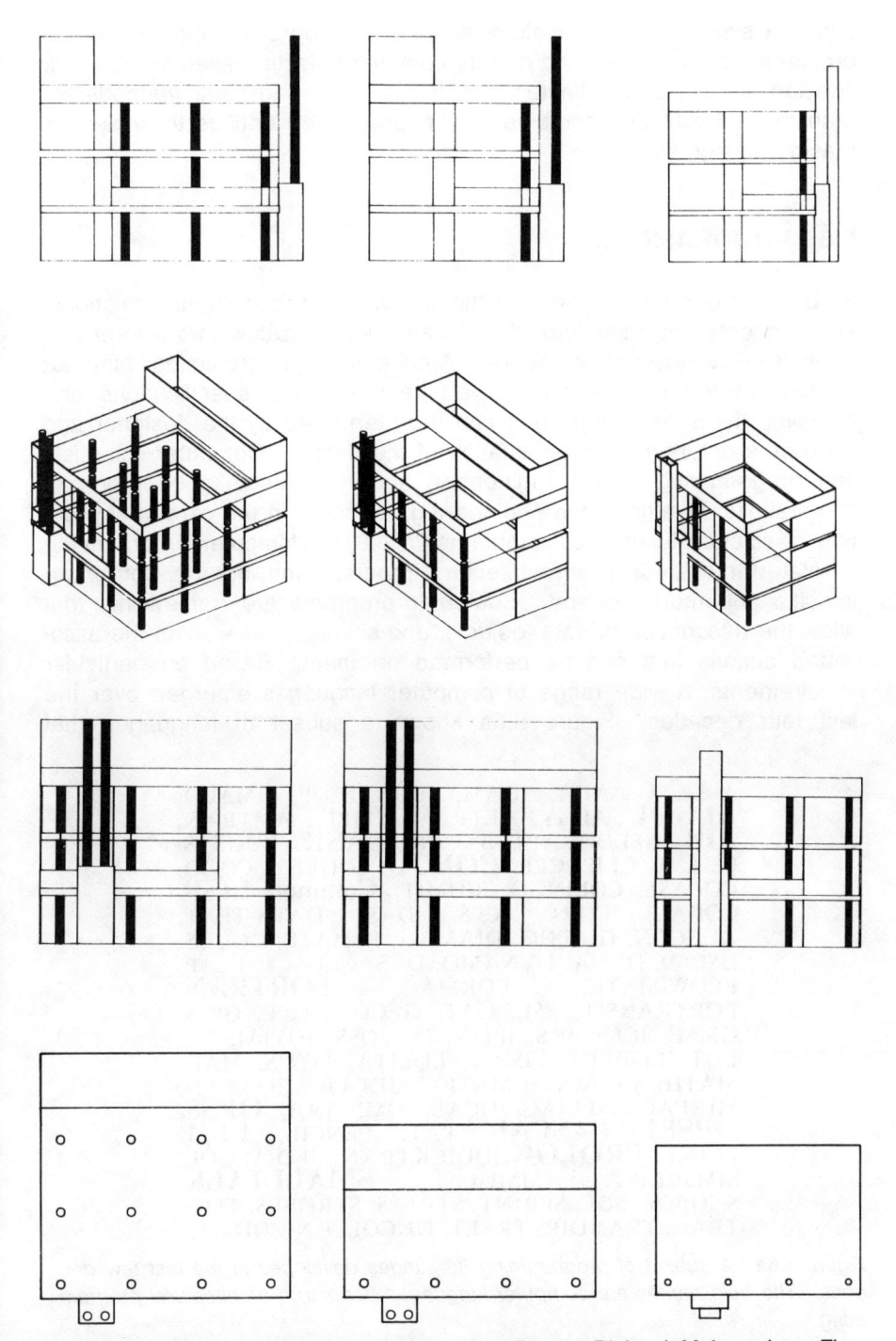

Figure 6.5f Shape grammar to design according to Richard Meier rules. The resulting buildings resemble Richard Meier residences. Heng Jung Hsiung.

113

complex symbol, yet in traditional methods incongruities appear. Shape grammars allow the building of very complex objects based on very few "design words" and a limited set of rules. In traditional methods we tend to deal with and combine larger, predefined entities to achieve a feasible design solution.

6.6 PROGRAMMING

Programming is concerned with the analysis of requirements, relations, and concepts and their formalization and generalization into a form that is accessible to various users. Architectural programming aims at addressing the client's needs, requirements, and specifications and compiles them into a form that can be interpreted by the designer and used as a criterion in the evaluation of the design. Computer scientists see programming as an engineering activity. Hence, good programming, similar to other good engineering, is rooted in the careful application of science to practical problems [Wulf81]. Computer programming is related to the notion of architectural programming, but it is both more specific and more general. Computer programs are frameworks that allow the description of data, objects, and situations as well as the associated actions that can be performed on them. Based on particular requirements, a wide range of computer languages emerged over the last four decades. Figure 6.6a shows a subset of languages that

A-2 & A-3, ADA, ADAM, AED, AESOP, AIMACO, **ALGOL**, ALGY, ALTRAN, AMBIT, AMTRAN, **APL**, APL/360, APT. BACAIC, **BASIC**, BUGSYS. **C**, C-10, CLIP, CLP, **COBOL**, COGENT, COGO, COLASL, COLINGO, COMIT, **Common LISP**, CORAL, CORC, CPS. DAS, DATA-TEXT, DEACON, DIALOG, DIAMAG, DIMATE, DOCUS, DSL/90, DYNA, DYNAMO, DYSAC. FACT, FLAP, FLOW-MATIC, FORMAC, **FORTRAN**, FORTRANSIT, FSL. GAT, GECOM, GPL, GPSS, GRAF. ICES, IDS, IPL-V, IT. JOSS, JOVIAL. L6, LDT, LISP 1-5, LISP 2, LOLITA, LOTIS. MAD, MATHLAB, MATH-MATIC, META5, MILITRAN, MIRFAC. NELIAC. OCAL, OMNITAB, **OPS5, OPS83**. **PASCAL**, PAT, PENCIL, **PL/1**, PRINT, **PROLOG**. QUICKTRAN. SFD-ALGOL, SIMSCRIPT, SIMULA, **SMALLTALK**, SNOBOL, SOL, SPRINT, STRESS, STROBES. TMG, TRAC, TRANDIR, TREET. UNCOL, UNICODE.

Figure 6.6a A subset of programming languages developed in the last few decades. The bold names are computer languages popular in architectural programming.

evolved. Although even in the eyes of scientists they are a subject that has considerable "emotionalism and mystique associated with it" [Horowitz84], most of them share a few essential concepts: variables, expressions, statements, typing, scope, procedures, data types, exception handling, and concurrency. In design and architecture, we construct complex representations out of points, lines, and polygons. Similarly, it is possible to construct high-level, structured languages such as Pascal [Cooper82] or C [Schustack85], [Kernighan78], from machine or low-level languages such as assembler.

Very early in the development of CAD languages emerged that allowed the representation of knowledge and the encoding of inferencing processes needed to arrive at solutions. With the development of Artificial Intelligence, computational tools were created to represent rules in a form readable by the computer. One of the first languages developed to represent rules in a computer-readable form was LISP (LISt Programming) [Winston84]. Later followed Prolog (PROgramming in LOGic), OPS5 (Official Production System 5), and OPS83 [Forgy85]. Although any programming language is capable of encoding the necessary inferencing mechanisms, expert system frames and shells are popular because they already have the inferencing mechanisms built in. OPS5 and OPS83 fall into this category. With the advent of expert systems, and the practical applications of rule-based programs, a growing number of expert system frames and shells were developed.

Previous sections addressed the issue of design languages and their definition in terms of vocabulary, relations, rules, and grammar. Given the existence of a variety of computer languages, it seems logical to create a mapping between design and computer languages. During the first wave of office and drafting automization, this has happened to some extent. Many of the basic skills, representational and manipulative techniques described in the first part of this book, have been formalized to a high degree, converted into a machine understandable form, and are being used by all new microcomputer systems. This applies particularly for the representational techniques that can be automated almost entirely, provided special manual effects are not desired. It is necessary to keep in mind, however, that none of the existing programming languages were developed specifically for the purpose of design automation. Therefore, the mapping between design languages and computer languages is restricted. For the same reason, general-purpose programming languages are easier to adapt to specific architectural design needs than highly specialized programming languages, unless the domains have strong conceptual correlations.

An interesting phenomenon in graphic programming is the achievement of identical graphic result through different means. To clarify this assertion, three different programs are presented that produce the same

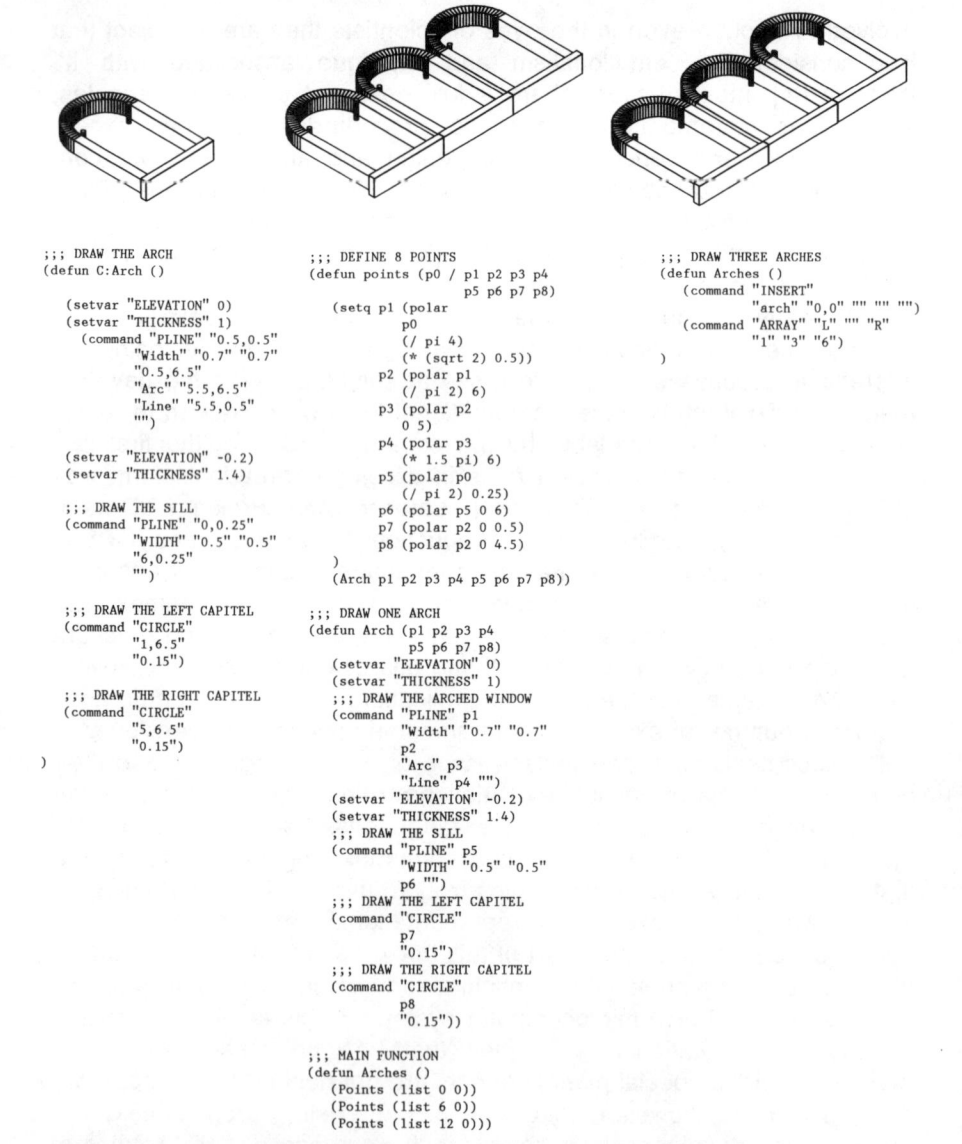

```
;;; DRAW THE ARCH                ;;; DEFINE 8 POINTS                ;;; DRAW THREE ARCHES
(defun C:Arch ()                 (defun points (p0 / p1 p2 p3 p4    (defun Arches ()
                                                 p5 p6 p7 p8)          (command "INSERT"
    (setvar "ELEVATION" 0)          (setq p1 (polar                            "arch" "0,0" "" "" "")
    (setvar "THICKNESS" 1)                       p0                     (command "ARRAY" "L" "" "R"
    (command "PLINE" "0.5,0.5"                   (/ pi 4)                        "1" "3" "6")
                    "Width" "0.7" "0.7"          (* (sqrt 2) 0.5))   )
                    "0.5,6.5"                 p2 (polar p1
                    "Arc" "5.5,6.5"              (/ pi 2) 6)
                    "Line" "5.5,0.5"          p3 (polar p2
                    "")                          0 5)
                                              p4 (polar p3
    (setvar "ELEVATION" -0.2)                    (* 1.5 pi) 6)
    (setvar "THICKNESS" 1.4)                  p5 (polar p0
                                                 (/ pi 2) 0.25)
    ;;; DRAW THE SILL                         p6 (polar p5 0 6)
    (command "PLINE" "0,0.25"                 p7 (polar p2 0 0.5)
                    "WIDTH" "0.5" "0.5"       p8 (polar p2 0 4.5)
                    "6,0.25"                )
                    "")                    (Arch p1 p2 p3 p4 p5 p6 p7 p8))

    ;;; DRAW THE LEFT CAPITEL         ;;; DRAW ONE ARCH
    (command "CIRCLE"                 (defun Arch (p1 p2 p3 p4
                    "1,6.5"                        p5 p6 p7 p8)
                    "0.15")             (setvar "ELEVATION" 0)
                                        (setvar "THICKNESS" 1)
    ;;; DRAW THE RIGHT CAPITEL          ;;; DRAW THE ARCHED WINDOW
    (command "CIRCLE"                   (command "PLINE" p1
                    "5,6.5"                             "Width" "0.7" "0.7"
                    "0.15")                             p2
)                                                       "Arc" p3
                                                        "Line" p4 "")
                                        (setvar "ELEVATION" -0.2)
                                        (setvar "THICKNESS" 1.4)
                                        ;;; DRAW THE SILL
                                        (command "PLINE" p5
                                                        "WIDTH" "0.5" "0.5"
                                                        p6 "")
                                        ;;; DRAW THE LEFT CAPITEL
                                        (command "CIRCLE"
                                                        p7
                                                        "0.15")
                                        ;;; DRAW THE RIGHT CAPITEL
                                        (command "CIRCLE"
                                                        p8
                                                        "0.15"))

                                        ;;; MAIN FUNCTION
                                        (defun Arches ()
                                            (Points (list 0 0))
                                            (Points (list 6 0))
                                            (Points (list 12 0)))
```

Figure 6.6b   Graphic images and listing of LISP programs to generate them within a general-purpose drafting package.

result. The programming language is LISP where the utilities of a drafting program are used to display the result of the programs. The goal is to draw an arched window, its sill, and two small capitals. The commented programs are explained in detail in the appendix.

Figure 6.6b on the left displays the program listing and the graphic result. The objective was to define the thickness of an extruded polyline and then connect the appropriate points with straight lines or an arch. The program looks rather long and does not allow any syntax errors. It will always produce the same graphic result in the same location.

Figure 6.6b in the center shows an even longer program to produce the same figure. This program, however, is more generalized and is referred to as a parameterized program. It accepts the points that will be connected to produce the figure from a LISP function called Points. The Points function calculates all the point values in relation to a point of origin that must be passed to the function. The program uses polar coordinates to define a point relative to another point. The input sequence is original point, angle from original point (counting counterclockwise), and distance from original point. The third LISP function, called Arches, calls the Points function three times and shifts the origin by six units in the x direction with each call.

Figure 6.6b on the right shows a third program to produce the same figure. The program is much shorter and easier to understand than the previous ones. It assumes that the window is stored as a block in a library of building parts. The program calls this block from the library and inserts it in the desired location. The program then uses a second command, called Array, to produce a row of three windows. Once the user knows the high-level commands such as Insert or Array, she or he can concentrate on the design rather than on the low-level implementation of programs.

Figure 6.6c substantiates the assertion that the length of the program is unrelated to the complexity of the resulting representation. The seemingly complicated figure was created with a short, recursive C function. Similar recursive LISP functions will appear in the next chapter and in the appendix.

Figure 6.6d indicates the relative performance of computer languages for particular tasks. The three building types, church, cathedral, and monastary, increase in complexity from left to right. The graph compares the file creation time for each type using C versus TOPSI, an expert system shell.

The examples suggest that once a process has been understood and explained, it can be expressed in another form—in this case, a formal computer language. Early programs required the user to communicate with the computer in a very low level language, such as assembler or machine language, that the machine could directly understand. Later

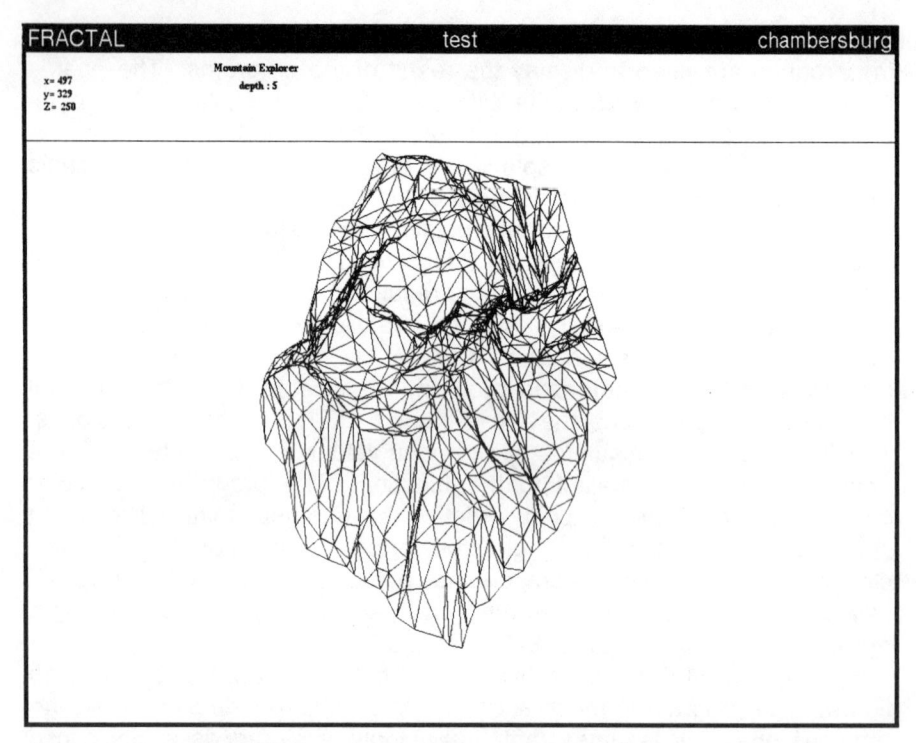

Figure 6.6c An image resembling a mountain produced with a short recursive C function. Gen Shong Lo.

developments produced high-level languages with interfaces of a natural-language character, taking care of the translation into machine-understandable code through compilation. Recent developments are natural-language interfaces that translate the user's input into high-level languages and then into machine-readable code. These interfaces are already available for spread sheet and database management programs, and it is only a matter of time before they will be available for microcomputer-based CAD systems.

Regardless of the level of language, the user should be able to program. Programming once required the orderly top-down organization of sequential procedures. The top-down organizational requirements have been eased by using expert system shells and production system languages. However, programming still requires the capability to organize thoughts clearly and logically, as programming is a form of even higher abstraction than natural or architectural languages.

Programming has made many manual tasks in architectural drafting obsolete. Programming could also eliminate many traditional tasks in architectural language development and eliminate the need for some

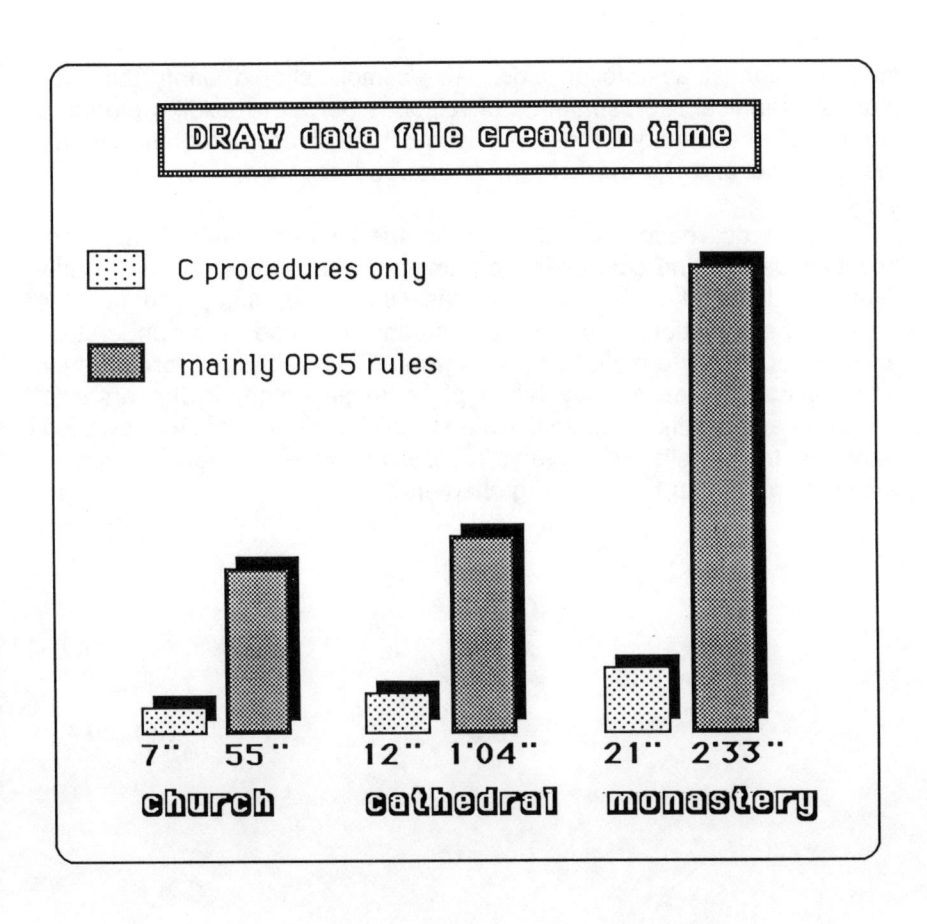

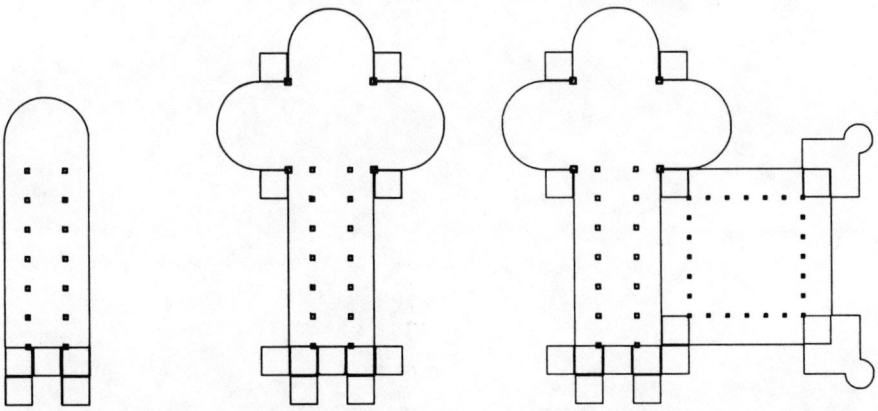

Figure 6.6d Applying different computer languages to different tasks based on performance requirements. Computed objects, church, cathedral, monastery (bottom, from left to right) and associated computing time (top). Jean Christophe Robert.

kinds of manual abstraction aids. An example should clarify this: The manual graphical representation of relations between building elements is not really necessary if those relations can be directly programmed into the machine and the elements are arranged accordingly and automatically.

There is no reason to assume that the development of mappings between design and computer programming will be confined to the relatively low level of architectural utilities such as drafting, if in fact the notions of abstraction, discovery, and creativity can be better understood and consequently formalized to a degree. This process of formalization and application has already taken place to an extent in the areas of structural and engineering analysis and building performance evaluation. Attempts to formalize discovery, creativity, and evaluation techniques will be described in the following chapters.

7
Discovery

What, in fact, is mathematical discovery? It does not consist in making new combinations with mathematical entities that are already known. That can be done by anyone, and the combinations that could be so formulated would be infinite in number, and the greater part of them would be absolutely devoid of interest. Discovery consists precisely in not constructing useless combinations, but in constructing those that are useful, which are in infinitely small minority. Discovery is discernment, selection [Poincaré52].

Poincaré's definition of mathematical and scientific discovery is applicable for discovery in architecture as well. The traditional discovery process in architecture does not occur by producing all possible solutions to a design problem and then selecting the most promising one. This strategy is also useless in microcomputer-aided architectural design because it is computationally too expensive and complex even for the most advanced mainframe computers. It is necessary, then, to develop a framework to employ the new machines effectively for the discovery process.

Chapter 6 covered architectural language as an important form of abstraction. The discussions revealed ways to represent and manipulate the syntactic aspects of architecture computationally. It is now appropriate to explore and discover the meaning or semantics of architectural design in light of and with the support of the new machines.

Research findings by Akin and Flemming suggest that the architectural discovery process can be approached and supported by scientific methods [Akin86], [Flemming86b]. Key elements in the description of computer-aided architectural discovery are search systems, a prominent term in Artificial Intelligence (AI). Computer-aided search is an important method in problem solving and consequently in architectural design. In addition to search strategies, ways to represent architectural design in its different stages in a form appropriate for computation will be discussed. Equipped with this knowledge, it is possible to begin addressing the problem of inferencing and reasoning in the design process by presenting three inferencing methods.

The reader should not be intimidated by the use of AI terms. Most are self-explanatory and, after all, AI is first and foremost an attempt to model human intelligence and thinking. The description of techniques in computer-aided search, representation, and reasoning could stimulate the reader to think of new ways to employ computers in the design process. AI research and applications rely on knowledge of experienced designers and planners. Similarly, planners can use AI techniques in their design process.

7.1 SEARCH IN ARCHITECTURAL DESIGN

Architectural discovery is, in most cases, the result of an attempt to solve a design problem. In some cases, it results from an informal interaction between graphical representations and the designer. This section will concentrate on the exploration of design discovery as a result of problem solving and search.

Search as an AI technique consists of three main components [Barr81]. The first component, the database, describes the current domain-dependent situation as well as the goal. The second component is a set of operators that are employed to manipulate the database. The third component is the control strategy that decides which operators to apply in which sequence. An equivalent architectural database example would consist of the building program, the site description, and the client's particular needs and requirements as the database. The architect's knowledge of how to transform a program requirement into the description of a three-dimensional space are the operators. The design strategy the architect chooses to produce a final solution is equivalent to the AI control strategy.

One design problem statement can produce an infinite set of solutions and, vice versa, there is an infinite number of ways to arrive at the one particular design solution, given a problem statement or the database. Although this statement is true, it is not particularly helpful or interesting to solve design problems practically. Therefore, architects have developed efficient methods to quickly arrive at a limited set of solutions, and have built teaching and analysis methods to describe a particular instance of architecture in a logical way. The notions of search, databases, operators, and control strategies are therefore nothing new to the experienced architect. In fact, the capacity of human designers to infer knowledge by studying existing architecture and integrate this knowledge in the next design problem in some manner, is an intriguing and still unsolved problem in AI. Another difference between the human design process and AI techniques to solve design problems is equally important: It seems that experienced human designers commit themselves relatively early to particular design strategies and problem-solving paths (called greatest commitment in AI terms), whereas AI-based design systems often make a design commitment as late as possible (called least commitment in AI terms) [Gero87b]. The reasons for this are not clear, but two possible answers come to mind. The first is that few, if any, experienced architects have developed computer-aided discovery tools. The least commitment behavior is typical for less experienced architects. The second reason could be that computers can easily produce a larger set of alternatives than the human designer and that the greatest commitment strategy is therefore seen as too limiting in the early design stages. David Pye describes the related process of invention and concludes that it "can only be done deliberately, if the inventor can discern similarities between the particular result which he is envisaging and some other actual result which he has seen and stored in his memory. An inventor's power to invent depends on his ability to see analogies between results and, secondarily, on his ability to see them between devices" [Pye64]. This conclusion supports the earlier statement that design discovery is based on discernment and selection and not on random generation of alternatives. Akin describes several of the paths taken to arrive at architectural discovery [Akin86]. He divides the search methods used by architects into two categories: global search methods described as depth-first search and breadth-first search, and local search methods such as generate-and-test, hill-climbing, and heuristic search. Without endorsing this particular view of the design process, it provides an interesting framework and offers the opportunity to inspect different search methods and their applicability for CAD. The reader must keep in mind that none of these methods were originally intended for architectural or design search and discovery, rather, they apply to this domain due to their general character:

1. **Depth-first Search.** This method uses the analogy of an inverted tree with branches that connect nodes. A parent node is one from which several branches connect to lower nodes. As a consequence of expanding the deepest node first, the search follows a single path from the start node. An alternate path is only considered if it reaches a state that has no successors [Barr81]. Experienced architects use this method to quickly explore a design solution from a high to a low level of abstraction. An example would be the sequence of exploring a site

plan, placing a massing model on it, developing some sample floor plans and details, and presenting the results to the client. A computer implementation of this process that could yield comparable results would be extremely difficult. Most computer programs lack the important constraint knowledge and the experience or meta knowledge to select the appropriate prototype and search path through the search space in reasonable time. The depth-first search method becomes very inefficient when the branches of the tree become very large or contain cyclical paths. The method is also not well suited to guarantee design optimization because each decision is influenced by the constraints of the previous decisions.

2. **Breadth-first Search.** In breadth-first search, the designer tends to focus attention on nodes of the same depth before moving to the next parent node. In architectural terms breadth-first search is related to the activity of exploring many possible design alternatives on one particular level of abstraction before moving on to the next level. A typical application in design is the selection of a solution from a few prototypes that adhere to the most critical constraints of the design problem. In practice, the breadth-first search is followed by depth-first search after a feasible solution has been identified. Once a field is well defined or the designer has acquired significant knowledge in a particular domain and has thus become a domain expert, modified breadth-first search seems to be the preferred method [Akin86].

On a local level, specific design problems can be solved with an array of possible search strategies, three of which will be described:

1. **The Generate-and-Test (G-A-T) Method.** The G-A-T method is the simplest and conceptually attractive. However, the G-A-T method is thought to be "weak" because it merely requires a procedure to generate possible candidates for a solution and a procedure to test whether the candidates are indeed solutions. The generator requires information concerning a set and then produces elements of that set one by one. The tester determines whether some condition or a predicate is true of its input and presents the output as satisfied or unsatisfied. The difficulty in finding a solution is proportional to the size of the set and therefore not feasible for large design problems. Since complete solutions must be generated before they can be tested, the G-A-T method is also a depth-first search procedure [Rich83]. In its most systematic form, G-A-T is an exhaustive search of the entire problem space. Architectural researchers use this method for the exhaustive enumeration of possible building layouts [Flemming86b]. Figure 7.1a shows a simplified application. The "problem space" is a rectangle representing the private zone in one of Richard Meier's residential designs. The constraints for the generation of solutions are as follows: The corridor occupies the

SEARCH IN ARCHITECTURAL DESIGN   125

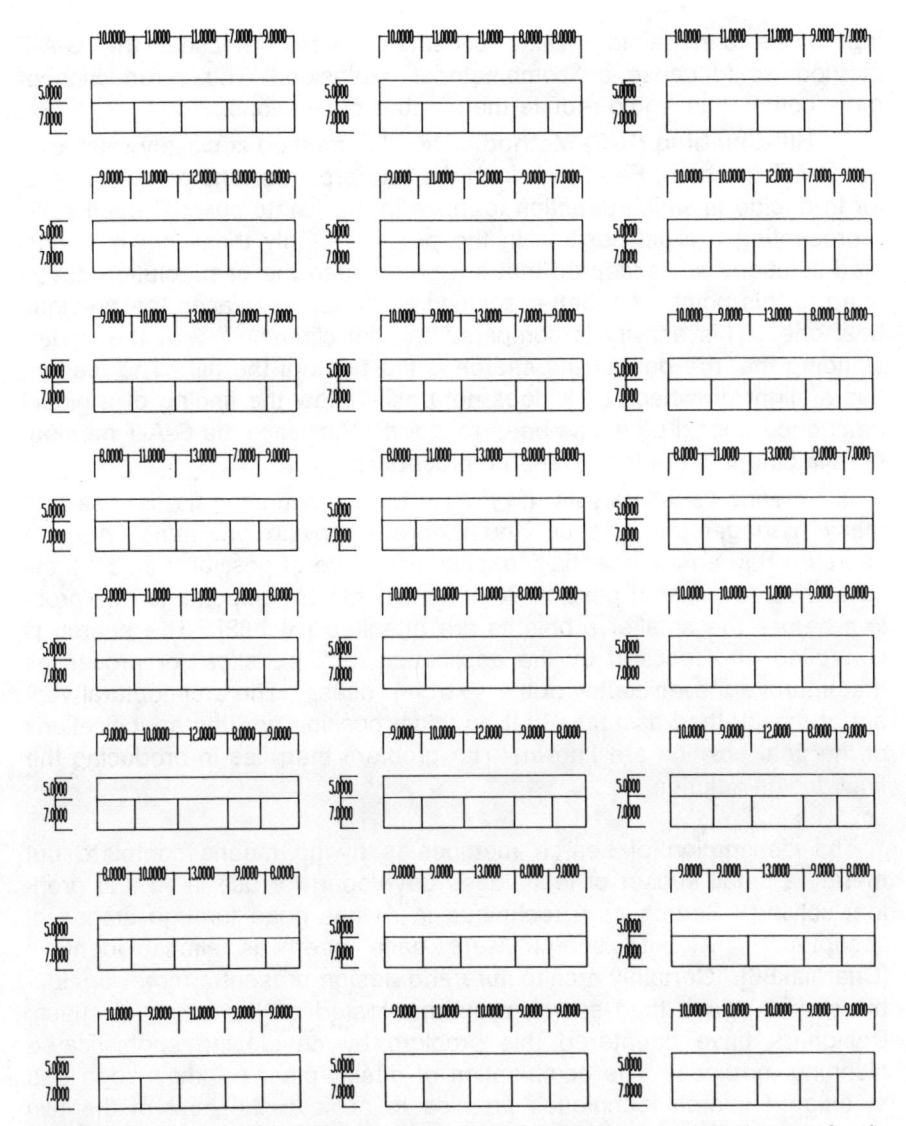

Figure 7.1a   Using the generate-and-test (GAT) method to produce layouts for the private zone of Richard Meier residences. The subdivided rectangles are only a small subset of all possible solutions.

top part of the rectangle; bedrooms, bathrooms, kitchen, and two other support functions occupy the bottom part of the rectangle; the corridor width is 5 feet, the room width is 7 feet; the minimum room depth is 7 feet, the maximum room depth is 13 feet. Even with these constraints, the number of possible solutions for placing the 5 rooms is overwhelming. Figure 7.1a only shows a very small subset of the solutions adhering to the constraints. If the constraints were released, the G-A-T method would cause a "combinatorial explosion." The introduction of more constraints would reduce the number of solutions.

2. **Hill-Climbing (H-C) Method.** The H-C method is closely related to the G-A-T method. Feedback from the test procedure helps the generator to decide in which direction to move in the "state space," each state representing a legal position in the process. Only those newly generated solutions are accepted that are better than the best solution developed to this point. If a better solution is found, it replaces the previous best one. This activity is compared to "hill climbing," with the understanding that the goal of the search is the peak of the hill. The method has a slight drawback as it does not easily allow the finding of a global peak once a local peak has been reached. Similar to the G-A-T method, hill climbing is a depth-first search procedure.

3. **Means-End-Analysis (M-E-A).** Means-end-analysis is used in many management science and theorem proving programs where a search within an exponentially expanding space of possibilities is necessary. M-E-A makes it possible to solve the major components of a problem before the smaller problems are attacked [Rich83]. The search is controlled and focused by the application of "heuristics" or processes that improve the efficiency of the search process. The architectural variant of the method assumes that an initial position and the specifications of the final position are known. The problem then lies in producing the final design solution.

The description of search methods is by no means complete but merely a small subset of techniques developed for use in AI and problem solving. Search as a technique in AI has gone through stages of acceptance. AI and search were once seen as almost identical [Charniak86]. Certainly architecture and design present a more formidable search space than search programs tested on the game of chess. Designers have countered this problem by developing sophisticated planning methods. The combination of design-planning knowledge and automated search techniques promise to achieve the best of the two worlds of design and AI. This combination could lead to the discovery of better design solutions in a shorter period of time.

7.2 REPRESENTATION OF ARCHITECTURAL DESIGN

Understanding the meaning of architectural representations is key to discovery in design. As the representations change, so does our ability for interactive architectural discovery. Chapter 3 dealt with traditional architectural representation methods and the use of microcomputers to facilitate external representation. This chapter addresses the problem from a fundamentally different perspective. Whereas the traditional external medium, such as paper, has no intelligence of its own, a computer program, representing the design, can have varying degrees of "design intelligence." The objective of design intelligence is to interpret the world around us and make meaningful decisions toward a design goal. In traditional design the external medium acts as a temporary or permanent storage device for design ideas. We interpret the drawing by looking at it and drawing meaningful conclusions from it. The semantic content is entirely supplied by the designer. Computers and computer programs, on the other hand, cannot simply "look" at the same external design representations and produce conclusions. In order to do so, they must be equipped with extremely sensitive vision systems and excellent domain knowledge. Both requirements are far from being met. Presently, computers perform better as design aids if the representation is tuned to their capabilities. In more advanced systems the program internal representation is hidden from the user with the result that the user feels "familiar" with the representation he or she is manipulating.

Microcomputers represent the geometric properties of objects extremely well and with growing ease. What used to require the building of a physical model can now be achieved by building a computer model. Both physical and computer model allow views of the object from different angles, distances, and perspectives. The computer model normally takes less time and fewer expenses to construct and to change. When we look at the program internal representation of the computer model, it seems to have little to do with the visual result on the screen or on the plotter. We also find that the same result on the screen can be achieved as the representation of different internal data models. This observation is interesting in three respects:

1. The traditional representation of an architectural object is one representation of an abstracted model of this object in the designer's memory. The exact representation of the mental model can take various forms (which are presently being researched). If these representations and the necessary operators can be thoroughly understood and formalized, it should be possible to build equivalent representations in the computer memory and manipulate them with operators similar to those of humans. Example: protocol analysis with designers [Akin86] shows that design decisions are made in different ways by different subjects, often arriving at similar solutions through different search and representation paths.
2. The computational representations used to define the geometric properties of objects are based on mathematics and algebra and may be different from the representation used in the human mind. The result, however, can be similar to the result produced with the human representation of design. Example: the intersec-

tion of two lines can be done by hand geometrically. It can also be calculated by the computer. The representation of the result, that is, the point of intersection, on an external medium such as a piece of paper is the same.

3. With the maturing of computer technology, it will be easier for users to represent human modeling and representation techniques on the computer—rather than tuning the representation and the operators to the computer's capabilities. Without contradicting the previous statement, presently it is more effective to adjust computer-based design representation to the machine capabilities. Example: the early computers required programming to be done in machine code. Since then, higher level languages have been developed such as FORTRAN, Pascal, C, LISP and Prolog, that allow a much more natural-language-like programming style. Natural-language interfaces to database management and other commercial programs go one step further in abstraction as an attempt to elevate the communication between machine and human to almost the same level in one specific domain.

The following three examples introduce representations of architectural design in the human memory according to Akin [Akin86]. In information processing terms, two basic modes of representation are available to the designer: the verbal-conceptual and the visual mode. An example for the verbal-conceptual mode would be the word "door," which could represent an infinite number of different doors. An example for the visual mode would be a specific view of a specific door with which we can associate only one verbal-conceptual schema, "door." There are several representational paradigms that are consistent with this distinction:

1. **Productions.** Productions are simple control structures with a left-hand side (LHS) and a right-hand side (RHS). The LHS contains a condition, the RHS the associated action. Productions are also known as if-then rules. We briefly introduced a production system in the section about rules in design (see Section 6.4). When many rules are combined to simulate more complex behavioral patterns, the resulting system is called a production system. A typical production system language is OPS5 [Forgy81]. Production systems are quite robust and generic and are developed in growing numbers for microcomputer applications [Schmitt86a].

2. **Conceptual Inference Structures.** Shank developed the idea of conceptual inference making in 1975 [Shank75]. Conceptual inference structures address the fact that not all inferences must obey logical rules (like production systems) in order to be valid. Rieger identifies four

important characteristics of conceptual inference structures: (a) They are spontaneous and automatic; (b) They are subconscious for the most part and not subject to conscious control; (c) They are performed in the parallel, associative part of our brain; and (d) They have little goal direction until certain criteria are met [Rieger75]. Architecture seems to offer an abundance of opportunities to apply conceptual inference structures.

3. **Chunks.** In problems dealing with spatial arrangements, chunks have proven to be the most robust information structure. Chunks are defined as organizers of hierarchical, multiassociative links in memory [Chase73]. The human memory organizes tokens into clusters or chunks that have one or more common relationships binding them together. The associative links, spatial or symbolic, are always stronger between information belonging to the same chunk than between information belonging to different chunks. By nesting chunks within chunks, multileveled hierarchies can be achieved. Commercial database management programs make use of a related organizational principle by assigning common and foreign keys to the relations or tables. Microcomputer drafting programs provide somewhat related structures to chunks in their "block" structures that allow the buildup of chunks and multiple hierarchies.

The most developed and formalized representations are productions and chunks. The description of the representation of design in the human mind is not complete; research in this area is ongoing. However, many of the findings have been consciously taken up by computer program developers and can either directly or indirectly be applied to microcomputer-aided architectural design.

The last three examples of architectural design representation are closely linked to developments in computer-aided design and computer graphics.

7.3 INFERENCE AND REASONING IN ARCHITECTURE

Architectural design involves several forms of inferencing. Charniak describes inferencing as "believing a new fact on the basis of other information" [Charniak86]. Knowingly or intuitively inferencing plays a role in most design decisions and explorations. AI contributes by formalizing inferencing and providing mechanisms that allow inferencing with computers. Three kinds of inferencing are of particular interest: deductive, abductive, and inductive inferencing. Deduction is the best known and most formalized form and means "logically correct inferencing" [Charniak86]. An example: If the envelope and the structural system of a residence are made of concrete, then we can deduct that the building is of heavy construction type (since the building's main elements consist of concrete, and since concrete is relatively heavy as compared to wood or brick, the building is heavy). Deductions are handled computationally with "predicate calculus," a method that allows the calculation of the truth of the predicate or proposition (in the previous example, the proposition is that the building is of heavy construction type). As a simplification, predicate calculus may be seen as a language that can express propositions and contains rules for inferring new facts or propositions from those we have already established. The reader may compare this description of predicate calculus as a language with the notion of an abstract design language in the previous chapter. In fact, predicate calculus is used in many experimental architectural systems that exploit the deductive qualities of some design decisions [Gero85].

Architects know, however, that in design few pure deductions are possible. The limitation of deduction becomes evident in attempting to design a floor plan deductively, given even the simplest building program. Consequently, programs based on deduction only are often inadequate for CAD. A second form of inferencing, "abduction" is a process that generates explanations and has the following structure [Charniak86]:

From: b

(if a b)

Infer a

Or, to cite an architectural example:

From: the public zone of this residence is facing the best view.
(Richard Meier's residences, for example, are divided in public and private zones, the public zones facing the best view.)

Infer: Richard Meier designed this building.

Obviously, this explanation can lead to wrong conclusions because it takes into account only one characteristic of Meier residences that is shared by many other buildings. Abduction is therefore not a legal inference, but nevertheless useful and an often-used inferencing technique. If, for example, someone mentions a large shell-shaped building in Australia, we immediately abduct Jorn Utzon's Sydney Opera House; and because there are not too many shell-shaped buildings in Australia, our guess will probably be correct.

The last form of inferencing is called induction, and it seems to be particularly interesting for design applications [Akin86]. A common form is [Charniak86]

From: (P a), (P b), . . .

Infer: (forall (x)(P x))

An architectural example for induction would be

From: if House A has a roof and the roof material is wood and House B has a roof and the roof material is wood.

Infer: all houses have wooden roofs.

The reader will realize that this is not a sound but again a very interesting and important kind of inference. Induction is more commonly known as learning and is extremely difficult to achieve with computers. A more convincing example would be that of residential design:

From: studying many instances of residential floor plans over the last 500 years anywhere in the world, some form of a kitchen may be found in each one of them.

Infer: all residences built in the last 500 years have a kitchen, or more importantly, every residence should have a kitchen.

Although these examples sound trivial seen in isolation, they can produce very powerful induction systems in combination.

The architectural design process involves inductive reasoning. The search techniques and the representational schemes described in the previous sections support induction. Assuming that research findings will provide the foundations for a satisfactory model of design [Chan87], they can be formalized and translated into a program. An inductive reasoning package would be the beginning of a design machine or at least the beginning of the development of a design support system.

It is at this point not feasible to design and build an inductive architectural reasoning machine that would come close to or outperform an experienced architect. In areas, however, where design relies heavily on deduction and abduction, such as analysis, computer programs may exceed human performance. Inductive reasoning is extremely knowledge intensive. The knowledge must be acquired selectively with human help or may be generated within the machine (using search) and then interpreted for its usefulness. The knowledge types are descriptive or representational, transformational, and procedural.

Akin proposes a system for machine reasoning called AIM [Akin86].

AIM has three major components: working memory space, rewriting rule space, and heuristic rule space. The working memory space contains room for a temporally ordered record of actions of the system and an object representation space to record all information about the object being examined. The rewriting rule space is necessary for reasoning or conceptual inferences. It rewrites the information gathered about the object into another form with the help of if-then rules. The THEN part describes the probable relation in case the IF part is applicable. The heuristic rule space, finally, consists of individual operations executing the G-A-T method described earlier. These operations are encoded in the form of rules that provide mechanisms for directing the focus of attention, searching, hypothesizing, input, parsing, output, saving, inferring, and stopping. AIM has been successfully tested and demonstrated its value as an experimental tool.

Gero proposes and has built a prototype of an induction program that infers a grammar from reading a plan [Gero87a]. The program is capable of detecting the grammar by "looking" at a representation of a building. It works for a well-defined domain with sufficient domain knowledge available to the machine.

This section introduced deductive, abductive, and inductive reasoning. Deduction is well handled by predicate calculus and a useful and frequently applied method in CAD. Abduction or explanation of design or design decisions is attracting growing attention. The most interesting form of inference is induction or learning. It is computationally the least explored method but bears the greatest potential for building a true CAD system.

8
Creativity

Typically, we apply fairly stringent criteria in judging creativity. In most cases, we require an act to pass three tests before we call it creative. First, we must believe that the act is *original*. Second, we must believe that it is *valuable*. And third, it must suggest to us that the person who performed the act has special mental *abilities*. For example, when we see what the person has done, we ask ourselves, "How did she ever think of that?" or, "How did he have the patience to work all that out?" [Hayes81]

Creativity is the art of causing to exist original or imaginary ideas or objects. This definition is open to interpretations that range from the layman's view of creativity as a mystical activity to Shank's provocative statement that creativity is mechanical [Shank86]. In either case, it is a skill attributed to a limited group of people. Imagination and intuition are related capabilities, often considered the skill of the same limited group of people. Creativity is an area in design that has very little formalization. It is therefore difficult to find computational models that allow imitation or improve upon human creativity. If we accept the point of view that creativity is not something mystical, but a function of understanding, learning, and inferencing, we can begin to accept computers as tools in the formalization and application of creative processes. This chapter will touch on some issues important for the understanding of this view of creativity.

Creativity is fundamental to the development of society, but the creative act or creative people are not always appreciated. According to Koberg and Bagnall:

It is simple enough to list those "attributes of creativity" which are needed by the designer and to point out the reasons for their inclusion. But actual development of such behavioral characteristics is difficult since society makes it a relentless battle, an often thankless and rarely positively reinforced chore, to maintain such behavior. The same society which readily accepts the creative "product" will chastise or deny the creative "activity" required for such production because of its non-typical nature [Koberg81].

This observation is comparable to Shank's definition of "creativity through the misapplication of explanation patterns," a suspect activity for many people [Shank86].

Creativity is situated on a different level of abstraction than design languages or design discoveries. It certainly needs the results of both language abstraction and search for its high-level and associative inferences. It is elevated occasionally to an unjustified, mystical level. The fact that it cannot be formalized at the present does not exclude this possibility in the future. Past experience shows that every step toward explanation of a phenomenon—and at the moment creativity is a phenomenon—has led to an increase of new and creative ideas. Therefore, the exploration of creativity with all means, especially with microcomputers, will help to improve rather than discourage our creative skills.

8.1 ARCHITECTURAL CREATIVITY

The observations made on creativity as a phenomenon may apply to architectural creativity as well. Every creative act in built architecture becomes subject to an extensive evaluation over time. If it is found useful, interesting, or an improvement over the status quo, it will be accepted by other designers and find its following. Creativity in architecture is easily evaluated because of the physical nature of built architecture. This allows direct comparison of performance, visual quality improvement, and cost between old and new (creative) architecture. Architecture is the physical product of creativity. It may simplify forms and arrangements of objects, but it will not subject architecture to backward development. This quality distinguishes architecture from creativity in other fields, such as human behavior, where the physical evidence of invention and creativity has a relatively short life span and, with few exceptions, ceases to exist with the person.

As stated in the Preface, one of the purposes of this book is the demystification of the use of computers in design. In doing so, and to explore the computer's capabilities to its fullest, it becomes necessary to also demystify some of the traditional notions about design and creativity. This is not to say intentions are to completely formalize and computerize creativity; this would be a contradiction in terms. But it is necesis applied to an abstract model. The effect of creativity is monitored and simulated through all the techniques described in the previous chapters. There seems to be no danger that computer tools will hamper this process. In fact, the faster feedback of results and the immediate visual control will enhance creativity. For intelligent users, computers will provide more opportunities for creativity.

Monitoring the development of architectural creativity through history reveals its interdependence with cultural and technological progress and the invention of new tools. Examples are Greek and Roman architecture, the architecture of the Renaissance, and industrial architecture. The technological breakthroughs of computer technology will improve abilities to create in two fundamental ways: They will enable the creation of a large number of visual alternatives in a short period of time, making selections and new associations possible, and they will be able to execute the aspects of creative behavior that are definable and explainable. Both possibilities will be explored in the next sections.

8.2 SUPPORT UTILITIES

If creativity can be defined and explained as an activity based on rationality, it is possible to identify an array of options to support creativity. Although the creative act has not been formalized, we can assume that it has some underlying conceptual framework. Whatever is known of this framework today can be made available to support architectural creativity.

In his metamagical themas, Douglas Hofstadter concludes that variations on a theme are the essence of imagination and creativity:

> Newton said that if he saw farther than others, it was only because he stood on the shoulders of giants. Too often, however, we simply indulge in wishful thinking when we imagine that a clever or beautiful idea was somehow due to unanalyzable, magical, transcendent insight rather than to any mechanisms, as if all mechanisms by their very nature are necessarily shallow and mundane. My own mental image of the creative process involves viewing the organization of a mind as consisting of thousands, if not millions, of overlapping implicospheres, at the center of which is a conceptual skeleton. The implicosphere is a flickering, ephemeral thing, rather like the electron cloud, with its quantum-mechanical elusiveness, around an atomic nucleus [Hofstadter82].

What are the necessary utilities that can support creativity? Although there is no guarantee that a combination of circumstances and sophisticated tools will result in creative design, they can improve the probability of creativity on a rational base. In accordance with our previous definition attempt of creativity, utilities to support architectural creativity sary to explore design and the processes that lead to new, creative design solutions, as systematically as possible. Only then it will be possible to take advantage of the computer beyond its being a mere drafting tool. Knowing that the following definition of creativity will cause controversy, it will nevertheless be presented as a point of departure for better definitions:

1. Architectural creativity depends on having a set of precedences in the envisioned domain. In computer terms, this requires an intelligent database of existing buildings and building elements with extraordinary indexing capabilities. This condition is close to being met by object-oriented databases.
2. Architectural creativity depends on the designer's ability to explain the precedents and their reason for being. In computer terms, this is related to the capacity of machines to perform abductive inferencing or explanation. The problem is far from being solved in general, but is handled successfully for small domains.
3. Architectural creativity relies on heuristics of finding applicable solutions of the past and adapting them to new design problems. In computer terms, this is related to heuristic search and inductive reasoning, as discussed in the previous chapter.
4. Architectural creativity relies on the capacity of the designer or an external critic to ask questions—often very uncomfortable and seemingly unrelated questions. In computer terms, this capability has no equivalent yet. It is related to abductive and inductive reasoning and is almost the inverse of deductive inference. As questions arise, it allows the designer to view the problem in a larger context. Computers presently do not have contextual knowledge of satisfactory dimensions.
5. Architectural creativity relies on the idiosyncracy of individual designers. In computer terms, this means the necessary building of idiosyncratic machines, or exposure to similar machines with different inductive processes.

Whereas the first three points show that the capability to learn, remember, and apply knowledge are necessary to be creative, the last two items demonstrate the necessity of questioning and individual discovery. In examining the present stage of computer hardware and software, particularly for microcomputers, the outlook for computer-aided creativity in the near future seems bleak. However, it is possible that designers and architects will be the first ones to build creative machines as they have, through design education, a strong knowledge base in the teaching of creativity.

Creativity can develop in its best form in the design process, where it fall into four categories: physical and psychological utilities, background information utilities, visualization tools, and reasoning tools. The following is a description of each of the instruments for creativity.

1. **Physical and Psychological Environment.** The physical and psychological environment for creative behavior can differ from an environment for routine or training activities. A good example is the physical and psychological context of design and architecture studios, which is radically different from the context of lecture and laboratory classes. There seems to be a relation between an informal atmosphere and the ability to create. This observation is related to the fact that creativity is enhanced by evaluating the present from an external standpoint by means of stepping out of the routine environment.

2. **Extensive Background Knowledge Utilities.** The creation of an idea or an object has limited positive impact if the same creation has occurred previously. The knowledge of architectural history, relations between architecture and society, state-of-the-art knowledge in structures, building related energy research and applications, financial conditions and possibilities, and special regional conditions, will be of benefit. Knowledge of the relation between the historic precedence and the present situation will facilitate creativity. An extensive background knowledge allows the construction of associations and new combinations, possibly leading to new creations. Various kinds of database management systems with extensive indexing capabilities are the first computer tools to support this process. Microcomputers, utilizing local databases or functioning as terminals of national and international databases, have a growing impact in the acquisition and distribution of background knowledge.

3. **Tools for Visualization of Synthesis and Analysis.** It is difficult to predict what impact the availability of a powerful microcomputer would have had on the creativity of Leonardo da Vinci, Michelangelo, or Einstein. It is safe to assume that a good computerized visualization tool will reduce the feedback time between the development of an idea, its representation on an external medium, and its realization. Thus, a larger number of variations can be observed and invalid solutions can be discarded quickly. With the advent of powerful workstations, microcomputers are on the verge of becoming useful visualization tools.

4. **Effective Tools for Architectural Reasoning.** This includes tools for reasoning on different levels of abstraction: reasoning about concepts and preliminary design ideas, reasoning about specific configurations and layouts, reasoning about various systems in the building and their impact on the overall performance, and reasoning about material assemblies and elements and their geometrical relations. [Woodbury87] These instruments go beyond visualization because they are capable of making decisions. Tools of this kind are in their infancy

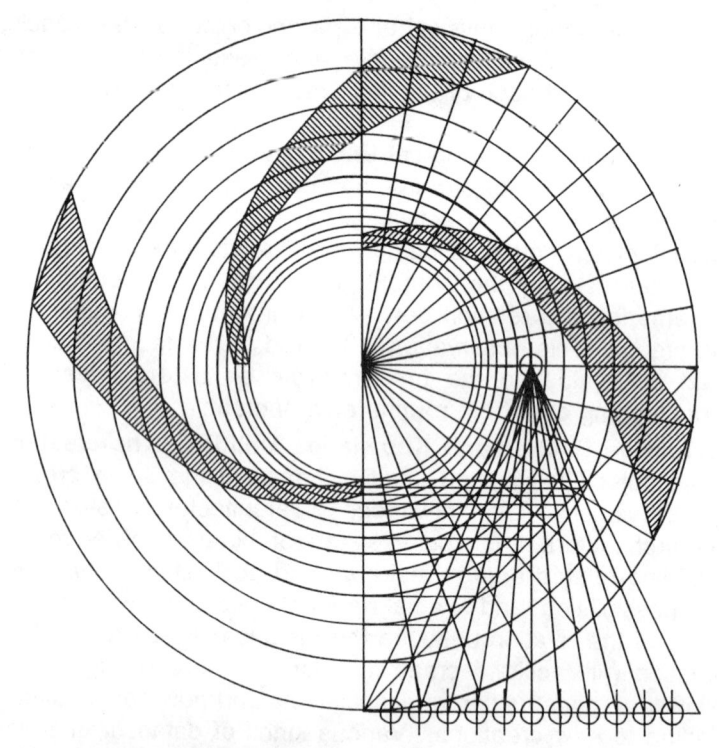

Figure 8.2a Advanced CAD systems offer all capabilities of traditional manual geometric construction. In addition, they allow automation, display, and high-quality reproduction of constructions on external media.

and far from being practical at the moment. However, their further development is crucial for a comprehensive computational environment to support creativity.

Providing these utilities in combination with a physical and psychological environment open to creativity will lead to new solutions that are unexpected, attractive, and useful. The development of computer-animated logos in the film and television industry is an example of the creative application of a new technology. A particular strength of the new technology is the fact that the objects meant to be recognized from representations do not necessarily have an equivalent in real life. The abstract character of computer representation leads to the creation of new objects of different quality. Figures 8.2a to 8.2f illustrate this point. In Figure 8.2a a traditional construction method is used to produce a set of circles whose radius diminishes in perspective. The spiral is then constructed by connecting circle and radius intersections. Figure 8.2b creates the same spiral by using the shape grammar approach, greatly

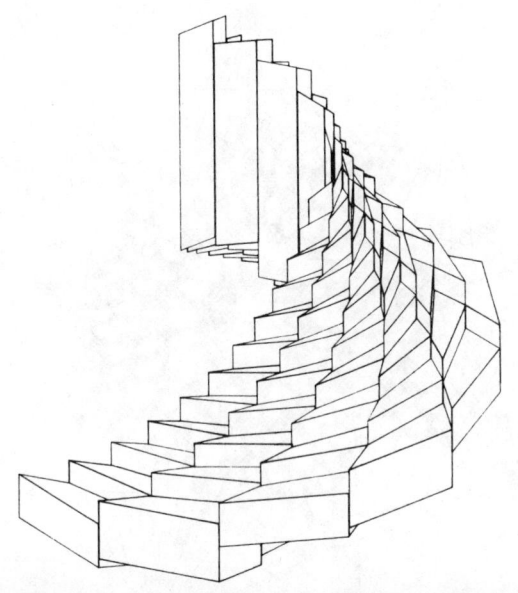

Figure 8.2b Object created by combining manual construction (defining the basic shape) and automated construction (writing a function that controls the shape and location transformations).

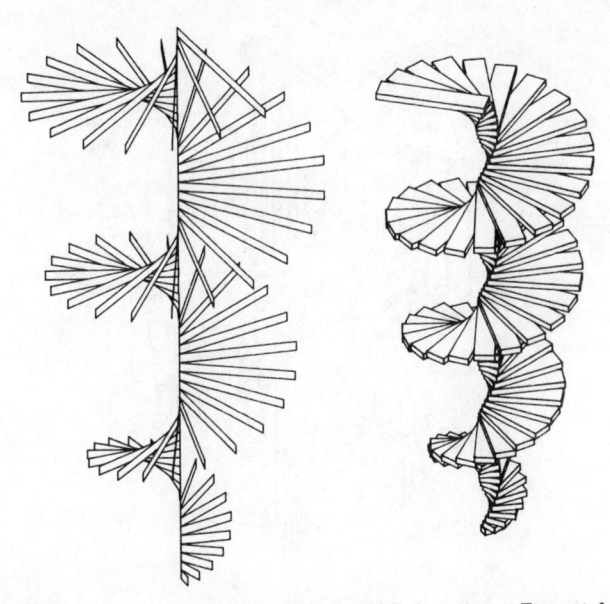

Figure 8.2c Objects created entirely with a LISP function. Except for the object that undergoes shape and location transformations, the figures are identical. The difference in the basic shapes is controlled by the function.

Figure 8.2d Mixing manual construction (basic shape), and automated mirroring, rotation, and diameter-dependent extrusion.

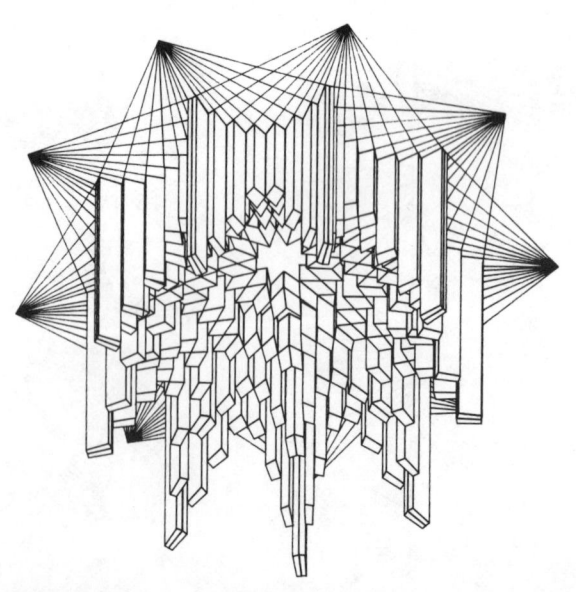

Figure 8.2e Mixing manual construction (basic shape), and automated mirroring, rotation, and diameter-dependent extrusion. Axonometric view of the object seen from below.

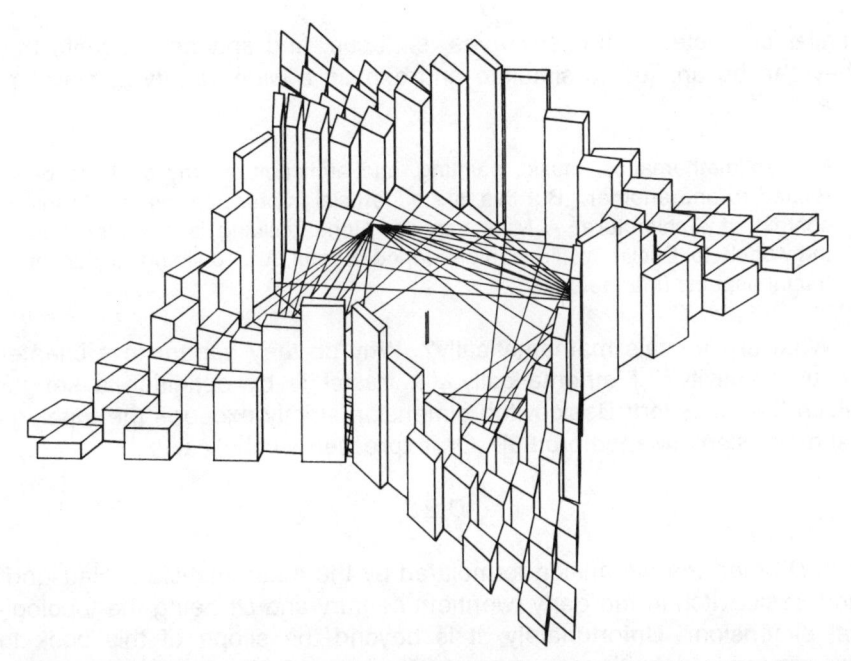

Figure 8.2f Parts of the previous object scaled and rotated individually in an interactive session.

simplifying the process after the initial shape and the generating algorithm are defined. Figure 8.2c, again using a simple shape grammar implemented in LISP, resembles a stair in one form, a plant or an organism in another form. Figure 8.2d, created through a combination of manual methods to construct the basic shape and automated transformations, appears as a floor pattern. Figure 8.2e, the same object but extruded differently, resembles Islamic room enclosures. Figure 8.2f finally, created by selecting parts of the previous shapes and rearranging them differently, presents new and unexpected shapes. The examples show the application of microcomputers as a quick visualization tool to support creativity. In these examples, all the background information ("resembles or characterizes . . ."), and the reasoning utility (selecting only extrusions and transformations that "make sense"), are the responsibility of the user.

8.3 FRACTALS

The term "fractal" has been coined to describe curves and surfaces of space-filling character. Fractal surfaces are increasingly used in computer graphics to simulate natural patterns. The recursive and self-similar character of fractal curves, surfaces, and spaces suggests that they can be applied to simulate and explain a wide variety of phenomena.

> Modern mathematics, music, painting, and architecture may seem to be related to one another. But this is a superficial impression, notably in the context of architecture: A Mies van der Rohe building is a scalebound throwback to Euclid, while a high period Beaux Arts building is rich in fractal aspects [Mandelbrot83].

What are fractals mathematically? Why do they appear in a chapter about creativity? Mathematically, "a fractal is by definition a set for which the Hausdorff Besicovitch dimension strictly exceeds the topological dimension" [Mandelbrot83]. Or, expressed symbolically:

$$D \geq D_t$$

with D being the dimension formulated by the mathematicians Hausdorff and Besicovitch in the early twentieth century and Dt being the topological dimension. Unfortunately, it is beyond the scope of this book to explore these definitions in more depth, but as a hint the reader may try to compare the fractal or Hausdorff dimension D with the Euclidian or topological dimension Dt. Euclid gives a line the dimension one, a plane the dimension 2, and a volume the dimension 3. Hausdorff proposed calculating the linear measure of a polygon by adding its sides' lengths without transforming them or by raising them to the power $D = 1$, which is, as we stated before, the Euclidian dimension of a line. Similarly, the surface of a closed polygon is calculated by paving the polygon with squares and by adding the square's sides raised to the power $D = 2$, which corresponds with the Euclidian dimension of a plane. What happens if the dimension is neither 1 or 2 or 3 but a fraction or an integer greater than the topological dimension? Mandelbrot proposes calling curves for which the fractal dimension D exceeds the topological dimension Dt "fractal curves." In the following, the expression "fractal" is used both as a noun and as an adjective, and in a broader sense than Mandelbrot's original definition.

The discussion of fractals under creativity is appropriate for two reasons. The first one, according to the previous definition of creativity, states the probability of creative design acts is improved with broadening and generalizing the knowledge base while increasing expertise in specific areas. The reader will with no doubt recognize relations between fractals and shape grammars and will find that the same graphic result is possible with either technique. But the real purpose of the discussion is to encourage planned experiments with fractals and to explore the potential of fractals in architecture.

Figure 8.3a   Fractal exploration of wheatlike forms. The algorithm manipulates individual pixels on a bit-mapped display. Gen Shong Lo.

The second reason is more intuitive. Is it pure coincidence that at the time when several mathematicians proposed some of the ideas that the French mathematician Mandelbrot later expanded and formalized was also the time of Beaux Arts and historicism, both relying heavily on studying nature and incorporating natural forms and ornaments? And is it coincidence that the American architect Eisenman claims that he never saw fractals before designing projects that can be clearly expressed as fractals? Eisenman suggests that fractal thinking may be a way to design creatively [Eisenman87].

Typically, fractals are used to represent natural forms. Examples are coastlines [McGregor86], trees (see Figure 8.3b), clouds, texture (see Figure 8.3a), and mountain ranges [Oppenheimer86]. But fractals also have properties that make them particularly appropriate for representing architecture. Fractal properties such as self-similarity and structure in spite of an apparently chaotic appearance for higher levels of recursion have interesting parallels in architectural examples of the past and the present. Figure 8.3c shows two buildinglike objects that were produced with the same algorithm as the trees in the previous figure. The object in Figure 8.3d was inspired by architect Peter Eisenman's Fin d'Ou T Hou S project [Eisenman85]. From left to right, the recursion depth increases from 1 to 4. The top two rows show the buildings with and without hidden lines removed, the lower two are elevations and floor

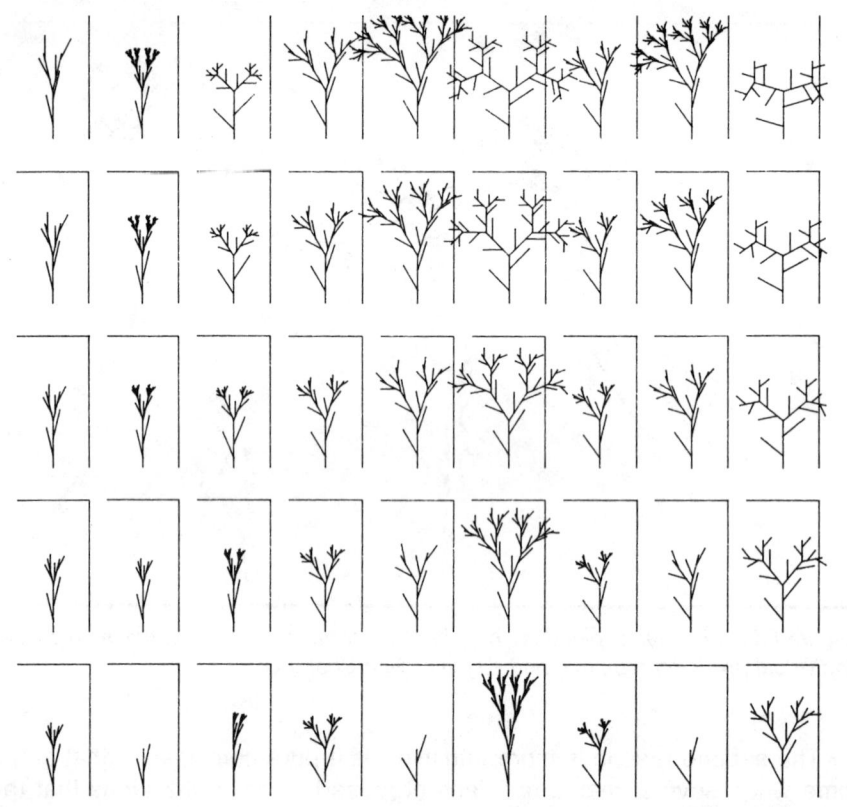

Figure 8.3b Developing fractals to represent natural forms. All trees and bushes are based on the same parametric fractal algorithm.

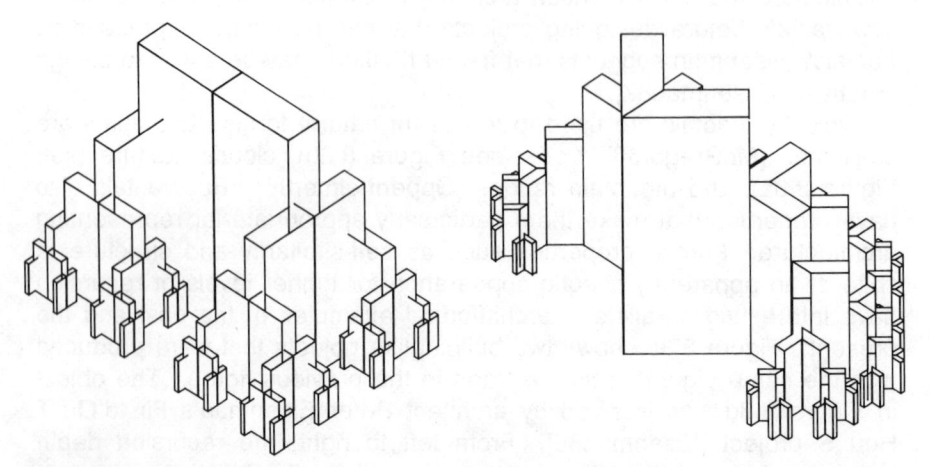

Figure 8.3c Approaching abstract architectural representations: a variation of the fractal tree algorithm.

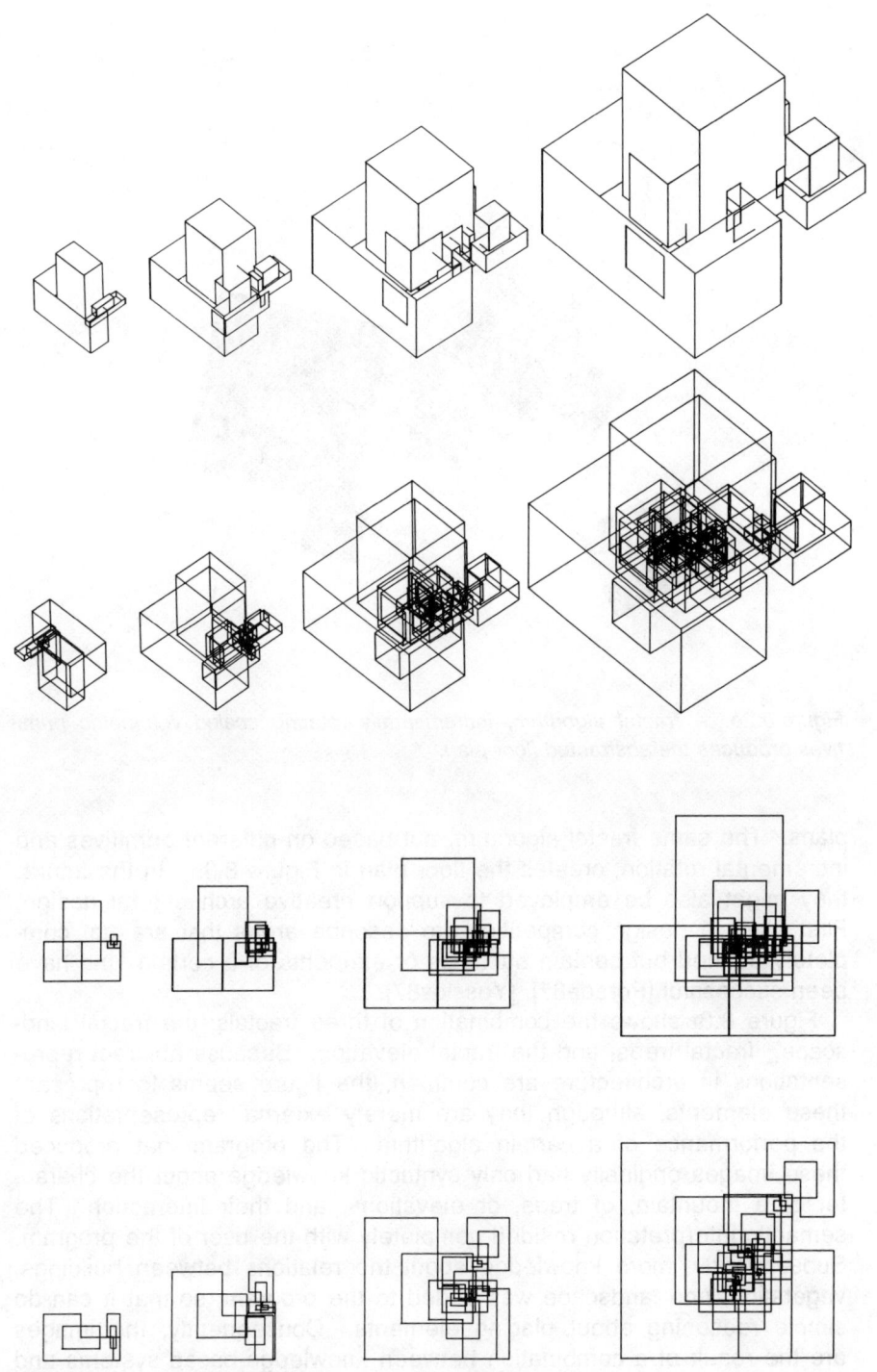

Figure 8.3d Supporting creative architectural design through fractal recursion. Axonometric views (top), elevations, and plans (bottom).

146   CREATIVITY

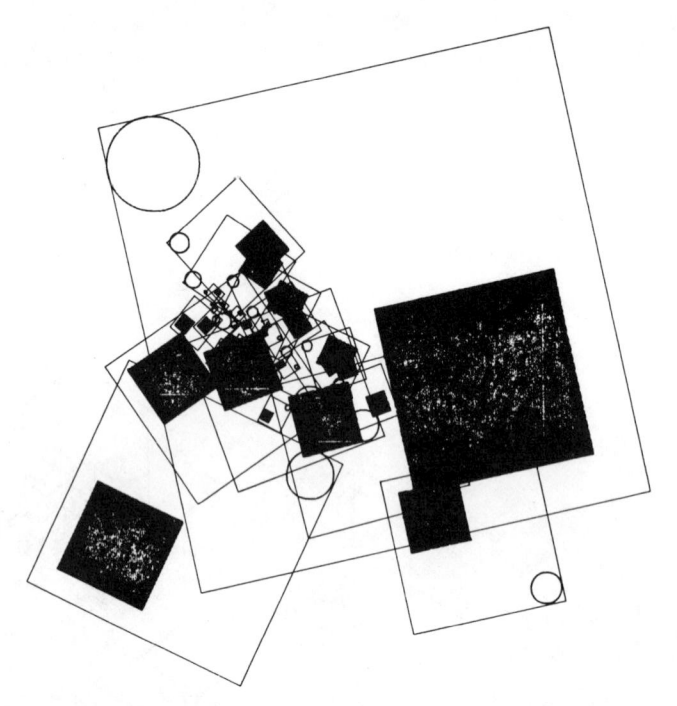

Figure 8.3e A fractal algorithm, incrementally rotating scaled volumetric primitives produces the abstracted floor plan.

plans. The same fractal algorithm, but based on different primitives and incremental rotation, creates the floor plan in Figure 8.3e. In the future, they might also be employed to support creative architectural design. First uses in design competitions to describe areas that are not completely defined but contain buildings or elements of a certain kind have been successful [Porada87], [Yessios87].

Figure 8.3f shows the combination of three fractals: the fractal landscape, fractal trees, and the fractal elevation. Because abstract representations in architecture are common, the figure seems to represent these elements, although they are merely external representations of the performance of a certain algorithm. The program that produced these images originally had only syntactic knowledge about the character of a mountain, of trees, or elevations, and their interaction. The semantic interpretation resided completely with the user of the program. Subsequently, more knowledge about the relations between buildings, vegetation, and landscape was added to the program, so that it can do simple reasoning about placing elements. Consequently, the images are the result of a combination between knowledge-based systems and fractal algorithms, a research area that is beginning to emerge.

The explanation of existing buildings in terms of the fractal geometry

Figure 8.3f Architectural fractals used to create landscape, trees, and building.

147

Figure 8.3g   Architectural fractals used to re-create existing architecture: Ukrainian church floor plan and axonometric. Fang Yuan Chih.

148

of architecture has just begun. Figure 8.3.g illustrates a Ukrainian church floor plan and axonometric created by a fractal algorithm. The first level of generation depth places an octagon at the center. The next level of generation adds 8 octagons and produces the image shown. The following level (depth of three, not shown) surrounds the original octagon with 24 more octagons, thus creating a very complex object. It is interesting to discover that the generating algorithm can easily be modified to generate examples of ideal Renaissance churches.

The preceding examples are the first in the exploration of the fractal geometry of architecture.

9
Evaluation

The final test for the quality of a building is its physical appearance, its quantitative performance, and the degree of satisfaction it provides for users and owners. In the past, these qualities were assessed through post occupancy evaluation. Results of the evaluation were collected and could serve in published form as feedback for new designs. Although these case studies are a useful tool to avoid major design mistakes of the past, they do not offer the direct individual feedback and advice the architect needs in the design process. Simulation, on the other hand, attempts to reach better design solutions interactively before the building is actually constructed. Computerized evaluation is a recent method in the assessment of design solutions, based on a long historical development. The following is a brief list of methods that support and lead to design evaluation and shows the increasing formalization of evaluation over time.

Ad hoc building with available materials and construction methods, 5000 B.C. – today.
Learning from failures and successful experiences, 5000 B.C – today.
Building a knowledge base of case studies—what works and what does not [Rudofsky64].
Formal analysis of existing buildings [Vitruvius26].
Formalization and generalization of analysis results [Placzek65], [Alberti66].
Formalization of underlying principles: geometry [Flemming77]; thermodynamics [Clarke85]; meaning [Alexander77], [Coyne86].

Simulation of design based on underlying principles [Clarke85].
Prediction of design performance and evaluation of alternatives [DOE-2-80].
Local optimization of design aspects, partial automation [Gero85].
Global, multicriteria design optlmization, total automation [Radford88].

This chapter will focus on the computer-supported evaluation of different design aspects. Evaluation is the process of applying judgment to the result of analysis according to a set of criteria. The more comprehensive the criteria, the more complete and useful the analysis. Criteria are developed according to different categories considered important for the use of the product; the quality of a product can be measured by its quantitative and qualitative performance. Judgment is based on high-level knowledge that reaches beyond the limited domain of the criteria. In computer terms this knowledge is referred to as meta knowledge.

In the process of rational decision making applied to design, solutions are generated, alternatives evaluated, and the optimal solution decided upon. In this process, we apply analysis and evaluation to a design product that has already reached an analyzable stage. It could be argued that this is not the ideal way to find optimal solutions because it involves many traditional ad hoc decisions that are sometimes difficult to defend. If, however, the desired performance of the building was known from the outset, all design decisions could be made accordingly and a set of optimal design solutions would result. In fact, this approach of multicriteria optimization, once perfected, would subsume both simulation and evaluation [Radford86]. Interactive real-time multicriteria design optimization is a goal for the future and exceeds today's microcomputers' capacity of speed and memory. An effort will therefore be made to concentrate on the more traditional method of generating a design solution and then analyzing and evaluating it with microcomputer programs.

Microcomputer analysis programs can facilitate the comparison of design alternatives and increase the efficiency of design analysis along selected criteria. The existing microcomputer analysis programs address only a limited set of criteria and therefore must be treated with caution. They are able to find an optimal solution for a certain aspect of the design, such as first cost or energy performance, but they are not able at this point to find an overall optimized design solution. The problem is related to the hill-climbing-search method described earlier; the different analysis programs can find "local peaks," but not the overall best solution, the "global peak." Computerized evaluation and selection according to the above definition requires high level design and decision knowledge. Knowledge-based evaluation systems begin to address this problem.

The chapter begins with the description of three selected analysis areas: energy analysis, cost analysis, and structural analysis. It ends with addressing a fundamental concern of design evaluation—the integration of different analyses.

9.1 ENERGY PERFORMANCE EVALUATION

Energy performance evaluation is a crucial step toward responsible design. Independent from the price or temporary availability of energy, one of an architect's goals should be to achieve energy efficiency for the proposed building. Before the energy crisis of 1973 designers relied on indicative calculation methods for energy performance evaluation, those that were based on experience and simplifying assumptions such as steady state behavior and perfect temperature control [Clarke85]. Since then, new simulation and evaluation models have emerged that deal by explicit means with the dynamic behavior of buildings in response to climatic conditions, user behavior, and environmental control systems. These programs, dynamic as opposed to static, will eventually replace the questionable practice of assigning prescriptive window percentages and U-values rather than striving for an energy consumption optimization of the building. Powerful microcomputers are beginning to support this simulation and optimization process.

Energy consciousness in architecture is a phenomenon that becomes particularly visible in times of energy scarcity. The period subsequent to 1973 and the first oil crisis confirm this observation. Energy-conscious design gained momentum, energy-related courses were introduced into architectural curricula, and insulation and consumption thresholds became a part of building codes. Parallel to a growing consciousness about the limits of growth, the first energy performance computer models were developed. The computer proved to be an excellent tool in solving complex heat transfer equations and handling elaborate weather data. The first energy simulation programs were developed on mainframes, the largest programs contained well over 300,000 lines of code and required several minutes of CPU time. Well-known examples are DOE-2 and BLAST, which provide accurate hour-by-hour simulations (see Figure 9.1a). With the introduction of cheaper microcomputers, some of the mainframe programs were converted and reduced to more compact versions. Still, a computer simulation with DOE-2 that took 5 minutes of CPU time on a mainframe would require more than 6 hours of CPU time on a typical microcomputer. Consequently, microcomputer versions were developed, resulting in the simplification of simulation methods and thus a reduction in the accuracy of prediction. Several strategies evolved to overcome this problem:

1. **Mainframe-Generated Databases.** This method is the fastest and most accurate for a restricted set of buildings. A large number of possi-

154   EVALUATION

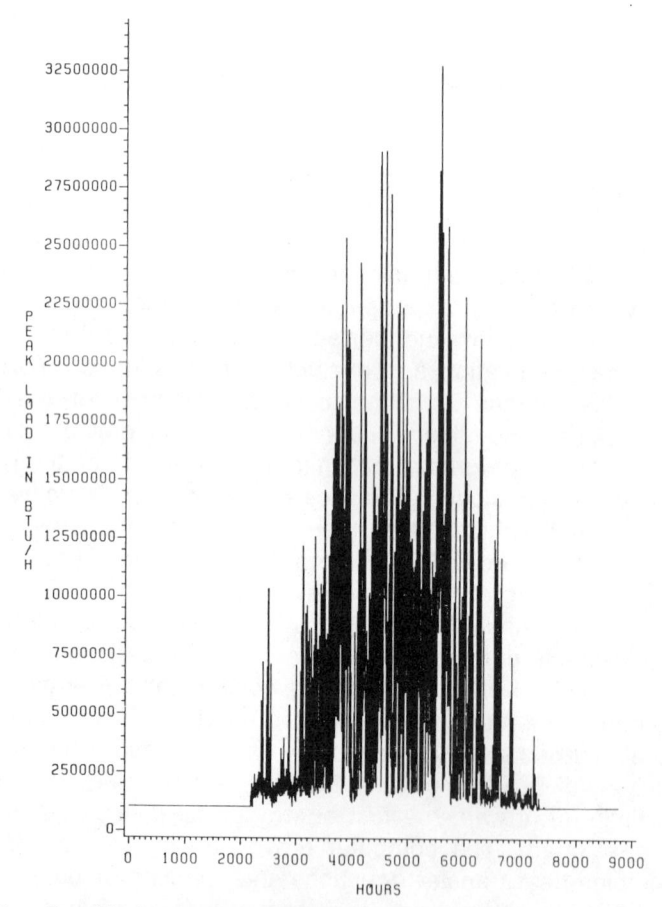

Figure 9.1a   Graphical output of energy simulation data: The graph shows the peak plant cooling load of a hospital over the course of one year on an hour-by-hour basis. January 1 is on the left, the results were computed with DOE-2.1B.

ble configurations of one building type, such as single-family residences, is generated and analyzed with a mainframe program. The most sensible parameters are varied in many parametric runs. A database, containing all the input parameters, and the associated output parameters, is generated and stored. A microcomputer program is used to search the database and to supply the user with mainframe accuracy. The user is restricted by the scope of the database. If results are not directly found, interpolations to the next closest case occur. The method is quite efficient for simulating standard building types, though it is weak if applied to complicated building configurations or building types other than those in the database.

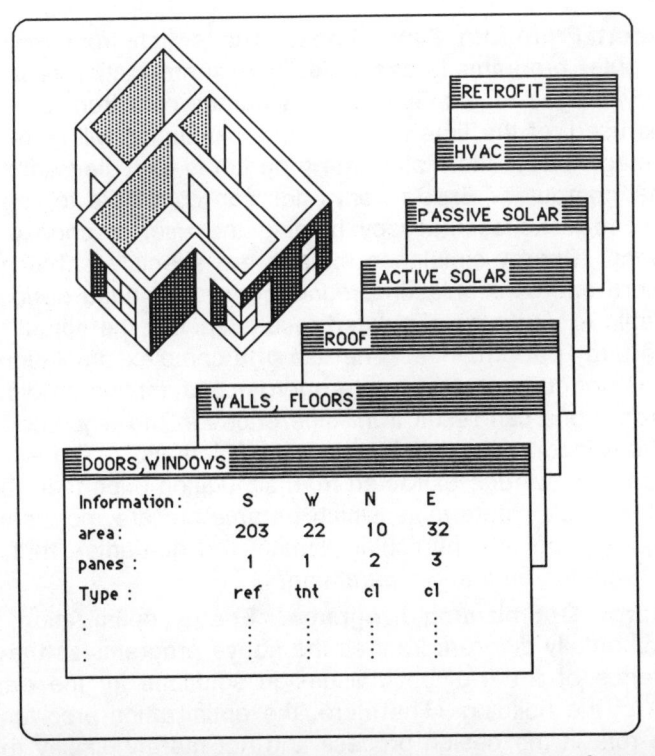

Figure 9.1b Combination of architectural input and energy performance output. A system of this kind can be built with programs that have windowing capabilities and is facilitated by an operating system that allows the concurrent execution of several processes, such as UNIX.

2. **Simplified Methods for Microcomputers.** This method is acceptable for preliminary energy performance analysis when few detailed design decisions have been made. The overall decisions, such as building volume, orientation, thermal zoning, and operation schedules must be known in order to make valid assumptions for the overall performance of the building. Weather data is less detailed than for the large hour-by-hour simulations, which require up to 14 different data for every hour of each day. Normally, one typical design day in each month is selected. Simplified microcomputer-based energy performance simulation programs appear in different forms: in spread sheet format, as stand alone numeric input programs, or with graphic front ends [EEDO84]. Figure 9.1b illustrates the prototype graphic front end of an energy program that facilitates numeric input and simultaneously displays the design [Schmitt85].

3. **Expert Front-End Simulations.** The switch from mainframe to microcomputer programs is desirable for decentralization reasons. Certain disadvantages result: Simulation accuracy can drop, if a simplified method is used, or the time spent on one simulation will increase by an order of magnitude if the mainframe program is executed unmodified on a personal computer. Expert front ends can contribute to combine calculation speed and accuracy by helping the user to choose the right assumptions. Energy simulation experts are specialists that have used one or more energy simulation programs over extended periods of time and are able to verify the simulated results against the actual measured building energy performance. The use of a complex simulation program alone does not guarantee accurate energy consumption prediction; inaccurate predictions can result from differences in the algorithms used as well as from inconsistencies in the input [Clarke85]. The expert front-ends contain knowledge extracted from simulation experts in the form of rules. These rules determine which parameters are most sensible for each building type in a particular climate and guarantee that the input work concentrates on the key parameters.

4. **Energy Optimization Programs.** Energy optimization programs are fundamentally different from all the above programs as they assume the existence of a set of optimal design solutions for the energy performance of the building. Therefore, the optimization program will play an active role in the design process and not merely display the energy performance of a given design [Radford86]. If all the objective functions for the energy optimization could be defined, the traditional computer simulations would appear as trial-and-error approaches in comparison. However, this potential strength of optimization is also one of its weaknesses; it is very difficult to develop an objective function for all energy-related issues in a building. For the near future, this technique will be useful for clearly defined local optimization problems.

The integration of energy performance programs with drafting programs is underway. An example of this approach is shown in Figure 9.1c. The program focuses on quantifiable parameters such as heating load, electricity cost, window percentage, circulation percentage, and total cost. The algorithms for calculating these data are taken from the ASHRAE handbook [ASHRAE85]. The user asks the program for explanations of certain performance criteria. The program will respond and give advice for improvement if a parameter falls below the threshold of acceptability. The advice is based on recommendations from the *Passive Solar Energy Handbook* [Mazria79].

Although programs of this kind are still in prototype stages and rarely applied in practice, they promise to become a source for designers to make responsible design decisions in the early design phases. The future development will combine these utilities with other evaluation programs, such as structural and cost evaluation packages.

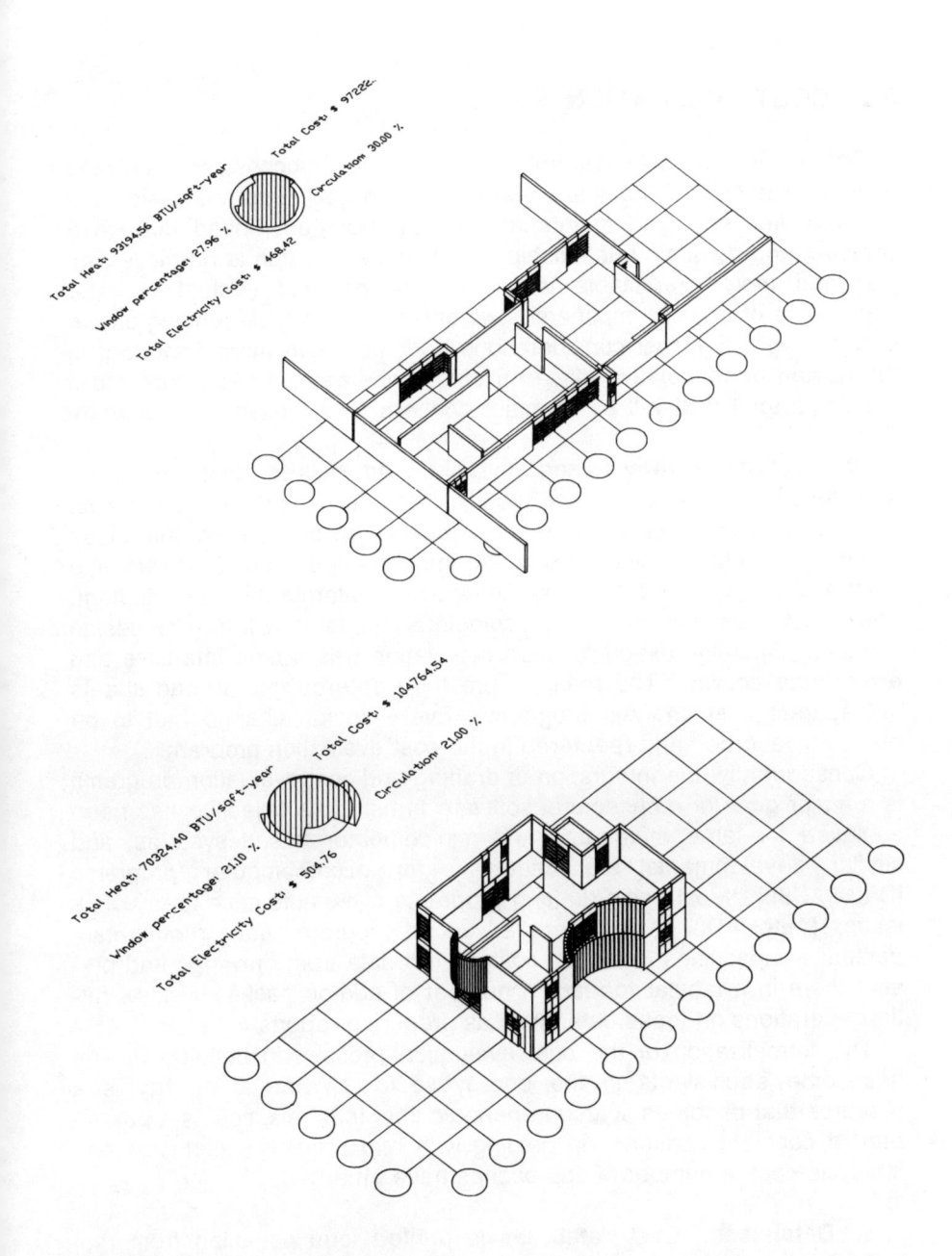

Figure 9.1c Automatic energy performance analysis during the design process and integration with a drafting program. The AutoLISP program monitors the designer's space and window allocation and plots the performance diagram upon request. Top: automatically generated building, using the shape grammar program described earlier. Bottom: manually designed building.

157

9.2 COST EVALUATION

Cost evaluation is fundamental to the financial success of a building project. The cost of a building may be broken down into two basic components: first cost and maintenance cost. Both are linked through a complex and dynamic relationship. First-cost evaluation is normally simpler and more predictable than maintenance cost evaluation. The importance of either component is weighted differently depending on the building type; first-cost considerations become much more important in the design of speculative office buildings, whereas life-cycle cost and a building's total cost will be of major concern for hospitals and laboratories.

Architects have always used state-of-the-art tools for cost evaluation. It is therefore no surprise that specification writing and simple first-cost analysis were the first design-related activities to become computerized in an architectural office. Computer-implemented spread sheets and database management programs helped to accelerate this development. These activities, however, were completely separated from the design process. Quantity takeoff for area calculation was a time intensive and error-prone activity. The results were then entered into spread sheets or separate cost analysis programs. Every design change had to be manually recorded and reentered in the cost evaluation program.

Consequently, the integration of drafting and cost evaluation programs is a major goal for architectural software firms. This objective has been achieved for large mainframe and minicomputer based systems, and similar developments are underway for microcomputer programs [DataCAD86]. Most basic drafting programs allow automatic area calculations [AutoCAD87]. The more advanced programs have rudimentary database capabilities to extract cost-related data from drawings and present them in a tabular format. A number of add-on packages allow further operations on these data, such as preparing reports.

The formalization of the cost evaluation process in building design has some equivalents in the energy sector. Whereas energy is a resource that becomes scarce in periodic time intervals, cost is a parameter of constant concern. In dealing with and predicting first cost and life-cycle cost, a number of approaches have emerged:

1. **Databases.** Cost databases in printed form compiled from real building cost data are a major tool in architectural offices and in university courses [Means87]. These databases are available for the full range of computers from mainframes to microcomputers. The user typically performs quantity take-offs from the drawings and then performs a table lookup on the appropriate cost data. The first step of automating this process is the computerization of the calculation process and the establishment of a material and quantity database. The second, more

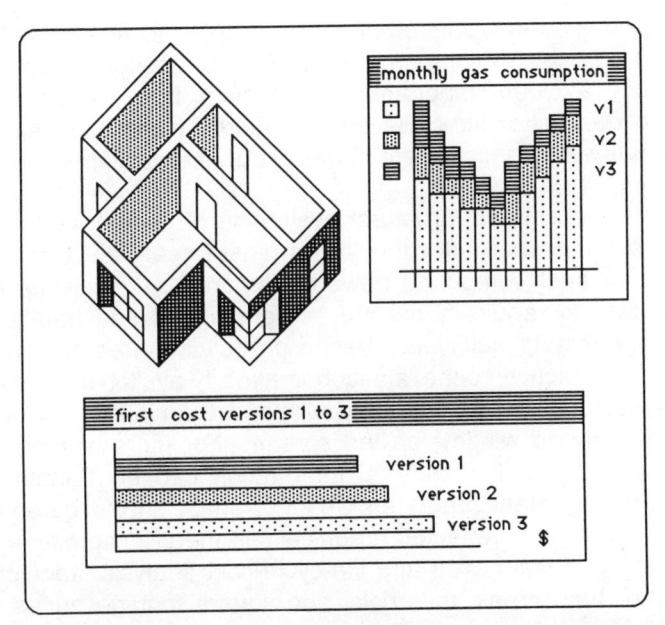

Figure 9.2a Cost estimation: relationship between first cost and energy consumption. The lowest first cost does not guarantee lowest lift-cycle costs.

promising approach is the direct integration of drafting and cost estimation and evaluation of different alternatives. Figure 9.2a shows a prototypical relation between first cost and energy consumption. In this case, the low first-cost design solution results in overall higher energy consumption. Cost evaluation is also part of other analysis and simulation programs, such as DOE-2 [DOE-2-80], which models the cost-effectiveness of different design solutions with regard to first cost and life-cycle cost of energy conservation options.

2. **Simplified Estimation Methods.** Simplified estimation methods are used in the early design process and occur in both manual and computerized form. Evolving expert systems simulate the rule-of-thumb calculations of cost-estimating experts. Prototypes of interactive simple architectural cost estimation programs that work in conjunction with drafting and design packages are under development at different universities [Bollinger86].

3. **Cost Optimization Methods.** Cost optimization is one of the earliest applications of optimization techniques. In fact, many projects are the result of cost optimization attempts, often resulting in architecturally unsatisfactory design solutions, particularly if only first-cost considerations are taken into account. This must not necessarily be so because good architecture is not directly proportional to high design and building

costs. However, the same problems that apply to energy optimization may occur for cost optimization: A single parameter optimization will automatically exclude important other factors from consideration. To optimize a design for life-cycle costs requires more complex objective functions but will also produce a richer set of alternatives.

Similar to energy and structural evaluation of design, cost evaluation in real time rather than after the fact is most beneficial. Obviously, this requires additional computing power. For first-cost analysis, however, the programming requirements are straightforward and traditional algorithmic programs are sufficient. Based on building area and per square foot prices, interactive cost evaluation is already available. Typically, the programs calculate areas automatically and then allow a view on the costs in a separate window on the screen. For more complex applications, area and building material information can be transferred to a database management program. Changes made in the database management program are reflected graphically in the drafting package.

For building maintenance and life-cycle-cost analysis, additional information other than areas, materials, and square footage prices are necessary. Each building requires the modeling of a different scenario that is computationally best handled in different domain models. These financial domain models, similar to energy and structural domain models, need a substantial knowledge base. Hybrid systems consisting of knowledge-based programs and database management programs are therefore appropriate tools for life-cycle-cost analysis.

9.3 STRUCTURAL EVALUATION

Basic structural evaluation of the design should not be completely delegated by the architect. The architect must have a reasonable understanding of the structural system and the structural performance of the design. While some university curricula place heavy emphasis on the teaching of structures, others allow the development of "structurally neutral" buildings in which the structural system is of little concern to the student. Knowledge about the structural system, however, is one of the basic responsibilities of the architect.

As structural evaluation is based on mathematical models and requires extensive calculations, computers were strong in this field from the beginning. Structural engineers have long since taken advantage of computational models, certainly before architects. In recent years several microcomputer-based structural analysis programs were developed and marketed. Commercial structural evaluation programs typically offer the following features:

Analysis capabilities:

- Two- or three-dimensional analysis using, for example, the matrix displacement or stiffness method for solution.
- In-core or out-of-core solutions.
- Analysis of beam, truss, thin shell/plate, bending/plane, stress elements with fixed, pinned, or offset connections.
- P-Delta or standard linear analysis.
- Analysis of displacements, reactions, and member forces. Section forces and minimum and maximum force envelopes.
- Design of concrete beams and columns according to building code requirements.
- Checking of structure for completeness or stability.

Graphical capabilities of commercial microcomputer-based structural analysis packages include:

- Basic graphical representation of two- and three-dimensional structures.
- Manipulation of structural geometry through editing functions to correct input errors.
- Zoom, sectioning, and structural member list features to allow the user different views of the structure.
- Member and joint numbering that can be activated and deactivated during the analysis.
- Display of deflected shapes, bending moment, and shear force diagrams based on specific loading conditions. Variable deflection scales to allow better visualization.

The specific analysis method is of peripheral interest to the architect, particularly to the student. The main concern is whether or not the building will stand up and at what cost. There is a need for interactive tools that monitor the designer's decisions in structural terms and display warning messages as soon as certain thresholds are exceeded. This real-time evaluation, though very computing intensive, has advantages over after-the-fact analysis. It will allow truly interactive competent structural design. Knowledge-based systems allow a quick prototyping and implementation of structural design programs. The domain knowledge that such a system requires is different from the domain knowledge needed for interactive energy analysis, but both systems should be based on the same conceptual building model and both require an agreement on a general representation model for design.

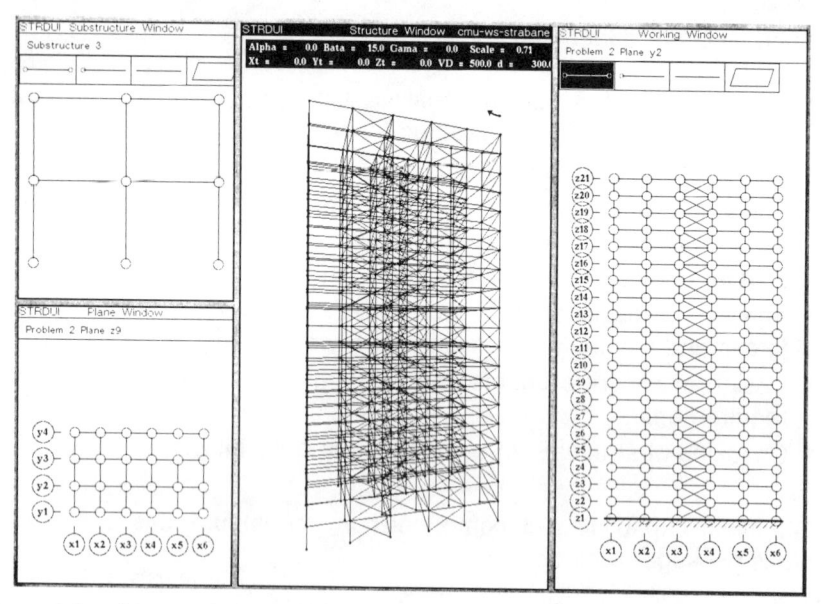

Figure 9.3a Input screen for the structural analysis program SDU displaying working window and windows for structure, substructure, and planes. Weiguang Zhang.

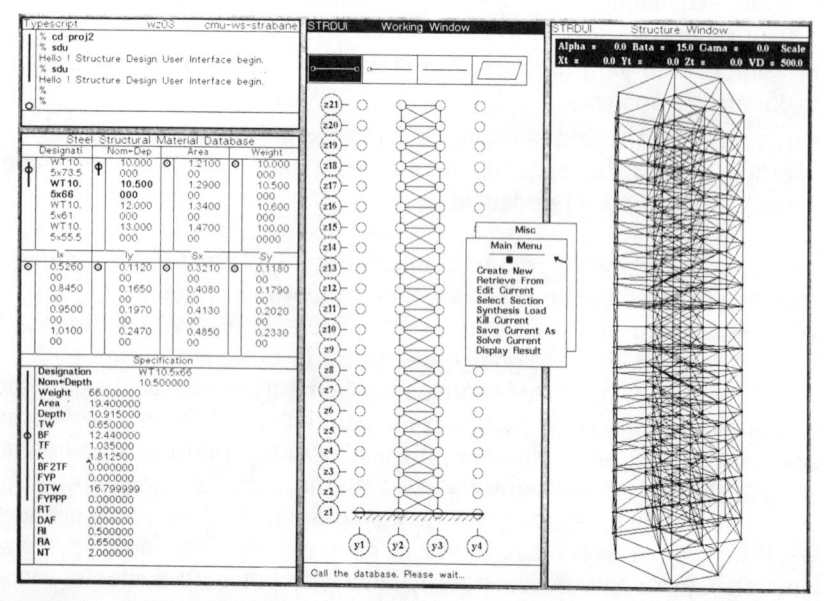

Figure 9.3b Input screen for the structural analysis program SDU displaying working window and windows for structure and structural material database. Weiguang Zhang.

162

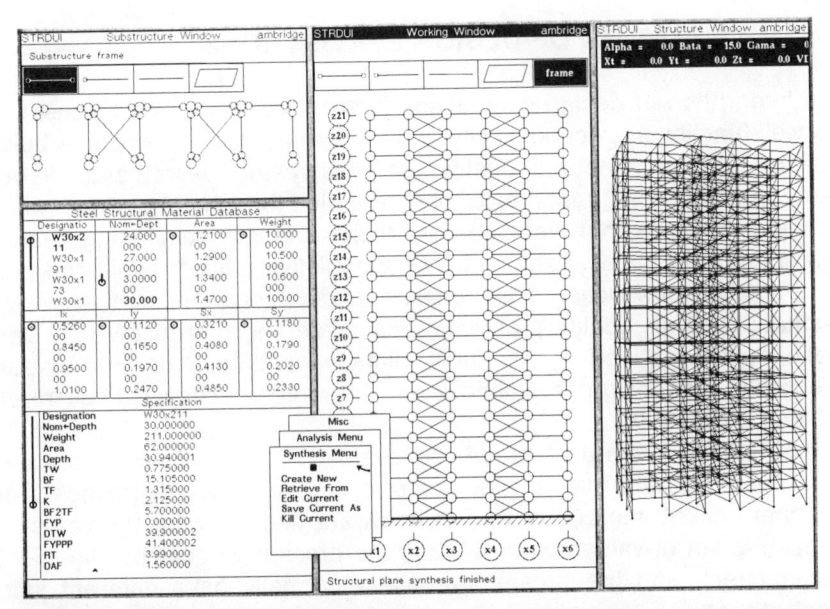

Figure 9.3c Input screen for the structural analysis program SDU displaying working window and windows for structure, substructure, structural material database, and specification. Weinguang Zhang.

Of particular interest to designers are programs that support structural system synthesis in true three-dimensional space. Such a program should feature full graphical input and output, check the structure for completeness or stability, and allow easy editing of entered data. On the analysis side, a program of this kind must feature finite element analysis, substructuring, display of stresses and deflections, model floor and wind loads, model and analyze shear walls, and have access to the appropriate design databases.

Figures 9.3a to 9.3c demonstrate that programs of this kind are feasible for microcomputer work stations. They display the SDU (Structural Design User Interface) developed by Weignang Zhang and used in the architectural curriculum at Carnegie Mellon University [Zhang86]. Figure 9.3a is one user's view of SDU. The display is divided into four windows: substructure window, plane window, structure window, and working window. Changes to any one of the windows is immediately reflected in the other windows. Figure 9.3b displays a structure window, a working window, and a material database for structural steel. The user can interactively select values from the material database. Figure 9.3c shows numerical and graphical information of a structure with the same number of floors but with a larger floor area.

9.4 INTEGRATION OF DESIGN EVALUATIONS

The integration of design evaluations is a crucial step toward constructing well-functioning, economically and environmentally appropriate buildings of high architectural quality that satisfy the users' and clients' requirements. The importance of integration becomes obvious when studying buildings that were designed with a single dominating evaluation criterion in mind. Examples are speculative offices, evaluated only for low first construction cost; energy efficient residences that create aesthetic and air quality problems; and museums that follow only aesthetic guidelines and ignore local climatic conditions or user needs. Integration of design evaluations is therefore necessary but rarely achieved [Rush86].

Why is the integration of design evaluations so difficult to realize? The main reasons lie in the nature of the design process, the designer – client interaction, and in hardware and software problems. A competing set of values characterizes the process of design: The client, the architect, and the prospective users normally have different judgment criteria for evaluation. The completed building is the result of a compromise between those groups. The criteria do not only differ, but they have varying weights. The same criterion might be applied by the architect, the user, and the client, but the priority they assign to this criterion may be completely different. On the other hand, different criteria from different groups might have the same priority and weight, so that a decision must be made in favor of one group or one criterion.

Every attempt to computerize the design evaluation process must take these conditions into account. There is however, parallel to qualitative and subjective criteria, a standard set of criteria and evaluations that are objective and quantitative. A subjective criterion is the perceptual or the conceptual quality of a design. An objective criterion may be the amount of heat lost on a certain design day. Microcomputer programs are presently better prepared to handle the objective criteria, as they are built on known algorithms and can be executed sequentially. The subjective criteria, often as important or even considered more important for the outcome of a successful design solution, are difficult to formalize. Expert systems allow, for the first time, the integration of subjective criteria into the evaluation process. This integration, however, comes at a price. The knowledge necessary to evaluate a building design grows exponentially with the number of criteria. Even if optimization will eventually replace generation and simulation of alternatives, there seems to be a limitation in the number of criteria against which a design can be optimized [Radford88].

These observations do not diminish the value of single-criterion evaluations if they can eventually be integrated into a larger system. The knowledge gained in writing these programs will not be lost. Due to the algorithmic and sequential nature of most microcomputer analysis programs, they are known as vertically integrated programs. They are capable of exploring, evaluating, and sometimes optimizing one particular aspect of a problem in great depth. These evaluations are important and necessary. There is, however, the need for a horizontal integration of computer evaluation programs. This horizontal integration, working with different criteria and values from different areas simultaneously, requires mature judgment and intelligence that microcomputers do not presently offer. A related problem is lack of standardization in describing and representing the criteria from different disciplines in a form understandable to all evaluation programs. Another difficulty arising for the integration of design evaluations is the time factor and the dependency on local conditions. The same building program will result in different buildings, depending on the time and the place the building was designed.

The computerization of the evaluation process requires its formalization, which forces us to research and to define the criteria of evaluation. This process will also facilitate the integration of design evaluations. The necessary steps are as follows:

1. Definition of the appropriate quantitative and qualitative design analysis criteria.
2. Development of a general evaluation language, able to communicate with the building design in different stages as a design critic.

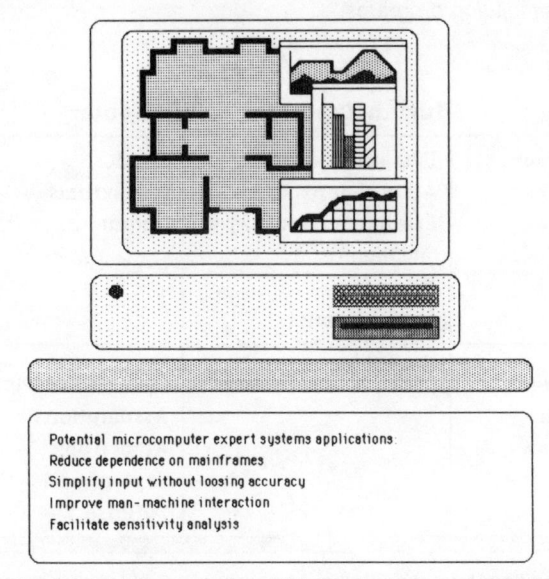

Figure 9.4a Vision of an interactive, real-time design evaluation system from the user's view.

Task II

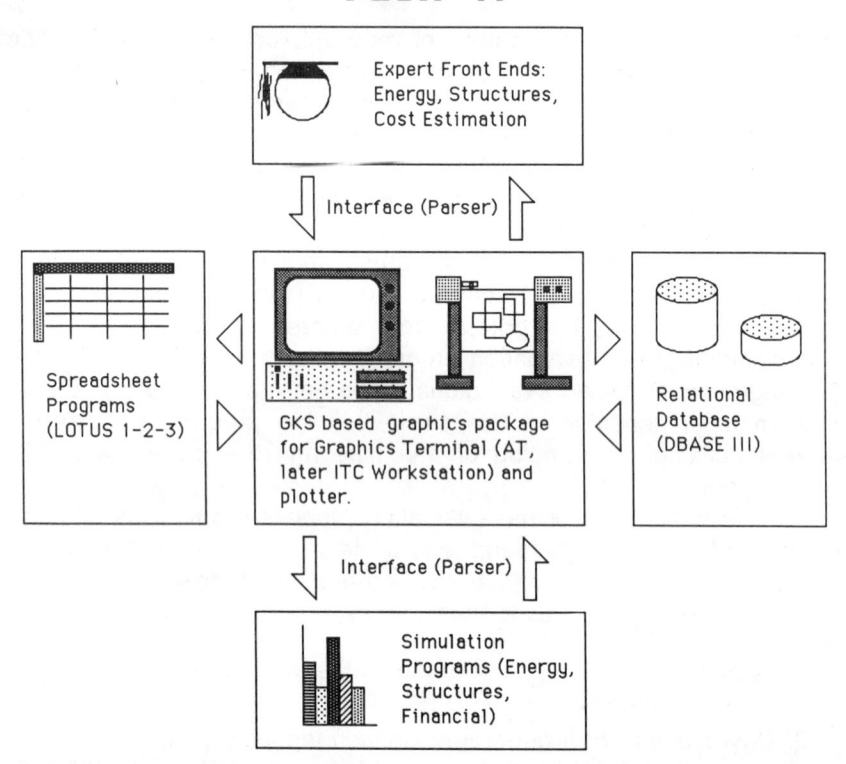

Figure 9.4b An integrated microcomputer-based evaluation system including expert front ends, commercial spread sheets, relational database management programs, and simulation programs.

	Human Expert	**Computer**
Traditional Computer Evaluation	Domain Knowledge Assumptions Extensive Input Judgement Priorities Interpretation	Input Algorithms Output
"Intelligent" Computer Evaluation	Creative Interaction	Domain Knowledge Assumptions Algorithms Explanation Defense

Figure 9.4c Traditional versus intelligent computer evaluation programs. Areas of human expertise become integral parts of computer programs.

3. Definition of a general building design representation language that understands and reacts to the evaluation language.
4. Development of a mechanism that allows the coexistence and interaction of evaluation and optimization in the design process.

A possible scenario for an interactive integrated design evaluation environment, which already exists in prototype form, is shown in Figures 9.4a to 9.4e. Figure 9.4a is an example for a system that lets the user design interactively and shows the results of design decisions on different performance criteria. Performance graphs and design representation appear on the same screen. The user makes design decisions based on visual feedback from the evaluation graphs. This requires the application of high-level design knowledge on the user's part. Figure 9.4b describes a practical prototype of an integrated microcomputer-based evaluation system. Commercial spread sheet, database management, and analysis programs are grouped around an interactive graphic user interface. Expert front ends or small knowledge-based systems are able to exercise various levels of control: They monitor input, interpret output, and are able to explain results. The system has been used for preliminary residential design [Schmitt85]. The shift from traditional methods of computer evaluation toward intelligent computer evaluation is characterized in Figure 9.4c. The development assigns growing responsibility in the handling of traditionally human evaluation activities to the computer, with the intention of

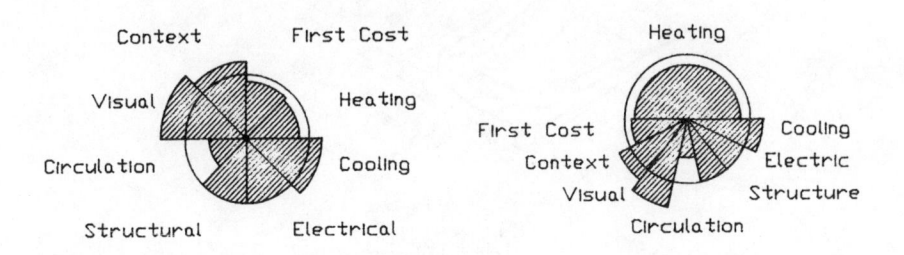

Figure 9.4d Comparing automatically generated diagrams to monitor the performance of a building in different areas. Circle sector diagram (left) and weighted circle sector diagram (right). The circle represents a threshold. A smaller sector radius signifies below standard performance, a larger radius signifies above standard performance.

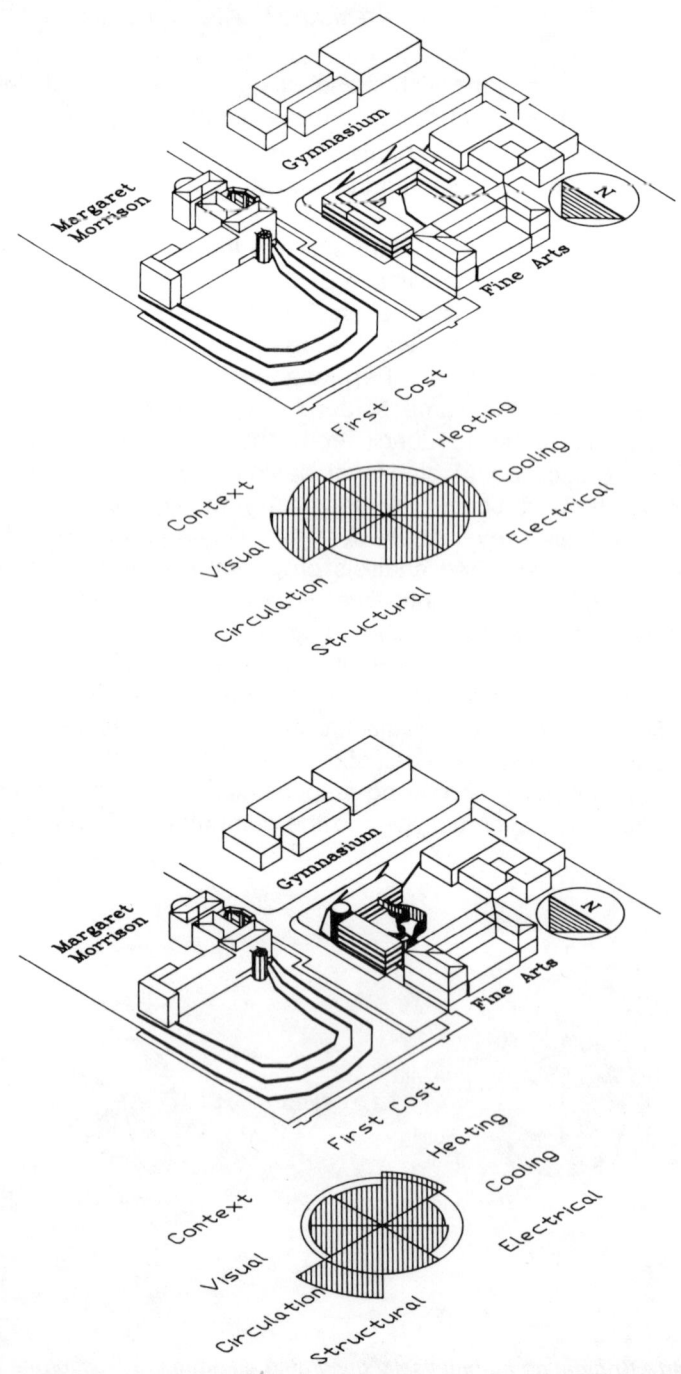

Figure 9.4e Design alternatives for a given site and parallel display of the performance of alternatives. A U-shaped solution, forming a courtyard with the existing building (type 1, top), and an L-shaped building, using the existing College of Fine Arts as a backdrop (type 2, bottom).

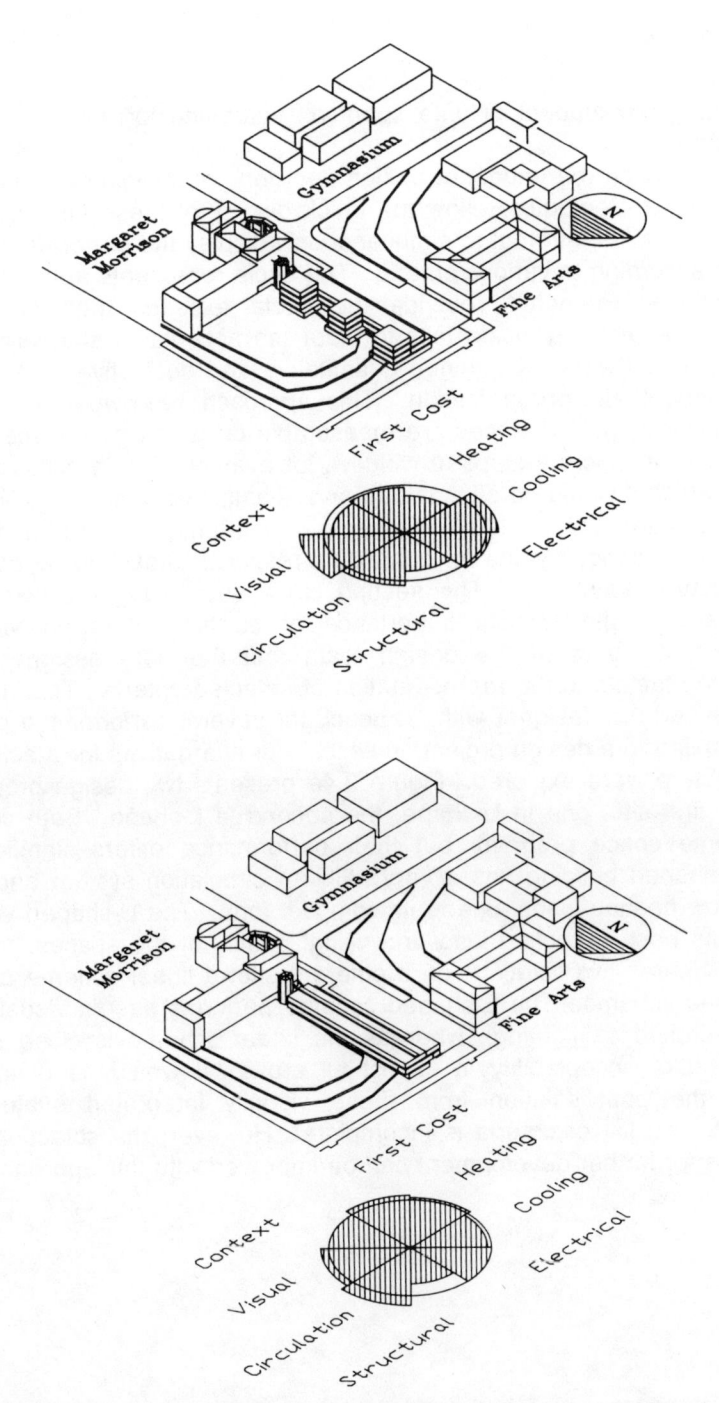

Figure 9.4f Design alternatives for a given site and parallel display of the performance of the alternatives. An E-shaped proposal (type 3, top), and a linear building (type 4, bottom). Trade-offs between the different schemes become obvious.

increasing the amount of time spent on searching for superior design solutions.

Feedback on the impact of design decisions on building performance is essential. Computers allow the quick display of these impacts. Figure 9.4d is a first attempt to simultaneously display the performance of a design according to various criteria. The circle represents a threshold of acceptability: Everything outside the circle exceeds the acceptable standard, everything inside fails to meet the acceptable standard. The circle sector diagram combines quantitative and qualitative criteria and normalizes their representation. This approach has two major drawbacks: Not all performances are measurable on a continuous scale, but may occur in discrete steps (a window, for example, has a minimal area below which it would be eliminated), and quantitative and qualitative performances are represented in the same normalizing method (it is difficult to assign a numeric value for contextual responsiveness, visual comfort, or structural feasibility). The second circle sector diagram takes into consideration the relative importance of certain criteria in view of different members of the design team and therefore assigns visual weighting factors to the representation of selected criteria. This method of providing the designer with feedback for several performance criteria was applied to a design project, in which four alternatives for a school of architecture were explored. Figure 9.4e presents two design proposals on the first site, one in U-shape, the second in L-shape. Both contain the same space program, but their performance differs significantly. The L-shaped building has a very efficient circulation system and relatively low heating loads, due to its compact form. The U-shaped version performs best in cooling load and visual quality of the spaces. Figure 9.4f compares two solutions on a different site: a linear scheme and an E-shaped scheme. The E-shaped scheme performs best in visual quality (controlled daylighting), whereas the linear scheme is close to the threshold of acceptability in almost all areas. It would be difficult to select the best solution from these visually integrated evaluations because the list of criteria is incomplete. However, the selection of a scheme for further development can be improved with this approach.

APPENDIX A

Sample Programs in AutoLISP

This appendix presents programs that were used to produce some of the figures in this book, mostly those in Part Two. These programs are written in AutoLISP, a programming language available with the AutoCAD drafting program [AutoLISP87]. The introductory book by Touretzky [Touretzky84] and the more advanced text by Winston [Winston84] are highly recommended texts for learning more about the LISP programming language. AutoLISP is a subset of the Common LISP programming language that has become a de facto standard for microcomputer applications. Although the approach of writing LISP programs within a particular graphics program is somewhat restrictive, it allows the user to build programs on a high level of abstraction on top of an industry standard commerical CAD program that provides a solid computational infrastructure and user interaction. It also results in the production of objects that can be manipulated similar to other manually produced drawing objects. Most importantly, it gives users immediate graphic feedback of their programming skills. The necessary prerequisites for using this appendix successfully are:

- Interest in doing more than mechanical drafting.
- Some knowledge about the DOS operating system: copying, renaming, and erasing files, creating and changing directories.
- AutoCAD version 2.6 or more recent and a word processor to generate and edit text files.
- Some basic understanding about programming—or enough curiosity and persistence to learn it from the above sources.

The programs presented in the next sections are available to the reader in print and as files on a disk that contains these and other, more complex programs and drawings. The disk is available separately.

The easiest way to test the sample programs and to experiment with them, is to copy the disk into the current directory. All menu files have the extension .mnu, all AutoLISP program files have the extension .lsp. The next step is to start AutoCAD and enter a new or existent drawing file. Once in the desired file, load the included menu by typing the command MENU and supplying the appropriate menu name (WINDOW, CCURVE, SHAPE, or 3D). The AutoLISP programs are then loaded, executed, and manipulated from the menu.

The second way to experiment with the programs is to type them in the word processor directly from this book. This way, begin with a simple program and explore the more complex ones later. The menus are also typed in as text files. The format must follow exactly that in the book. If the menu is not typed in, then load the LISP files separately within AutoCAD. For loading, executing, and manipulating the program parameters, the menu commands must be typed exactly as they appear printed for each application.

The purpose of writing the programs was not to produce the most elegant and efficient LISP code but to give the user a step-by-step understanding of the programs through extensive commenting. The programs use many AutoCAD commands, macros and AutoLISP functions that are not available in standard LISP. These macros allow the construction of very complex objects with very short programs. Output from the programs, in some cases complemented by manual additions, accompanies each program listing.

A.1 THREE PROGRAMS TO DRAW WINDOWS

The following three programs are AutoCAD macros written in AutoLISP. They draw figures that resemble arched window or door frames. The programs are loaded and executed from the menu listed below. To access the window, type MENU and then WINDOW. Now, all three window drawing options are available from the menu. If the menu is not typed in or copied and loaded into AutoCAD, load and initiate the programs by typing exactly what is listed after the [ ] in the menu file.

```
***SCREEN
[*DRAWING]
[*WINDOWS]
[       ]
[**WIN1**]
[Load Wi1](load "window1")
```

```
[ DrawWi1]Arch
[ BlockAr]ELEV 0 0 BLOCK arch 0,0 W 0,0 7,10;;
[         ]
[**WIN2**]
[Load Wi2](load "window2")
[ DrawWi2]Arches
[         ]
[**WIN3**]
[Load Wi3](load "window3")
[ DrawWi3](Arches)
[         ]
[ACADMENU]MENU Acad
```

A.1.1 WINDOW1.LSP: A LISP Macro to Draw a Window.

WINDOW1.LSP is a simple LISP program that will draw a window frame and sill. The window is constructed as if it were laying flat on the ground. All elements are generated by extruding basic shapes. The program uses the PLINE and CIRCLE drawing commands and sets the system variables of ELEVATION and THICKNESS. To load the program, click to the [Load Wi1] option. To draw the window, the [DrawWi1] option is selected. After this, store the window as a BLOCK by choosing the [BlockAr] item. This BLOCK is necessary for program WINDOW3.LSP.

```
;;; PROGRAM WINDOW1.LSP
;;; LISP FUNCTION TO DRAW AN ARCHED WINDOW FRAME AND THE SILL
;;; ALL COMMENTS START WITH THREE SEMICOLONS

(defun C:Arch ()                    ;;; DEFINES THE FUNCTION NAME

   (setvar "ELEVATION" 0)           ;;; SETS THE ELEVATION OF THE ARCH
   (setvar "THICKNESS" 1)           ;;; SETS THE THICKNESS OF THE ARCH

   ;;; DRAW THE ARCHED WINDOW
   (command "PLINE" "0.5,0.5"       ;;; POLYLINE COMMAND, STARTING POINT
            "Width" "0.7" "0.7"     ;;; ASSIGNS STARTING AND ENDING WIDTH
            "0.5,6.5"               ;;; END POINT OF FIRST LINE
            "Arc" "5.5,6.5"         ;;; BEGINS AND ENDS AN ARC
            "Line" "5.5,0.5"        ;;; CONTINUES WITH LINE TO THE END POINT
            "")                     ;;; ENDS THE POLYLINE COMMAND

   (setvar "ELEVATION" -0.2)        ;;; SETS THE ELEVATION OF THE SILL
   (setvar "THICKNESS" 1.4)         ;;; SETS THE THICKNESS OF THE SILL
```

APPENDIX A

```
        ;;; DRAW THE SILL
        (command "PLINE" "0,0.25"        ;;; POLYLINE, STARTING POINT OF SILL
                "WIDTH" "0.5" "0.5"      ;;; ASSIGNS STARTING AND ENDING WIDTH
                "6,0.25"                 ;;; END POINT OF SILL
                "")                      ;;; ENDS THE POLYLINE COMMAND

        ;;; DRAW THE LEFT CAPITAL
        (command "CIRCLE"                ;;; INVOKES THE CIRCLE COMMAND
                "1,6.5"                  ;;; CENTER POINT OF CIRCLE
                "0.15")                  ;;; RADIUS OF CIRCLE

        ;;; DRAW THE RIGHT CAPITAL
        (command "CIRCLE"                ;;; INVOKES THE CIRCLE COMMAND
                "5,6.5"                  ;;; CENTER POINT OF CIRCLE
                "0.15")                  ;;; RADIUS OF CIRCLE

)                                        ;;; END OF FUNCTION ARCH
```

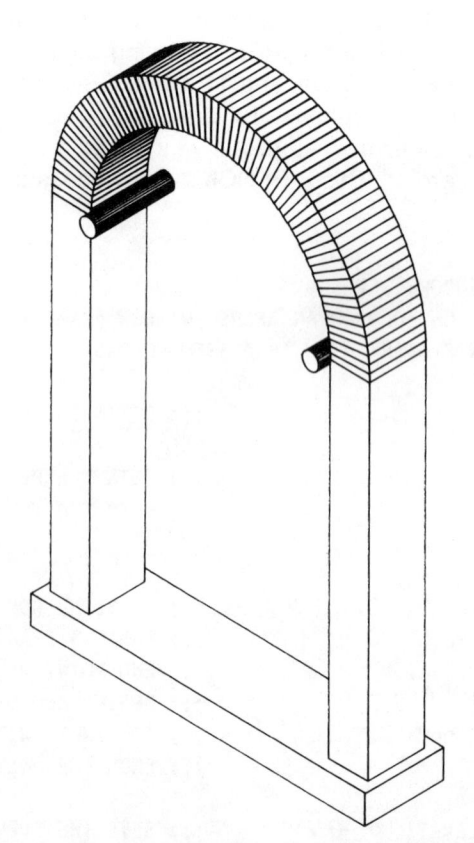

Figure A.1.1a   Window produced with program WINDOW1.LSP.

It is now possible to plot the window (see Figure A.1.1a). It is advisable to study the above code listing, to try some changes, and to watch the effects. Remember to make a copy of the original file and to manipulate the copy only. A change of the ELEVATION and THICKNESS variables, and of the PLINE width will have interesting results.

A.1.2 WINDOW2.LSP: A Program to Draw Three Windows.

The following program draws three identical adjacent windows. The main function is named ARCHES, which calls the POINTS function. This procedure then accepts the desired lower left-hand corner of the window as input (the global variable p0) and calculates the remaining eight points necessary to define the window and the capital (p1 – p8) (see Figure A.1.2a). The eight points are calculated using polar coordinates that

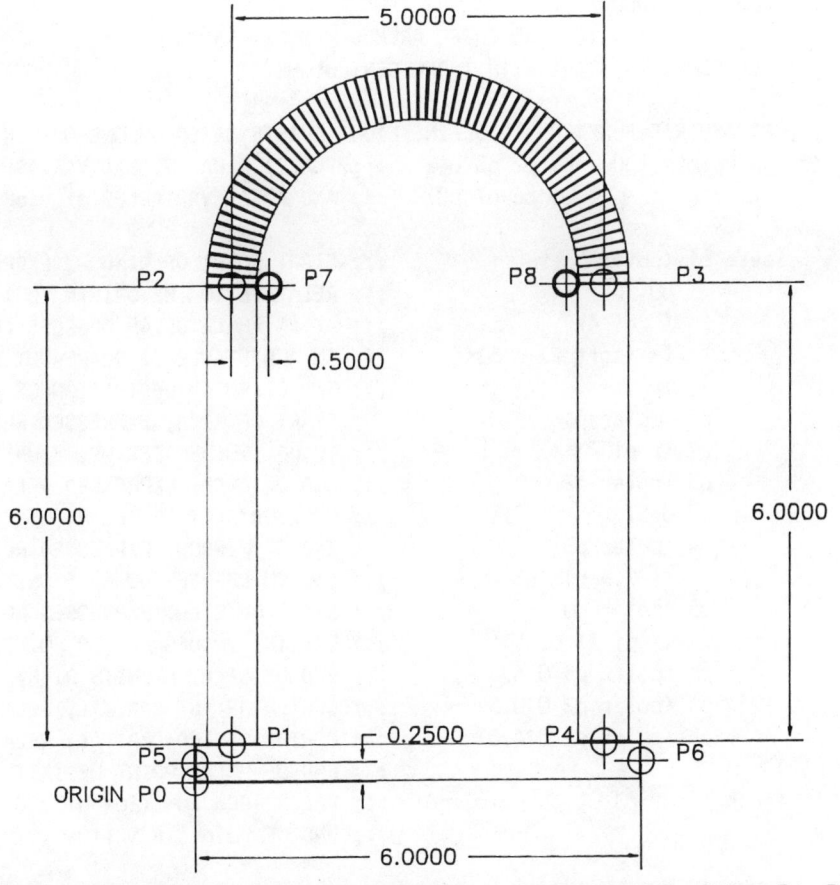

Figure A.1.2a Window produced with program WINDOW2.LSP. Points P1 – P8 refer to the AutoLISP code.

176 APPENDIX A

allow the user to define a new point, given an angle and a distance from an existing point. As these points are of interest only during the generation of the window, they are treated as local variables. The POINTS function, after calculating the appropriate point coordinates, calls the ARCH function. The WINDOW2.LSP program is similar to the WINDOW1.LSP program in the previous example, but note that it accepts variables (p1 – p8) instead of absolute coordinates or constants. The ARCHES function begins to execute once the program is loaded and ARCHES is typed. In its present form, the points of origin for the arches are defined as (0 0), (6 0), and (12 0) in the ARCHES function. Should a change of these global points be desired, for example to (0 10), (10 10), and (20 10) in the file WINDOW2.LSP, execute and save the changes, load the program again, and review the results. The windows will appear now in different locations, and are no longer adjacent.

```
;;; PROGRAM WINDOW2.LSP
;;; LISP FUNCTION TO DRAW THREE ARCHED WINDOW FRAMES
;;; ALL COMMENTS START WITH THREE SEMICOLONS

;;; PARAMETRIC FUNCTION TO DEFINE EIGHT POINTS BASED ON ONE ORIGIN (p0)
(defun Points (p0 / p1 p2 p3 p4     ;;; FUNCTION HAS GLOBAL VARIABLE p0
                   p5 p6 p7 p8)     ;;; AND LOCAL VARIABLES p1 - p8

    (setq p1 (polar                 ;;; START POINT OF WINDOW, EXPRESSED
              p0                    ;;; RELATIVE TO THE ORIGIN (p0)
              (/ pi 4)              ;;; AT AN ANGLE OF 45 DEGREES FROM P0
              (* (sqrt 2) 0.5)      ;;; IN A DISTANCE OF SQAREROOT 2 * 0.
              )                     ;;; END OF POLAR DEFINITION OF p1
          p2 (polar p1              ;;; START OF ARCH, EXPRESSED RELATIVE
              (/ pi 2) 6)           ;;; TO p1, 90 DEGREES UP, 6 UNITS AWA
          p3 (polar p2              ;;; END OF ARCH, EXPRESSED RELATIVE T
              0 5)                  ;;; HORIZONTALLY TO THE RIGHT, 5 AWAY
          p4 (polar p3              ;;; END OF WINDOW, EXPRESSED RELATIVE
              (* 1.5 pi) 6)         ;;; p3, 90 DEGREES DOWN, 6 UNITS AWAY
          p5 (polar p0              ;;; START OF SILL, EXPRESSED RELATIVE
              (/ pi 2) 0.25)        ;;; ORIGIN, 90 DEGREES UP, 0.25 AWAY
          p6 (polar p5 0 6)         ;;; END OF SILL, 6 UNITS RIGHT OF p5
          p7 (polar p2 0 0.5)       ;;; CENTER OF 1ST CAPITAL, RELATIVE T
          p8 (polar p2 0 4.5)       ;;; CENTER OF 2ND CAPITAL, RELATIVE T
    )                               ;;; END OF POLAR POINT DEFINITION
    (Arch p1 p2 p3 p4 p5 p6 p7 p8)  ;;; CALLS ARCH FUNCTION WITH 8 PARAME
)                                   ;;; END OF Points FUNCTION

;;; PARAMETRIC FUNCTION TO DRAW ONE ARCHED WINDOW, GIVEN EIGHT POINTS
(defun Arch (p1 p2 p3 p4            ;;; DEFINES THE FUNCTION NAME AND
             p5 p6 p7 p8)           ;;; THE PARAMETERS (8 POINTS)
```

```
    (setvar "ELEVATION" 0)              ;;; SETS THE ELEVATION OF THE ARCH
    (setvar "THICKNESS" 1)              ;;; SETS THE THICKNESS OF THE ARCH

    ;;; DRAW THE ARCHED WINDOW
    (command "PLINE" p1                 ;;; POLYLINE COMMAND, STARTING POINT
             "Width" "0.7" "0.7"        ;;; ASSIGNS STARTING AND ENDING WIDTH
             p2                         ;;; END POINT OF FIRST LINE
             "Arc" p3                   ;;; BEGINS AND ENDS AN ARC
             "Line" p4                  ;;; CONTINUES WITH LINE TO THE END POINT
             "")                        ;;; ENDS THE POLYLINE COMMAND
    (setvar "ELEVATION" -0.2)           ;;; SETS THE ELEVATION OF THE SILL
    (setvar "THICKNESS" 1.4)            ;;; SETS THE THICKNESS OF THE SILL

    ;;; DRAW THE SILL
    (command "PLINE" p5                 ;;; POLYLINE, STARTING POINT OF SILL
             "WIDTH" "0.5" "0.5"        ;;; ASSIGNS STARTING AND ENDING WIDTH
             p6                         ;;; END POINT OF SILL
             "")                        ;;; ENDS THE POLYLINE COMMAND

    ;;; DRAW THE LEFT CAPITAL
    (command "CIRCLE"                   ;;; INVOKES THE CIRCLE COMMAND
             p7                         ;;; CENTER POINT OF CIRCLE
             "0.15")                    ;;; RADIUS OF CIRCLE

    ;;; DRAW THE RIGHT CAPITAL
    (command "CIRCLE"                   ;;; INVOKES THE CIRCLE COMMAND
             p8                         ;;; CENTER POINT OF CIRCLE
             "0.15")                    ;;; RADIUS OF CIRCLE

)                                       ;;; END OF FUNCTION ARCH

;;; MAIN FUNCTION WHICH CALLS THE Points FUNCTION THREE TIMES
(defun C:Arches ()                      ;;; FUNCTION NAME, NO PARAMETERS
   (Points (list 0 0))                  ;;; CALLS Points FUNCTION WITH p0 AT 0,0
   (Points (list 6 0))                  ;;; CALLS Points FUNCTION WITH p0 AT 6,0
   (Points (list 12 0))                 ;;; CALLS Points FUNCTION WITH p0 AT 12,0
)                                       ;;; END OF FUNCTION ARCHES
```

A.1.3 WINDOW3.LSP: Drawing Multiple Windows with the ARRAY Command.

The program WINDOW3.LSP is very short, but it leads to the same result as the previous program WINDOW2.LSP, under one important condition: The prototype of the window, named ARCH, must exist in the form of a BLOCK within the drawing file or as an external drawing file named ARCH.DWG (see Figure A.1.3a). For a more complete descrip-

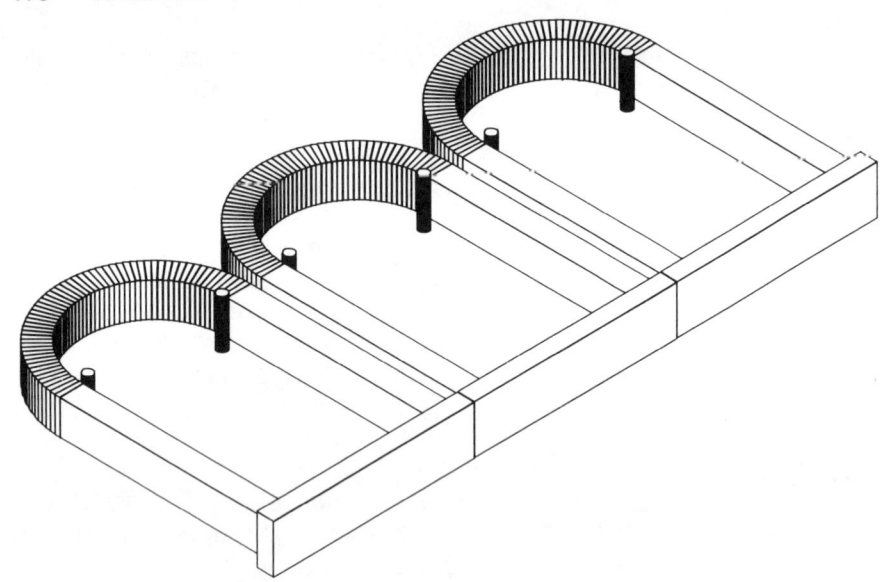

Figure A.1.3a   Windows produced with program WINDOW3LSP.

tion of the BLOCK, ARRAY, and INSERT commands, consult the user manual [AutoCAD87]. To execute the program successfully, create the appropriate window with the WINDOW1.LSP program and store it as a BLOCK named ARCH by selecting the [BlockAr] item from the menu.

The WINDOW3.LSP program works as follows: Once the program WINDOW3.LSP has been loaded and [DrawWi3] chosen, the INSERT command is invoked. INSERT asks for a file name and receives "ARCH", for an insertion base point, and receives "(0 0)". The following double quotes tell the INSERT command to accept the default scaling factors (1 in x, y, and z direction) and rotation angle (0) for the inserted object. The following ARRAY command asks for the selection of an object and receives "L" for "Last", because the inserted ARCH is to be repeated. The letter R signifies a rectangular ARRAY (as opposed to a polar ARRAY). The number 1 tells the command how many rows are required, the number 3 signifies the number of columns, and the number 6 specifies the distances between the windows.

This program only uses AutoCAD commands and supplies them with parameters. If the user is familiar with the command structure of AutoCAD, this becomes a very efficient drawing technique. A program of this kind is easily developed by going through the commands once manually (by typing INSERT or ARRAY and following the program prompts) and recording each answer on a piece of paper. The same answers are then integrated in the program. Experimentation with the program is encouraged. The same effect as changing the points of origin in the WINDOW2.LSP program to (0 10), (10 10), and (20 10) is achieved in the

WINDOW3.LSP program by changing the insertion point in the INSERT command from "0,0" to "0,10" and the distance between the window origins in the ARRAY command from "6" to "10".

```
;;; PROGRAM WINDOW3.LSP
;;; LISP FUNCTION TO DRAW THREE ARCHED WINDOW FRAMES
;;; ALL COMMENTS START WITH THREE SEMICOLONS

(defun Arches ()                      ;;; FUNCTION NAME, NO PARAMETERS
    (command "INSERT"                 ;;; INSERT A PRIMITIVE WITH THE NAME
             "arch" "0,0" "" "" "")   ;;; arch AT 0,0. NO SCALING OR ROTATION
    (command "ARRAY" "L" "" "R"       ;;; MAKE A RECTANGULAR ARRAY OF THE LAST
             "1" "3" "6")             ;;; OBJECT, 1 ROW, 3 COLUMNS, DISTANCE 6
)                                     ;;; END OF FUNCTION Arches
```

A.2 CCURVE.LSP: A PROGRAM TO BUILD C-CURVES

C-CURVE.LSP is a recursive program that begins with a set of parameters, executes, and calls itself with a set of changed parameters (see Figure A.2a). Self-similar and symmetric objects, important in architectural history, are easily created with recursive functions.

Begin by loading the CCURVE.MNU menu. The menu will display the various options available. Note that all commands in the menu file may

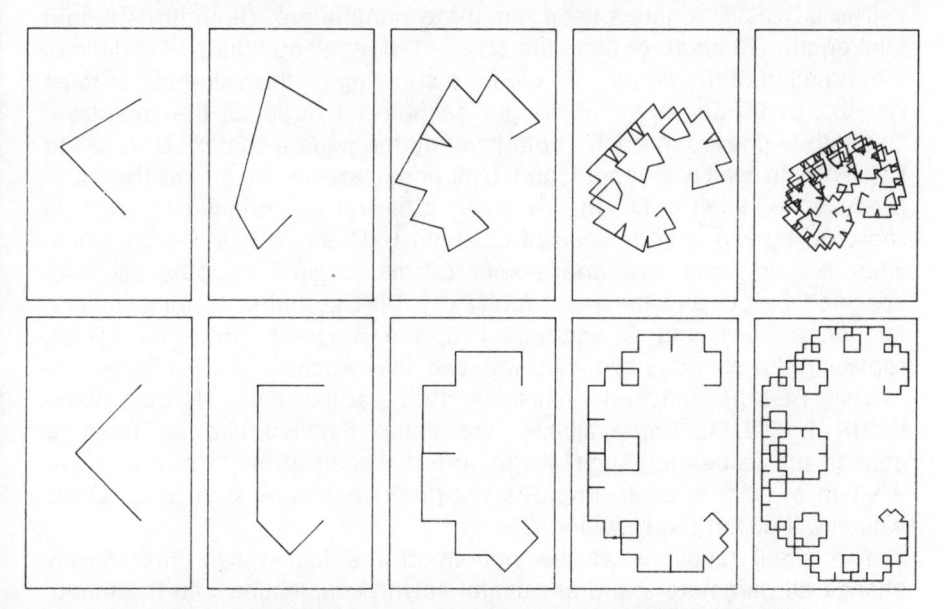

Figure A.2a C-curves produced with program CCURVE.LSP.

180 APPENDIX A

be typed in directly at the command prompt exactly as they appear in the file after the closing bracket.

```
***SCREEN
[*CCURVE*]
[**MENU**]
[           ]
[Load    CC](load "ccurve")
[ SetupCC](Setup)
[ Run    CC](ccurve CLength Tilt MinLength)
[           ]
[*CHANGE*]
[ Origin ](Origin)
[ Length ](OLength)
[ MinLeng](OMinLength)
[ Ang1   ](OAng1)
[ Ang2   ](OAng2)
[ Tilt   ](OTilt)
[           ]
[ACADMENU]MENU Acad
```

The core of program CCURVE.LSP is the CCURVE function. The SETUP function automatically initializes the necessary parameters, and the functions at the bottom of the listing interactively change all parameters.

The CCURVE function itself has three parameters: CLength, Tilt, and MinLength. CLength defines the size of the resulting figure. Tilt defines the direction of the figure. To create a standing C, the value of Tilt must be PI/2 or 90 degrees. Minlength defines the depth of the recursion: CLength is divided in each depth level by the square root of 2. A call to CCURVE in which CLength and MinLength are identical will therefore produce two lines only. In this case, a line of the original CLength is replaced by two shorter lines of CLength (/ CLength (sqrt 2.0)). These lines extend from the end points of the original hypothetical line, specified by pt1 and the point (polar pt1 Tilt CLength). If, for example, MinLength is 1 and CLength is two, the program draws four lines, replacing the previous two lines with two lines each.

The SETUP function initializes the parameters. If the menu CCURVE.MNU is not available, the setup function can be used to change the values for Ang1, Ang2, and the point of origin of the curve. A value of (/ pi 4) or 45 degrees will produce regular C-curves. Other values will distort the resulting C.

The small functions at the bottom of the listing can interactively change all parameters and are useful only in conjunction with the menu. They are well suited for experimentation and introduce (GETPOINT), one of AutoLISP's special functions to acquire input directly from the screen.

```
;;; PROGRAM CCURVE.LSP
;;; CCURVE FUNCTION TO RECURSIVELY BUILD C SHAPED CURVES

;;; SETUP FUNCTION
(defun Setup ()
   (setq pt1 '(0 0)          ;;; SETS UP THE POINT OF ORIGIN
         CLength 1           ;;; SETS UP THE ORIGINAL LENGTH
         MinLength 0.5       ;;; SETS UP THE MINIMUM LENGTH
         Ang1 (/ pi 4)       ;;; SETS UP THE ADDITION ANGLE
         Ang2 (/ pi 4)       ;;; SETS UP THE SUBTRACTION ANGLE
         Tilt (/ pi 2)       ;;; SETS UP THE TILT OF THE CCURVE
   ))

;;; THE RECURSIVE CCURVE FUNCTION
(defun ccurve (CLength Tilt MinLength)
   (cond (( < CLength MinLength)
          (command "LINE" pt1 (setq pt1 (polar pt1 Tilt CLength)) ""))
         (t (ccurve (/ CLength (sqrt 2.0))
                    (+ Tilt Ang1)
                    MinLength)
            (ccurve (/ CLength (sqrt 2.0))  ;;; SECOND CCURVE CALL
                    (- Tilt Ang2)           ;;; SUBTRACT 2ND ANGLE FROM TILT
                    MinLength)              ;;; MINLENGTH UNCHANGED
         )                                  ;;; END OTHERWISE OR ELSE
   )                                        ;;; END CONDITION
)                                           ;;; END DEFUN

;;; TO GET THE POINT OF ORIGIN OF THE CURVE
(defun Origin ()
   (setq pt1 (getpoint "\nPlease enter point of origin")))

;;; TO GET THE ORIGINAL LENGTH
(defun OLength ()
   (setq CLength (getreal "\nPlease enter the original length")))

;;; TO GET THE MINIMUM LENGTH
(defun OMinLength ()
   (setq MinLength (getreal "\nPlease enter the minimum length")))

;;; TO CONVERT DEGREES TO RADIANS
(defun dtr (a)
   (* pi (/ a 180)))
```

```
;;; TO GET THE FIRST ANGLE FOR ADDITIONS
(defun OAng1 ()
  (setq Ang1 (dtr (getreal "Onter the first angle in degrees"))))

;;; TO GET THE SECOND ANGLE FOR SUBTRACTIONS
(defun OAng2 ()
  (setq Ang2 (dtr (getreal "Onter the second angle in degrees"))))

;;; TO DEFINE THE TILT OF THE CCURVE: 90 DEGREES CREATE A STANDING C
(defun OTilt ()
  (setq Tilt (dtr (getreal "Onter the ccurve tilt in degrees"))))
```

The C-curve and related functions demonstrate the power of recursion. Changing one or more of the parameters produces infinite numbers of different curves. Interesting architectural symbols appear in recursion levels 1, 2, and 3: the pyramid, a flat roofed building, and a pueblolike structure. It is possible to replace the "LINE" command with any other drawing command, for example "PLINE", "CIRCLE", or "POLYGON". If, in addition to the horizontal recursion, ELEVATION and THICKNESS are changed with each function call, the variety of forms is unlimited.

A.3 THREE SIMPLE SHAPE GRAMMAR PROGRAMS

Section 6.5 introduces the notion of shape grammars in architecture. The following three small programs show the potential and problems associated with the implementation of shape grammars. SHAPE1.LSP sacrifices generality for compactness; the program is easy to understand and implement, but will not work in all cases. SHAPE2.LSP and SHAPE3.LSP are more generalized and provide additional features.

All shape grammar programs should be executed from the SHAPE.MNU file. The menu file is listed below and must be typed in exactly as shown or copied from the floppy disk. It is loaded by typing SHAPE in response to the MENU command. After the SHAPE menu appears on the screen, the three shape grammar programs can be loaded by clicking to the appropriate menu item. Shape1 and Shape2 must be initialized once. Rules 1, 2, and 3 apply to all three programs. The option ACADMENU retrieves the original AutoCAD menu.

```
***SCREEN
[GRAMMAR]
[       ]
[**ONE**]
[Load S1](load "shape1")
```

```
[Init S1](Init)
[        ]
[        ]
[**TWO**]
[Load S2](load "shape2")
[Init S2](Init)
[        ]
[        ]
[*THREE*]
[Load S3](load "shape3")
[        ]
[        ]
[**ALL**]
[ Rule 1](rule1)
[ Rule 2](rule2)
[ Rule 3](rule3)
[        ]
[        ]
[ACADMNU]MENU Acad
```

A.3.1 SHAPE1.LSP: A Very Simple Shape Grammar.

SHAPE1.LSP automates the graphical execution of three rules (see Figure A.3.1a). Rule 1 places an initial square, then allows the placement of a label on its lower edge, and marks the label with a circle. The following restrictions apply:

- The program should only be used in connection with the menu to get quick responses.
- The (init) function must be executed first and only once—to create and store block SQUARE1.
- The origin of the square and its lower right-hand corner must lie on a horizontal line.
- The label selected must be on the lower edge of the square, otherwise the subsequent squares will not appear in the correct locations.

If these conditions are fulfilled, rule 2 will place a second square within the first square. Rule 2 can be invoked as often as required, and will produce smaller and smaller squares. A special case is the placement of the label in the center of the lower edge. Applying rule 2 will create well-known architectural patterns. Rule 3, if executed after rule 2, will erase the marker.

The (rtd) function converts radians to degrees. It is required because

APPENDIX A

Figure A.3.1a   Image produced with program SHAPE1.LSP

the (ANGLE pt1 pt2) function in AutoCAD returns angles in radians, whereas the INSERT command by default accepts angles in degrees. If the angle input is set to radians with the UNITS command, (rtd) is not needed (see program SHAPE2.LSP).

```
;;; PROGRAM SHAPE1.LSP
;;; A SIMPLE MANUAL SHAPE MANIPULATOR WITH THREE RULES

;;; RULE 1 FUNCTION - PLACES THE INITIAL SQUARE
(defun rule1 ()
   (setq origin (getpoint "\nPlease enter origin: ")
      lowright (getpoint origin "\nEnter lower right corner of square: ")
      a (distance origin lowright) ;;; make sure lowright is on one
      )                             ;;; horizontal line with origin
   (command "INSERT" "square1" origin a "" "")
   (setq count 0
      mark (getpoint "\nPlease enter point on bottom side of square: ")
      c (- (car mark) (car origin))
      d (- a c)
      alpha (angle mark (list (car lowright) (+ c (cadr lowright))))
      b (sqrt (+ (* c c )(* d d)))
      reduction (/ b a)
   )
)
```

```
        (command "CIRCLE" mark (/ b 10))
)    ;;; END DEFUN

;;; RULE 2 FUNCTION - PLACES A SQUARE INTO A SQUARE WITH ONE VERTEX
;;; ON THE MARK
(defun rule2 ()
    (command "ERASE" "L" "")
    (setq nalpha (* (+ count 1) alpha)
    )
    (command "INSERT" "square1" mark b b (rtd nalpha))
    (setq
        mark (polar mark nalpha (/ (* b c) a))
        b (* reduction b)
        count (+ count 1))
    (command "CIRCLE" mark (/ b 10))
)    ;;; END DEFUN

; RULE 3 FUNCTION - REMOVES THE MARK
(defun rule3 ()
    (command "ERASE" "L" "")
)    ;;; END DEFUN

;;; THE INITIALIZATION FUNCTION TO BUILD SQUARE1
(defun init ()
    (setvar "BLIPMODE" 0) (setvar "CMDECHO" 0)
    (command "GRID" "ON") (command "SNAP" "ON")
    (command "UNITS" "" "" "1" "" "" "")
    (command "PLINE" "0,0" "1,0" "1,1" "0,1" "C")
    (command "BLOCK" "square1" "0,0" "L" "")
)

;;; TO CONVERT RADIANS TO DEGREES
(defun rtd (a)
    (/ (* a 180) pi))
```

A.3.2 SHAPE2.LSP: A Program to Draw Three-dimensional Shape Grammars.

The program structure of SHAPE2.LSP is similar to that of SHAPE1.LSP. The only significant addition is a three-dimensional option (see Figure A.3.2a). The accompanying menu SHAPE.MNU is required to guarantee a user-friendly interaction. The (init) function must be executed first as it constructs and stores CUBE1 as a block. The (init) function also sets appropriate system variables, changes the viewpoint, turns the grid and snap options on, and enables AutoCAD to read insertion angles in radians. Therefore, the (rtd) function is not needed. Similar to

186   APPENDIX A

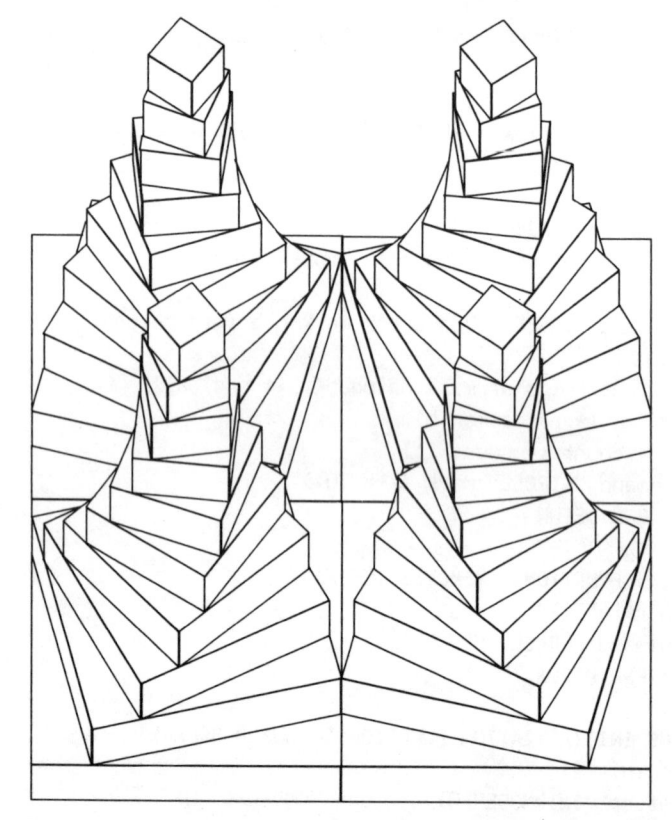

Figure A.3.2a   Image produced with program SHAPE2.LSP.

SHAPE1.LSP, the (init) function is basically a macro that executes AutoCAD commands automatically.

Rule 1 sets the elevation to 0, asks for the thickness of the first inserted element, and then for the height factor by which the height of the following elements will be multiplied. It also places a marker at the label. Rule 2 removes the previous label, places the new cube on top of the first in the appropriate rotation angle, and places a new label for the insertion of the next element. Rule 3 removes the last label if executed after rule 2. The same restrictions as in program SHAPE1.LSP apply.

```
;;; PROGRAM SHAPE2.LSP
;;; A SECOND SIMPLE SHAPE GRAMMAR

;;; RULE 1 FUNCTION - PLACES THE INITIAL SQUARE
(defun rule1 ()
    (setvar "ELEVATION" 0)
```

SAMPLE PROGRAMS IN AUTOLISP   187

```
        (setq heifac (getreal "\nPlease enter the height factor: ")
              basthi (getreal "\nPlease enter the basic thickness: ")
              origin (getpoint "\nPlease enter origin: ")
              lowright (getpoint origin "\nEnter lower right corner of square")
              a (distance origin lowright) ;;; make sure lowright is on one
        )                                  ;;; horizontal line with origin
        (command "INSERT" "cube1" origin "X" a a (* basthi heifac) "")
        (setq count 0
              mark (getpoint "\nPlease enter point on bottom side of square: ")
              c (- (car mark) (car origin))
              d (- a c)
              alpha (angle mark (list (car lowright) (+ c (cadr lowright))))
              b (sqrt (+ (* c c )(* d d)))
              reduction (/ b a))
        (setvar "THICKNESS" 0)
        (command "CIRCLE" mark (/ a 15))
)  ;;; END DEFUN

; RULE 2 FUNCTION - PLACES A SQUARE INTO A SQUARE WITH ONE VERTEX
; ON THE MARK
(defun rule2 ()
    (command "ERASE" "L" "")
    (setvar "ELEVATION" (* (+ count 1) heifac basthi))
    (setq nalpha (* (+ count 1) alpha))
    (command "INSERT" "cube1" mark "X" b b (* heifac basthi) nalpha)
    (setq
           mark (polar mark nalpha (/ (* b c) a))
           b (* reduction b)
           count (+ count 1))
    (command "CIRCLE" mark (/ a 15))
)  ;;; END DEFUN

; RULE 3 FUNCTION - REMOVES THE MARK
(defun rule3 ()
    (command "ERASE" "L" "")
)  ;;; END DEFUN

;;; INITIALIZATION - DRAWS AND STORES CUBE1 AS A BLOCK, RESETS ELEVATION
;;; AND THICKNESS, CHANGES THE VIEWPOINT, SETS GRID AND SNAP ON, TURNS
;;; COMMAND ECHO AND SCREEN BLIPS OFF
(defun init ()
    (setvar "ELEVATION" 0) (setvar "THICKNESS" 1)
    (setvar "BLIPMODE" 0) (setvar "CMDECHO" 0)
    (command "VPOINT" "-3,-4,5")
    (command "GRID" "ON") (command "SNAP" "ON")
```

188 APPENDIX A

```
        (command "UNITS" "" "" "4" "" "" "")
        (command "SOLID" "0,0" "1,0" "0,1" "1,1" "")
        (command "BLOCK" "cube1" "0,0" "L" "")
)
```

A.3.3 SHAPE3.LSP: A Program for Parameterized Shape Grammars.

Whereas SHAPE2.LSP and SHAPE1.LSP relied on the existence and insertion of a BLOCK, SHAPE3.LSP is more generalized. It accepts any four points to form a four-sided solid (see Figure A.3.3a). The basic height of this solid, originating at elevation zero, is multiplied by the height factor. The designer defines a label on the solid by drawing a random line that cuts through the first edge of the solid. The intersection of the line with the first edge is marked with a circle. Rule 2 places a second polygon on top of the first one. Its vertices touch the polygon edges. The location of the vertices is determined by the reduction factor that in turn is calculated from the location of the first label.

```
;;; PROGRAM SHAPE3.LSP
;;; A THIRD, SIMPLE PARAMETRIC SHAPE GRAMMAR FOR ANY FOUR EDGE POLYGON

;;; RULE 1 FUNCTION - PLACES THE INITIAL POLYGON
(defun rule1 ()
      (setq heifac (getreal "\nPlease enter the height factor: ")
            basthi (getreal "\nPlease enter the basic thickness: "))
      (setvar "ELEVATION" 0)
      (setvar "THICKNESS" (* heifac basthi))
      (four_points)
      (command "SOLID" p1 p2 p4 p3 "")
      (intersection)
      (setq count 0
            cirrad (/ (distance p1 p2) 15)
            reduction (/ (distance p1 mark) (distance p1 p2)))
      (setvar "THICKNESS" 0)
      (command "CIRCLE" mark cirrad)
)

;;; RULE 2 FUNCTION - PLACES A POLYGON INTO A POLYGON,
;;; STARTING AT THE MARK
(defun rule2 ()
      (command "ERASE" "L" "")
      (setvar "ELEVATION" (* (+ count 1) heifac basthi))
      (setvar "THICKNESS" (* heifac basthi))
```

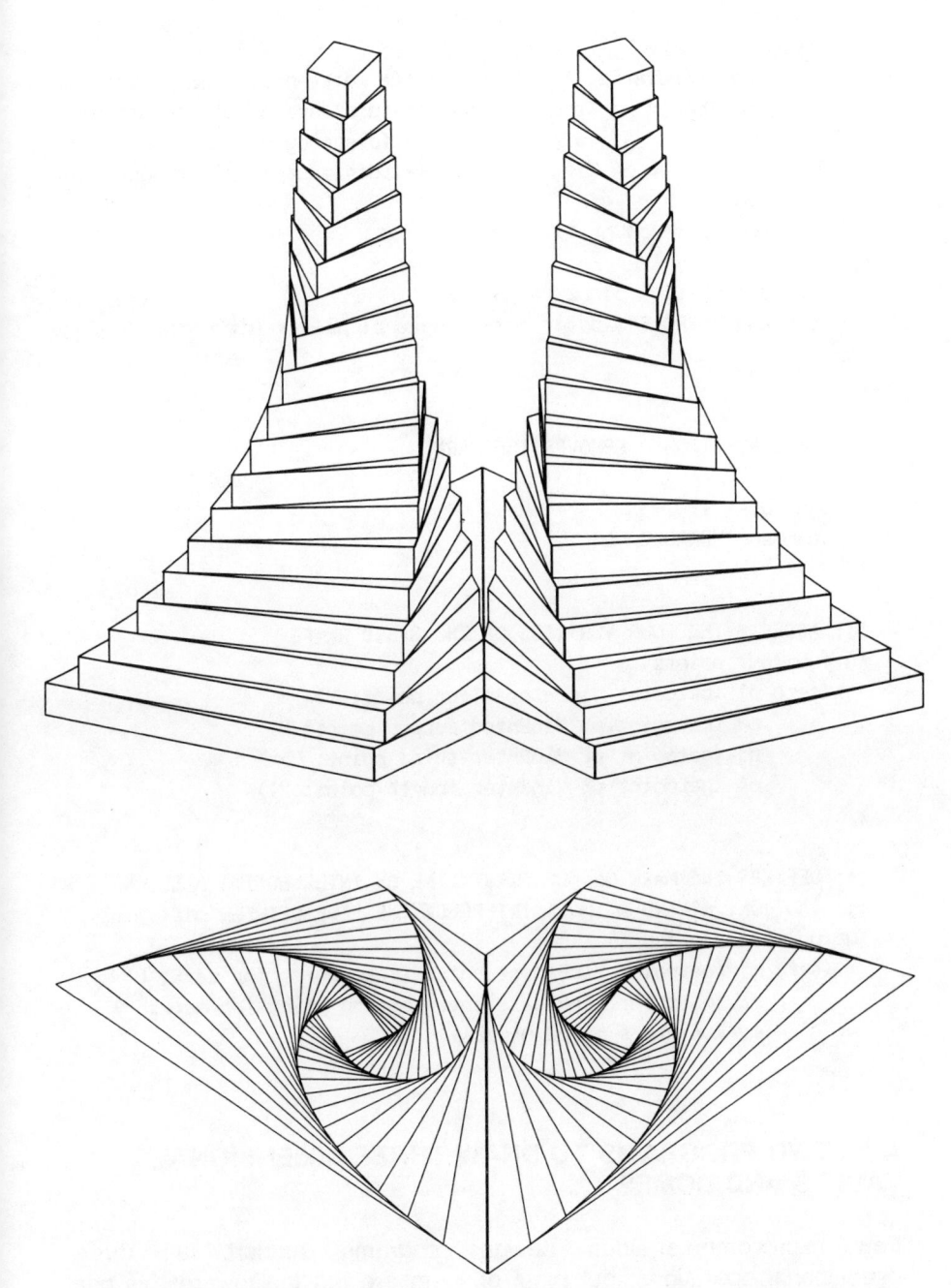

Figure A.3.3a   Floor plan (bottom) and axonometric view (top) of object produced with program SHAPE3.LSP.

190   APPENDIX A

```
(setq
    mark (polar p1 (angle p1 p2) (* (distance p1 p2) reduction))
    p2 (polar p2 (angle p2 p3) (* (distance p2 p3) reduction))
    p3 (polar p3 (angle p3 p4) (* (distance p3 p4) reduction))
    p4 (polar p4 (angle p4 p1) (* (distance p4 p1) reduction))
    p1 mark
    count (+ count 1)
)
(command "SOLID" p1 p2 p4 p3 "")
(command "CIRCLE" (polar mark (angle p1 p2) (* (distance p1 p2)
                                                reduction)) cirrad)
)

; RULE 3 FUNCTION - REMOVES THE MARK

(defun rule3 ()
    (command "ERASE" "L" "")
)

;;; ACCEPTS THE FOUR VERTICES OF THE BASIC SHAPE
(defun four_points ()
    (setq p1 (getpoint "\nEnter first point: ")
          p2 (getpoint p1 "\nEnter second point: ")
          p3 (getpoint p2 "\nEnter third point: ")
          p4 (getpoint p3 "\nEnter fourth point: "))
)

;;; DEFINES THE MARK ON THE FIRST LINE BY INTERSECTING A SECOND LINE
;;; CAUTION: m1 AND m2 MUST INTERSECT THE LINE BETWEEN p1 AND p2
(defun intersection ()
    (setq m1 (getpoint "\nPlease enter first point for mark: ")
          m2 (getpoint "\nPlease enter second point for mark: ")
          mark (inters p1 p2 m1 m2))
)
```

A.4 TWO PROGRAMS TO DRAW THREE-DIMENSIONAL VAULTS AND DOMES

Few microcomputer-aided design programs support full three-dimensional operations, but most of them are moving toward this goal [MEGACADD85], [VersaCAD86], [AutoCAD87]. The following programs use AutoCAD's 3DFACE command to position surfaces in three-dimensional space. The input for a 3DFACE requires the specification of three or four three-dimensional points: (setq p1 (list x1 y1 z1)), (setq p2 (list x2 y2 z2)), (setq p3 (list x3 y3 z3)), (setq p4 (x4 y4 z4)). Three or four of these points are then connected with lines that form the edges of three-dimensional surfaces. Tilted roof surfaces are easily input, but barrel vaults or domes are more difficult to input directly. The following two programs do the calculation work and allow specification of the desired object with few parameters.

The following 3DMENU.MNU menu should be copied exactly as it appears in the text. The same applies for 3DVAULT.LSP and 3DDOME.LSP. Subsequently, the vault and the dome function are loaded once and then executed.

```
***SCREEN
[*3DMENU*]
[          ]
[*VAULT**]
[Load Vau](load "3dvault")
[ SetVaul](SetVault)
[ BuildVa](Vault Radius Segments BeginAxis EndAxis)
[          ]
[**DOME**]
[Load Dom](load "3ddome")
[ SetDome](SetDome)
[ BuildDo](Dome Center Radius HoSegments VeSegments)
[          ]
[ACADMENU]MENU Acad
```

A.4.1 3DVAULT.LSP: A Program to Draw Barrel Vaults.

The 3DVAULT.LSP program draws vaults defined by the number of segments, radius, beginning point, and end point of the vault (see Figure A.4.1a). The designer specifies these parameters by clicking to the [SetVaul] menu item. The vault is drawn when the [BuildVa] item is selected. The number of segments determines the "roundness" of the vault: A large number (15) will produce a vault that approaches a semicircle in section. A small number (2) produces a tilted roof. After the vault is created, it can be moved, mirrored, copied, rotated, and used in an array. It is encouraged to modify the program after studying how it performs and to add more features. The presented method of specifying the three-dimensional faces that form the vault is only one of many possible methods.

```
;;; SETUP FUNCTION FOR THREE DIMENSIONAL TONS
(defun SetVault ()
    (setq Segments (getint "\nEnter number of segments for vault")
          Radius (getreal "\nPlease enter radius of vault")
```

192 APPENDIX A

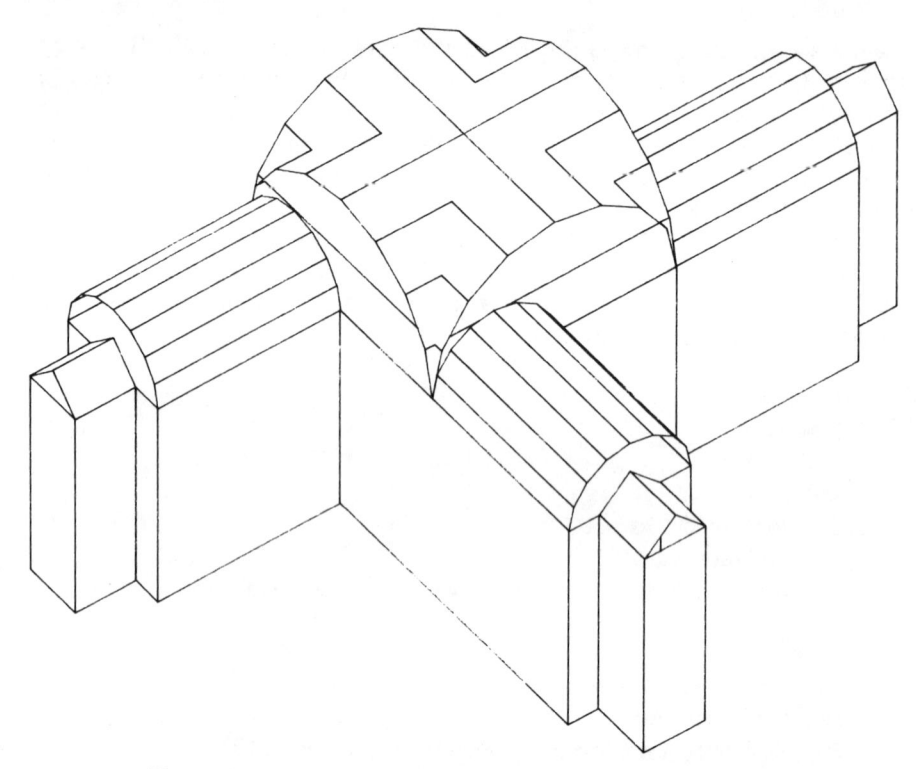

Figure A.4.1a   Object created with program 3DVAULT.LSP.

```
            BeginAxis (getpoint "\nEnter the begin of the axis")
            EndAxis (getpoint "\nPlease enter the end of the axis")
    )
)

;;; FUNCTION TO DRAW THREE DIMENSIONAL VAULTS IN ANY XY DIRECTION
(defun Vault (Radius Segments BeginAxis EndAxis)
    (setq Counter 0)
    (repeat Segments
    (setq p1 (list (+ (car BeginAxis)
                    (* (* Radius (cos (* Counter (/ pi Segments))))
                      (sin (angle BeginAxis EndAxis))))
                  (- (cadr BeginAxis)
                    (* (* Radius (cos (* Counter (/ pi Segments))))
                      (cos (angle BeginAxis EndAxis))))
                  (* Radius (sin (* Counter (/ pi Segments))))))
    (setq p3 (list (+ (car EndAxis)
                    (* (* Radius (cos (* Counter (/ pi Segments))))
                      (sin (angle BeginAxis EndAxis))))
```

```
                (- (cadr EndAxis)
                   (* (* Radius (cos (* Counter (/ pi Segments))))
                      (cos (angle BeginAxis EndAxis))))
                (* Radius (sin (* Counter (/ pi Segments))))))
   (setq Counter (+ 1 Counter))
   (setq p2 (list (+ (car BeginAxis)
                     (* (* Radius (cos (* Counter (/ pi Segments))))
                        (sin (angle BeginAxis EndAxis))))
                  (- (cadr BeginAxis)
                     (* (* Radius (cos (* Counter (/ pi Segments))))
                        (cos (angle BeginAxis EndAxis))))
                  (* Radius (sin (* Counter (/ pi Segments))))))
   (setq p4 (list (+ (car EndAxis)
                     (* (* Radius (cos (* Counter (/ pi Segments))))
                        (sin (angle BeginAxis EndAxis))))
                  (- (cadr EndAxis)
                     (* (* Radius (cos (* Counter (/ pi Segments))))
                        (cos (angle BeginAxis EndAxis))))
                  (* Radius (sin (* Counter (/ pi Segments))))))
   (command "3DFACE" p1 p3 p4 p2 "")
  )
)
```

A.4.2 3DDOME.LSP: A Program to Draw Three-dimensional Domes.

The 3DDOME.LSP program draws domes defined by the number of horizontal and vertical segments, radius of the dome, and center point. Specify these parameters by clicking to the [SetDome] menu option. The dome is drawn when the [BuildDo] item is selected. The minimum number of horizontal segments is 3, the minimum number of vertical segments is 1. A large number for both horizontal and vertical segments will produce an object resembling a half-sphere. Some typical cases are shown in Figure A.4.2a: The column from the top to the bottom right is created by increasing the horizontal segments from 3 to 7 and keeping the vertical segments constant at 1. This creates tentlike objects. Stepping from right to left, the number of horizontal segments increases by 1 in each column, reaching a maximum of 5 in the left-most column. The objects in the left most column resemble domes made of heavier materials, such as stone. As in the previous programs, experimentation will lead to many more surprising forms.

The algorithm uses two nested loops: The inner loop calculates and draws the surfaces on a horizontal layer; the outer loop steps through the vertical layers. Other types of algorithms are possible: The program could first calculate and draw the surfaces in one "slice" of the dome,

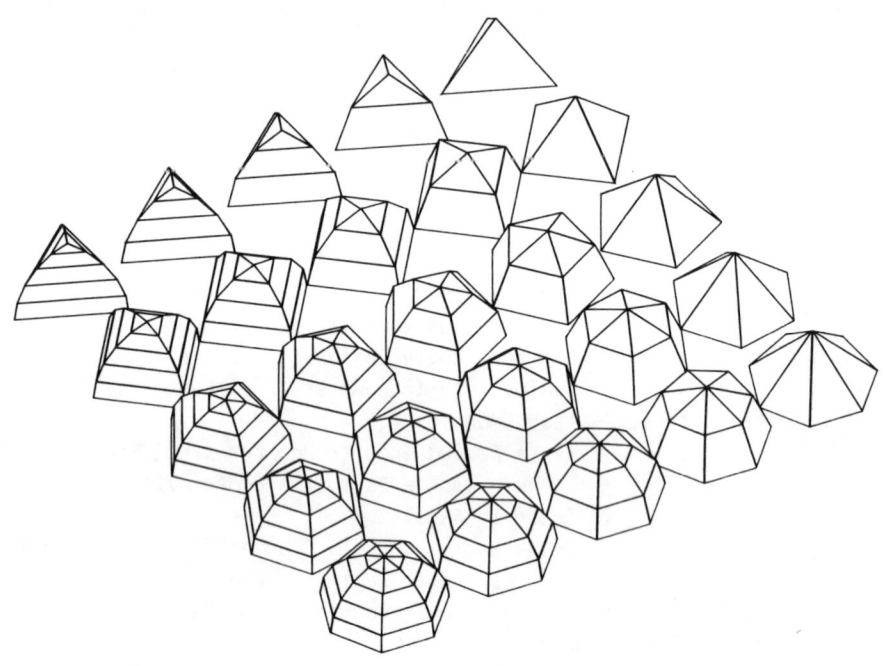

Figure A.4.2a   Objects created with program 3DDOME.LSP.

select them, and use the ARRAY function to rotate them around the center point.

```
;;; PROGRAM 3DDOME.LSP
;;; FUNCTIONS TO DRAW DOMES GIVEN THE CENTER, THE RADIUS, THE NUMBER
;;; OF VERTICAL AND THE NUMBER OF HORIZONTAL SEGMENTS

;;; SETUP FUNCTION FOR THREE DIMENSIONAL DOMES
(defun SetDome ()
   (setq HoSegments (getint "\nEnter number of horizontal segments")
         VeSegments (getint "\nEnter number of vertical segments")
         Radius (getreal "\nPlease enter radius of dome")
         Center (getpoint "\nPlease enter the center of the dome")
   )
)

;;; FUNCTION TO DRAW THREE DIMENSIONAL DOMES
(defun Dome (Center Radius HoSegments VeSegments)
    (setq H 0                         ;;; SETS HORIZONTAL COUNTER TO 0
          V 0                         ;;; SETS VERTICAL COUNTER TO 0
          Alpha (/ (* 2 pi) HoSegments)   ;;; HORIZONTAL ANGLE
          Beta  (/ (/ pi 2) VeSegments) ) ;;; VERTICAL ANGLE
```

```
      (repeat VeSegments                    ;;; BEGIN VERTICAL LOOP
      (repeat HoSegments                    ;;; BEGIN HORIZONTAL LOOP
      (setq p1 (list (+ (car Center)
                     (* (* Radius (cos (* V Beta)))(cos (* H Alpha))))
                     (+ (cadr Center)
                     (* (* Radius (sin (* H Alpha)))(cos (* V Beta))))
                     (* Radius (sin (* V Beta))) ) )
      (setq p2 (list (+ (car Center)
                     (* (* Radius (cos (* (+ V 1) Beta)))(cos (* H Alpha))))
                     (+ (cadr Center)
                     (* (* Radius (sin (* H Alpha)))(cos (* (+ V 1) Beta))))
                     (* Radius (sin (* (+ V 1) Beta))) ) )
      (setq p3 (list (+ (car Center)
                     (* (* Radius (cos (* (+ V 1)Beta)))(cos(* (+ 1 H)Alpha))))
                     (+ (cadr Center)
                     (* (* Radius (sin (* (+ H 1)Alpha)))(cos(* (+ V 1)Beta))))
                     (* Radius (sin (* (+ V 1) Beta))) ) )
      (setq p4 (list (+ (car Center)
                     (* (* Radius (cos (* V Beta)))(cos (* (+ 1 H) Alpha))))
                     (+ (cadr Center)
                     (* (* Radius (sin (* (+ H 1) Alpha)))(cos (* V Beta))))
                     (* Radius (sin (* V Beta))) ) )
      (command "3DFACE" p1 p2 p3 p4 "")      ;;; DRAW A 3-D FACE
      (setq H (+ 1 H))                       ;;; INCREASE HORIZONTAL COUNTER
      )                                      ;;; END HORIZONTAL LOOP
      (setq V (+ 1 V))                       ;;; INCREASE VERTICAL COUNTER
      )                                      ;;; END VERTICAL LOOP
)                                            ;;; END DEFUN
```

Bibliography

[Akin86] Akin, Ömer. *Psychology of Architectural Design.* Pion, London, 1986.

[Alberti66] Alberti, Leon Battista, Orlandi, Giovanni, and Portoghesi, Paolo. *L'Architettura—De Re Aedificatorica.* Edizioni Il Polifilo, Milano, Italy, 1966.

[Alexander77] Alexander, Christopher, Ishikawa, Sara, and Silverstein, Murray. *A Pattern Language.* Oxford University Press, New York, 1977.

[Andersen87] Andersen Corporation. *CADD-I Computer Aided Design and Drafting Manual.* Andersen Corporation, Inc., Bayport, MN, 1987.

[ASHRAE85] *1985 Handbook of Fundamentals.* American Society of Heating, Refrigerating and Air-Conditioning Engineers, Inc., Atlanta, GA, 1987.

[AutoCAD87] *AutoCAD Reference Manual.* Autodesk, Inc., Sausalito, CA, 1987.

[AutoLISP87] *AutoLISP Programmer's Reference.* Autodesk, Inc., Sausalito, CA, 1987.

[Axis87] *Axis Reference Manual, 2.3 edition.* Modern Medium, Inc., Amsterdam, The Netherlands.

[Barr81] Barr, Avron, and Feigenbaum, Edward A. *The Handbook of Artificial Intelligence.* William Kaufmann, Inc., Los Altos, CA, 1981.

[Bollinger86] Bollinger, Elizabeth, Hinton, Robert. *1986 CADD*

	Activities Survey, Technical Report. ACADIA, Association for Computer Aided Design in Architecture, March 1986.
[Chan87]	Chan, Chiu-Shui. *The Cognitive Processes in Architectural Design Problem Solving.* Ph.D. thesis proposal, Department of Architecture, Carnegie Mellon University, Pittsburgh, PA, 1987.
[Charniak86]	Charniak, Eugene, and McDermott, Drew. *Introduction to Artificial Intelligence.* Addison-Wesley, Reading, MA, 1986.
[Chase73]	Chase, William G., and Simon, H. A. "The Mind's Eye in Chess." In Chase, W. (Ed.), *Visual Information Processing.* Academic Press, New York, 1973.
[Clarke85]	Clarke, J. A. *Energy Simulation in Building Design.* Adam Hilger Ltd., Bristol and Boston, 1985.
[Cooper82]	Cooper, Douglas. *Oh! Pascal!* W. W. Norton, New York and London, 1982.
[Cooper83]	Cooper, Douglas, and Mall, Raymond. *Drawing and Perceiving.* Information Dynamics, Inc., Silver Spring, MD, 1983.
[Coyne86]	Coyne, R. D., and Gero, J. S. Semantics and the organization of knowledge in design. *Design Computing* 1(1):68–89, 1986.
[DataCAD86]	*DataCAD User's Guide.* Microtecture Corporation, Charlottesville, VA, 1986.
[dBASEIII84]	Pawluk, Hal. *dBASE III User Manual.* Version 1.1 edition, Ashton-Tate, 1984.
[DOE-2-80]	Building Energy Analysis Group. *DOE-2 Users Guide.* Lawrence Berkeley Laboratory, Berkeley, CA, 1980.
[EEDO84]	Burt, Hill, Kosar, Rittelmann Associates. *EEDO— Energy Economics of Design Options Reference Manual.* Burt, Hill, Kosar, Rittelmann Associates, Architects, Butler, PA, 1984.
[Eisenman85]	Eisenman, Peter. *Fin d'Ou T Hou S.* Architectural Association, London, 1985.
[Eisenman87]	Eisenman, Peter. *Discussions on Fractal Architecture.* Conversations with the author at Carnegie Mellon University on March 6, 1987.
[Emde87]	Emde, Helmut. "Geometrical fundamentals for design and visualization of spatial objects." In

Wagter, Harry, (Ed.), *CAAD Futures 87*. Eindhoven University of Technology, Eindhoven, The Netherlands, May, 1987.

[Filevision84] Metcalfe, Howard. *Business Filevision User Manual*. Telos Software, Santa Monica, CA, 1984.

[Flemming77] Flemming, Ulrich. *Automatisierter Grundrissentwurf. Darstellung, Erzeugung und Dimensionierung von dicht gepackten, rechtwinkligen Flaechenanordnungen*. Ph.D. thesis, Technical University of Berlin, 1977.

[Flemming86a] Flemming, Ulrich, Coyne, Robert, and Pithavadian, Shakunthala. *A Pattern Book for Shadyside*. Department of Architecture, Carnegie Mellon University, Pittsburgh, PA, 1986.

[Flemming86b] Flemming, Ulrich, Rychener, Michael D., Coyne, Robert F., and Glavin, Timothy J. *A Generative Expert System for the Design of Building Layouts*. Engineering Design Research Center, Carnegie Mellon University, Pittsburgh, PA, 1986.

[Foley82] Foley, James D., and Van Dam, Andries. *Fundamentals of Interactive Computer Graphics*. Addison-Wesley, Reading, MA, 1982.

[Forgy81] Forgy, Charles L. *OPS5 User's Manual*. Department of Computer Science, Carnegie Mellon University, Pittsburgh, PA, 1981.

[Forgy85] Forgy, Charles L. *The OPS83 User's Manual*. Production Systems Technologies, Inc., Pittsburgh, PA, 1985.

[Gero85] Gero, John, Radford, A. D., Coyne, R., and Akiner, V. T. "Knowledge-Based Computer-Aided Architectural Design." In Gero, J. S. (Ed.), *Knowledge Engineering in Computer-Aided Design*. Elsevier, NY, 1985.

[Gero87a] Gero, John. *Research at the University of Sidney*. Lecture at Carnegie Mellon University, Pittsburgh, PA, April 15, 1987.

[Gero87b] Gero, John. *Learning and Creativity in Knowledge-Based Design*. Lecture at Carnegie Mellon University, Pittsburgh, PA, April 22, 1987.

[Haider86] Haider, Gulzar S. "Implicit Intentions and Explicit Order in Sinan's Work." In *II. International Congress on the History of Turkish-Islamic Science and Technology*. 1986.

200 BIBLIOGRAPHY

[Hanks77]   Hanks, Kurt, Belliston, Larry, and Edwards, Dave. *Design yourself!* William Kaufmann, Inc., Los Altos, CA, 1977.

[Harrington83]   Harrington, Steven. *Computer Graphics—A Programming Approach*. McGraw-Hill, New York, 1983.

[Hayes81]   Hayes, John R. *The Complete Problem Solver*. The Franklin Institute Press, Philadelphia, 1981.

[Hearn86]   Hearn, Donald, and Baker, Pauline M. *Computer Graphics*. Prentice-Hall, Old Tappan, NJ, 1986.

[Heritage70]   American Heritage Publishing Co. *The American Heritage Dictionary of the English Language*. American Heritage, New York, 1970,

[Hofstadter82]   Hofstadter, Douglas R. Metamagical themes: variations on a theme as the essence of imagination. *Scientific American* **247**:20–28, 1982.

[Horowitz84]   Horowitz, Ellis. *Computer Software Engineering Series: Fundamentals of Programming Languages*. Computer Science Press, Rockville, MD, 1984.

[Kemper85]   Kemper, Alfred M. (Ed.). *Pioneers of CAD in Architecture*. Hurland/Swenson, Pacifica, CA, 1985.

[Kernighan78]   Kernighan, Brian W., and Ritchie, Dennis M. *The C Programming Language*. Prentice-Hall, Englewood Cliffs, NJ, 1978.

[Koberg81]   Koberg, Don, and Bagnall, Jim. *The All New Universal Traveler*. William Kaufmann, Inc., Los Altos, CA, 1981.

[Laseau80]   Laseau, Paul. *Graphic Thinking for Architects and Designers*. Van Nostrand Reinhold, New York, 1980.

[MacDraw84]   Stanton-Wyman, Pamela, and Espinosa, Christopher. *MacDraw User Manual*. Apple Computer, Inc., Cupertino, CA, 1984.

[MacPaint83]   Kaehler, Carol. *Macintosh MacPaint User Manual*. Apple Computer, Inc., Cupertino, CA, 1983.

[Maher84]   Maher, Mary Lou. *HI-RISE. A knowledge-based expert system for preliminary structural design of high-rise buildings*. Ph.d. thesis, Carnegie Mellon University, Pittsburgh, PA, 1984.

[Mandelbrot83]   Mandelbrot, Benoit B. *The Fractal Geometry of Nature*. W. H. Freeman, New York, 1983.

[Mauldin85]   Mauldin, John H. *Perspective Design*. Van Nostrand Reinhold, New York, 1985.

[Mazria79] Mazria, Edward. *The Passive Solar Energy Book.* Rodale Press, Emmaus, PA, 1979.

[McGregor86] McGregor, Jim, and Watt, Alan. *The Art of Graphics.* Addison-Wesley, Reading, MA, 1986.

[McKim80] McKim, Robert H. *Experiences in Visual Thinking.* Brooks/Cole, Monterey, CA, 1980.

[Means87] Horsley, William F. *Means Systems Costs 1987.* Robert Sturgis Godfrey, Kingston, MA, 1987.

[MEGACADD85] *Design Board Professional User Manual.* 3.3 edition, MEGA CADD, Inc., Seattle, WA, 1985.

[Mitchell77] Mitchell, William J. *Computer-Aided Architectural Design.* Petrocelli/Charter, New York, 1977.

[Mitchell87] Mitchell, William J., Liggett, Robin, and Kvan, Thomas. *The Art of Computer Graphics Programming.* Van Nostrand Reinhold, NY, 1987.

[Newman79] Newman, William M., and Sproull, Robert F. *Principles of Interactive Computer Graphics.* McGraw-Hill, NY, 1979.

[Oppenheimer86] Oppenheimer, Peter E. "Real time design and animation of fractal plants and trees." In Evans, David C., and Athay, Russel J. (Ed.), *Computer Graphics.* Association for Computing Machinery's Special Interest Group on Computer Graphics, August, 1986.

[Placzek65] Placzek, Adolf K. *Andrea Palladio: The Four Books of Architecture.* Dover, NY, 1965.

[Poincar] Poincar, Henry. *Science and Method.* Dover, NY, 1952.

[Porada87] Porada, Mikhael. "Digital image: a bridge towards mental images?" In Wagter, Harry (Ed.), *CAAD Futures 87.* Eindhoven University of Technology, Eindhoven, The Netherlands, May, 1987.

[Pye64] Pye, David W. *The Nature of Design.* Reinhold, NY, 1964.

[Radford88] Radford, Antony D., and Gero, John S. *Design by Optimization in Architecture, Building, and Construction.* Van Nostrand Reinhold, NY, 1988.

[Raker86] Raker, Daniel, and Rice, Harbert. *Inside AutoCAD.* New Riders Publishing, Thousand Oaks, CA, 1986.

[Rehak87] Rehak, Daniel, and Derrington, Patrice. "An overview of expert systems in civil engineering and architecture." In *Proceedings of ARECDAO '87*

Conference. Institut de Tecnologia de la Construccio de Catalunya, Barcelona, Spain, 1987.

[Rich83] Rich, Elaine. *Artificial Intelligence*. McGraw-Hill, NY, 1983.

[Rieger75] Rieger, C. J. "Conceptual Memory and Inference." In Schank, R. *Conceptual Information Processing*. Elsevier, NY, 1975.

[Rittel85] Rittel, Horst. *Expert Sytems in Design*. Statement in a seminar on expert systems at the National Bureau of Standards in Washington, D.C., 1985.

[Rudofsky64] Rudofsky, Bernard. *Architecture Without Architects*. Doubleday, Garden City, NY, 1964.

[Rush86] Rush, Richard D. *The Building Systems Integration Handbook*. Wiley, NY, 1986.

[Schank75] Schank, Roger C. *Conceptual Information Processing*. Elsevier, NY, 1975.

[Schank86] Schank, Roger C. *Explanation Patterns—Understanding Mechanically and Creatively*. Lawrence Erlbaum Associates, Hillsdale, NJ, 1986.

[Schmitt85] Schmitt, Gerhard. "Microcomputer based integrated energy design expert systems." In Osborn, Donald E. (Ed.), *First National Conference on Microcomputer Applications for Conservation and Renewable Energy*. University of Arizona, Tuscon, AZ, 1985, pp. 289–294.

[Schmitt86a] Schmitt, Gerhard. "OPS5 in Architecture: four applications." In Giraud Christian, (Ed.), *CAD and Robotics in Architecture and Construction*. Institute International de Robotique et d'Intelligence Artificielle de Marseille, Hermes Publishing, Paris, 1986, pp. 146–156.

[Schmitt86b] Schmitt, Gerhard. "Expert Systems in Design Abstraction and Evaluation." In Kalay, Yehuda (Ed.), *The Computability of Design*. Wiley, NY, 1987.

[Schmitt87] Schmitt, Gerhard. *ARCHPLAN: An Architectural Front End to Engineering Expert Systems*. Engineering Design Research Center, Carnegie Mellon University, Pittsburgh, PA, September, 1987.

[Schulze85] Schulze, Franz. *Mies van der Rohe—A Critical Biography*. The University of Chicago Press, Chicago, IL, 1985.

[Schustack85] Schustack, Steve. *Variations in C*. Microsoft Press, Bellevue, WA, 1985.

[Stiny80] Stiny, George. "Introduction to shape and shape grammars." *Environment and Planning* B7:343–351, 1980.

[Stiny85] Stiny, George. "Computing with Form and Meaning in Architecture." *Journal of Architectural Education* **39**(1), 1985.

[Stoller87] Stoller, Adam. CAD in Architecture—A Survey on the Use of Computer Aided Design Systems in the Architectural Profession. Comprehensive Examination and Independent Study, Department of Architecture, Carnegie Mellon University, Pittsburgh, PA, May 1987.

[ThunderScan85] *ThunderScan User's Guide.* Thunderware, Inc., Orinda, CA, 1985.

[Touretzky84] Touretzky, David S. *LISP—A Gentle Introduction to Symbolic Computation.* Harper & Row, NY, 1984.

[VersaCAD86] *Drafting System and Database Reference Manual.* VersaCAD Corporation, Huntington Beach, CA, 1986.

[Vitruvius26] Vitruvius Pollio. *The Ten Books on Architecture.* Oxford University Press, Oxford, England, 1926.

[Waterman78] Waterman, Donald Arthur and Hayes-Roth, Frederick. *Pattern-Directed Inference Systems.* Academic Press, NY, 1978.

[Winograd83] Winograd, T. *Language as a Cognitive Process.* Addison-Wesley, Reading, MA, 1983.

[Winston84] Winston, Patrick Henry, and Horn, Berthod Klaus Paul. *LISP.* Addison-Wesley, Reading, MA, 1984.

[Woodbury87] Woodbury, Robert F. *The Knowledge Based Representation and Manipulation of Geometry.* Ph.D. thesis, Department of Architecture, Carnegie Mellon University, 1987.

[Wulf81] Wulf, William A., Shaw, Mary, and Hilfinger, Paul N. *Fundamental Structures of Computer Science.* Addison-Wesley, Reading, MA, 1981.

[Yessios87] Yessios, Chris I., "A Fractal Studio." In Novitski, Barbara-Jo, (Ed.) *ACADIA Workshop '87*, University of Oregon, 1987.

[Zhang86] Zhang, Weiguang. Interactive Graphic User Interface for 3D Structural Design. Master's thesis, Department of Civil Engineering, Carnegie Mellon University, Pittsburgh, PA, March, 1986.

INDEX

Aalto, Alvar, 26
Abduction, 130
Akin, Omer, 121, 123, 124, 127, 128, 131
Abstraction, 34, 89, 90, 98
AI, 122, 123
Alberti, Leon Battista, 151
Alexander, Christopher, 151
Analysis, 137, 152
Andersen Corporation, 41
Ando, Tadao, 64, 65
Architectural:
    creativity, 134, 135, 138, 141
    drawings, 12
    firms, 10
    grammar, 107
    language, 65, 90, 94
    programming, 114
    reasoning, 129, 137
    vocabulary, 96, 97
Artificial Intelligence, 122, 123
ASHRAE, 156
AutoCAD, viii, 171
AutoLISP, viii, 171
AutoLISP programs:
    windows, 173, 175, 177
    C-curve, 179
    shape grammar, 182
    3d shape grammar, 185
    parameterized shape grammar, 188
    3d vaults and domes, 190
Axonometric projection, 52

Barr, Avron, 122, 123
Basic skills, 11
Blocks, 35
Botta, Mario, 26
Breadth-first search, 124
Brick module, 76, 77
Building:
    code checking, 103
    description language, 43, 167

C-curve, 179
Chambord, 49, 50
Chan, Chiu-Shui, 131
Charniak, Eugene, 126, 129
Chartres, 16
Chase, William G., 129
Chunks, 129
Clarke, J. A., 151, 152, 153, 156
Computer:
    cost, 17
    equipment, viii
    evaluation, 151
    graphics, vii
    modeling, vii,1
    programming, 114
    use, 10
Communication, 6, 8, 9
Cooper, Douglas, 34, 52, 59
Coordinate system, 30, 37
Copying, 27, 70

INDEX

Cost:
  estimation, 103, 158
  evaluation, 158
  life-cycle analysis, 160
  optimization, 159
Coyne, R. D., 90, 97, 151
Creativity:
  architectural, 133, 136
  support systems, 136, 137
Cutting plane, 40

Database, 86, 122, 153, 158, 163
DataCAD, 158
Decision-making, 1
Decision support systems, 7, 9
Deduction, 129
Depth-first Search, 123
Depth cues, 54
Design:
  alternatives, 7
  computer-assisted, 86
  development, 5
  evaluation, 6, 7, 164, 165
  framework, 1, 86
  ideas, 29
  intelligence, 127
  objectives, 6, 7
  process, vii, 5, 7, 29, 85, 135
  representation, 9
  students, vii
  selection, 6, 7
  stages, 6
  teaching, 2
  teachers, vii
Designers, viii
Decomposition, 58
Detail:
  level of, 32, 34
  sections, 42
Digitizing, 22, 23
Discovery, 121
Display, 17
DOE-2, 152, 153, 154
Drafting packages, 11
Drawing:
  3-dimensional, 53
  freehand, 28
  manual, 20
  media, 12, 17
  primitives, 18
  units, 30
  scale, 30

Eisenman, Peter, 143
Electronic pen, 27

Elevations, 44, 76
Energy:
  analysis, 155
  consumption prediction, 103
  performance evaluation, 153
  performance optimization, 156
Evaluation, 6, 151
Expert systems, 115, 156, 166
Extrusion, 52, 54, 79

Fachwerkhaus, 51, 55, 56, 57
Feedback, 170
Figure-ground, 51
Filling, 27
Flemming, Ulrich, 73, 101, 105, 121, 124, 151
Foley, James D., 70
Forgy, Charles L., 102, 128
Fractals, 141
Fractal:
  buildings, 146, 147, 149
  mountains, 146
  trees, 146, 144
Furniture, 76

Generate-and-Test (G-A-T), 124, 132
Gero, John S., 123, 130, 152
Golden section, 51, 57
Grammar, 107
Graphic:
  representation, 1
  symbols, 95
  programming, 115, 116
  vocabulary, 96, 97
  words, 98

Haider, Gulzar S., 37, 109
Hanks, Kurt, 69
Harrington, Steven, 70
Hatching, 17, 42, 43
Hayes, John R., 133
Hearn, Donald, 70
Hidden-line algorithm, 37, 53, 59
Hill-Climbing (H-C), 126, 152
Hofstadter, Douglas R., 136
Hornbostel, Henry, 21, 22, 31, 45, 48, 78
Horowitz, Ellis, 115

Induction, 130, 131
Inferencing, 115, 128, 129
Insulation studies, 56
Integration of evaluation, 164

Kemper, Alfred M., 5
Kernighan, Brian W., 115

Koberg, Don, 134

Language:
  architectural, 90, 94, 98
  computer, 91
  grammar, 107
  graphic, 91
  natural, 90, 98
  relations, 99
  rules, 102
  technical, 90
  vocabulary, 95
Laseau, Paul, 6, 25, 91, 107
Laser writer, 39
Layout:
  preliminary, 102
  generators, 103, 111
Layers, 32, 35, 39, 46, 47
Learning, 135
LHS, 102, 105, 128
Line:
  color, 13
  freehand, 13, 17
  intensity, 13, 15
  quality, 16
  resolution, 14
  thickness, 12
  type, 12
  weight, 21
Lines, 11, 12
LISP, 115, 116, 117, 172
LISP files, 173, 176, 179, 181, 184, 186, 188, 191, 194
Loos, Adolf, 58, 94

Mackintosh, Charles Rennie, 20, 21, 60, 61, 62
MacDraw, 27, 38
McGregor, Jim, 70, 143
McKim, Robert H., 90
MacPaint, 8, 26, 27
MacVision, 8
Mandelbrot, Benoit B., 142
Manipulation, 69, 75
Mauldin, John H., 59
Mazria, Edward, 156
Means, 158
Means-End-Analysis (M-E-A), 126
Meier, Richard, 36, 37, 113, 125
Menu files, 172, 180, 183, 191
Mirroring, 77, 78
Mitchell, William J., 70, 101
Model:
  abstract, 89, 98
  geometric, 127
  mental, 1, 89
  physical, 30, 127
  three-dimensional, 40
  solid, 41
Monotony, 28
Moving, 27, 70

Newman, William M., 70

Object:
  2-dimensional, 52
  3-dimensional, 53, 72
  transformation, 72
Oblique projection, 52
Office automation, 86
OPS5, 102, 115
Optimization, 152
Orthographic projection, 35, 39

Paint programs, 27
Painting, 27
Palladio, Andrea, 35, 37, 42, 53, 97
Panel architecture, 65
Passive solar quality, 57
Pelli, Caesar, 79
Performance diagram, 167
Perspective projection, 59
Pixels, 12, 19
Placzek, Adolf K., 37, 151
Plans, 34, 75
Plotting, 17, 34
Poincare', Henry, 121
Points, 11, 12
Porada, Mikhael, 146
Printing, 17
Problem-solving, 6
Productions, 128
Programming, 114, 116, 117, 171
Projections:
  axonometric, 52
  dimetric, 52
  isometric, 52
  oblique, 52
  orthographic, 29, 34, 39
  parallel, 29
  perspective, 29, 59
Prolog, 115
Proportion, 31
Pye, David, 123

Radford, Antony D., 152, 164
Realism of presentation, 59
Reasoning, 129
Recursive function, 118, 142

Relations:
    explaining, 101
    expressing, 99
    inquiring, 100
Repetition, 48, 75, 76
Representation:
    language, 167
    mathematical, 101
    of models, 29, 89
    of architectural design, 126
RHS, 102, 105, 128
Rich, Elaine, 124, 126
Rieger, Charles J., 129
Rotation, 70, 72, 73
Rubber-band:
    lines, 27
    rectangles, 27
Rules:
    general, 102
    graphical, 105
    shape grammar, 107, 182
Rule-based systems, 104, 106
Rush, Richard D., 164

Scale, 30, 31
Scaling, 70, 73
Scaling factors, 32
Scanning, 21
Schulze, Franz, 30, 79
Schustak, Steve, 115
Search, 123, 124, 125, 126
Sections, 39, 75
Shading, 45, 52
Shank, Roger C., 128, 133, 134
Shape grammar, 107, 108, 109, 182, 185, 188
Simulation, 156
Sinan, 37, 110
Site plans, 35, 37
Sketch:
    computer, 17, 25
    manual, 17, 29
    utilities, 27
Sketching, 12, 25
Spraying, 27
Stiny, George, 107, 108
Stoller, Adam, 5
Structural:
    analysis, 160
    evaluation, 160
    safety, 103
    system, 75
Symbols, 94
Symmetry, 48

ThunderScan, 20, 22
Timber frame house, 51, 55, 56, 57
Touretzky, David S., 171
Tracing, 11, 18, 22
Traditional:
    design process, 5, 6
    technology, 2
    tracing, 19
Transformation:
    concatenation of, 74
    matrix, 59
    perspective, 59
    rotation, 70, 72, 73
    scaling, 70, 73, 74
    translation, 70
Translation, 70
Transportability, 28

Urban Planning, 76

Van der Rohe, Mies, 79, 92, 106, 112
Vectorization, 23
Victorian houses, 105, 111
Viewing parameters, 52
Viewpoint, 32
Villa Rotonda, 19
Visualization, 137
Vitruvius, 151
Vocabulary:
    architectural, 95
    manipulative, 69, 70

Waterman, Donald A., 102
Winograd, Terry, 90
Winston, Patrick H., 115
Wireframe, 14
Worm's eye view, 57
Wright, Frank Lloyd, 42, 44
Wulf, William A., 114

Yessios, Chris, 146

Zhang, Weiguang, 162, 163
Zooming, 32, 33

NA
2728
.S36
1988

DATE DUE

APR 2 8 1996

DISCARDED

GAYLORD — PRINTED IN U.S.A.